Anna Karenina in Our Time

Russian Literature and Thought
GARY SAUL MORSON, SERIES EDITOR

Anna Karenina in Our Time
Seeing More Wisely

GARY SAUL MORSON

Yale University Press

New Haven and London

Set in Adobe Garamond type by Tseng Information Systems, Inc.
Printed in the United States of America.

Library of Congress Cataloging-in-Publication Data

Morson, Gary Saul, 1948–
"Anna Karenina" in our time : seeing more wisely / Gary Saul Morson.
p. cm. — (Russian literature and thought)
Includes bibliographical references and index.
ISBN 978-0-300-10070-9 (cloth : alk. paper)
1. Tolstoy, Leo, graf, 1828-1910. Anna Karenina. I. Title.
PG3365.A63M67 2007
891.73'3—dc22
2007013706

A catalogue record for this book is available from the British Library.

∞ The paper in this book meets the guidelines for permanence and durability of the
Committee on Production Guidelines for Book Longevity of the
Council on Library Resources.

10   9   8   7   6   5   4   3   2   1

For Alexander Morson and Emily Morson
and in memory of Aron Katsenelinboigen

Remember . . . that the chief work actuating man's whole life is not done by his hands, his feet, or his back, but by his consciousness. Before a man can do anything with his feet or hands, a certain alteration has first to take place in his consciousness. . . . Yet these alterations are always minute and almost imperceptible.

[The painter] Bryullov one day corrected a pupil's study. The pupil, having glanced at the altered drawing, exclaimed: "Why, you only touched it a tiny bit, but it is quite another thing." Bryullov replied: "Art begins where the tiny bit begins."

That saying is strikingly true not only of art but of all life. One may say that true life begins where the tiny bit begins—where what seem to us minute and infinitely small alterations take place. True life is not lived where great external changes take place—where people move about, clash, fight, and slay one another—it is lived only where these tiny, tiny, infinitesimally small changes occur. . . .

Tiny, tiny alterations—but on them depend the most immense and terrible consequences. . . . And boundless results of unimaginable importance may follow from the most minute alterations occurring in the domain of consciousness.

—TOLSTOY, "Why Do Men Stupefy Themselves?" R&E, 80–82

The aspects of things that are most important for us are hidden because of their simplicity and familiarity. (One is unable to notice something—because it is always before one's eyes.) . . . And this means: we fail to be struck by what, once seen, is most striking and most powerful.

—WITTGENSTEIN, *Philosophical Investigations,* paragraph 129

Contents

Acknowledgments

When the idea for this book was new, I benefited from extensive conversations with Jane Morson and with Aron Katsenelinboigen. Aron's ideas continue to inspire me, as do those of Stephen Toulmin, with whom I co-taught two courses, one on *Anna Karenina* and one on Wittgenstein and Bakhtin. Wayne Booth encouraged me and helped refine my ideas.

Over the two and a half decades during which I was thinking about Tolstoy's novel, I accumulated too many intellectual debts to acknowledge. I remember with gratitude dialogues with Elizabeth Cheresh Allen, Carol Avins, Marina Balina, Dan Ben-Amos, Fiona Björling, Jostein Bortnes, Bracht Branham, Frances Padorr Brent, Gary Browning, Elisabeth Calihan, Clare Cavanagh, Hillel Crandus, Freeman Dyson, Paul Edwards, Robert Edwards, Caryl Emerson, Joseph Epstein, Victor Erlich, Donald Fanger, Joseph Frank, Paul Friedrich, Susanne Fusso, Boris Gasparov, Marcia Gealy, George Gibian, Helena Goscilo, Gerald Graff, Thomas Greene, Robert Gundlach, Richard Gustafson, Norman Ingham, Robert Louis Jackson, Peter Jensen, Walter Jost, Aileen Kelly, George Kline, Diane Leonard, Robert Lerner, Daniel Lowenstein, Amy Mandelker, Kathe Marshall, Hugh McLean, Susan McReynolds-Oddo, Priscilla Meyer, Elliott Mossman, Seamas O'Driscoll, Donna Orwin, Clara Claiborne Park, Kathleen Parthé, Thomas Pavel, Roy Pea, Sarah Pratt, Martin Price, Gerald Prince, Thomas Remington, Alfred Rieber, Larissa Rudova, Peter Scotto, Kenneth Seeskin, James Sheridan, Frank Silbajoris, Jurij Striedter, Helen Tartar, Joanne Van Tuyl, Edward Wasiolek, Stevan Weine, Duffield White, Meredith Williams, Michael Williams, and the participants in the NEH Summer Seminars I conducted.

This book was also shaped, in style and content, by the experience of teaching it to many students whose thoughts proved, if proof were needed, that new insights occur to nonprofessionals who read attentively and think fearlessly: Kenley Barrett, Chase Behringer, Kolter Campbell, Wendy Cheng, Andrew Gruen, Belle Kleinberg, Ann Komaromi, Trevor Law, Shawn Anthony Levy, Adam Lurie, Jane Mackie, John Mafi, Dan Marlin, Sarah Kube Mohler, Matthew Morrison, Karthik Sivashanker, David Terry, Ryan Vogt, Cindy Wang, Jennifer Yeung, and many others. Former graduate students also contributed: Carla Arnell, Lindsay Sargeant Berg, Sara Burson, Mary Coffey, Leah Culligan, Michael Denner, Robert Gurley, John Kieselhorst, Michele LaForge, Timothy Langen, Joanne Mulcahy, Trish Suchy, Ruud Teeuwen, Peter Thomas, Justin Weir, James Wolfson, Pat Zody, and more. Nava Cohen, once a student, continues to teach me a lot. Lori Singer Meyer continues to surprise me.

Robert Belknap and William Mills Todd offered wisdom as well as insight, and Thomas Marullo heart as well as mind.

The final draft of this book benefited enormously from the suggestions offered by Frederick Crews, Robin Feuer Miller, and the three anonymous readers for Yale University Press. Andrew Wachtel, as always, read with care and offered important suggestions.

I cannot enumerate my many debts to Kenneth Mischel. For more than thirty-five years, Michael André Bernstein has been my co-conspirator in understanding much more than literature.

Jonathan Brent first proposed my doing this kind of book. Without his guidance, thought, and work, it would not have been written.

Alexander Morson and Emily Morson brought magic.

Katharine Porter must know the impossibility of stating what I owe to her.

References and Abbreviations

Citations from Russian works have occasionally been modified for accuracy.

Tolstoy

When page numbers alone are given, the reference is to Leo Tolstoy, *Anna Karenina,* the Garnett translation revised by Leonard J. Kent and Nina Berberova (New York: Modern Library, 1965).

CBY = *Childhood, Boyhood, and Youth,* trans. Alexandra and Sverre Lyngstad (New York: Washington Square Press, 1968).

D = "Drafts for an Introduction to *War and Peace,*" in the Norton Critical Edition of *War and Peace,* ed. George Gibian (New York: Norton, 1966), 1362–65.

GSW = *Great Short Works of Leo Tolstoy,* trans. Louise and Aylmer Maude (New York: Harper and Row, 1967).

Jub = *Polnoe sobranie sochinenii* [Complete works] in ninety volumes, ed. V. G. Chertkov et al. (Moscow: Khudozhestvennaia literatura, 1929–58).

P&V = The translation of *Anna Karenina* by Richard Pevear and Larissa Volokhonsky (New York: Viking, 2000).

R&E = "Why Do Men Stupefy Themselves?" in Leo Tolstoy, *Recollections and Essays,* trans. Aylmer Maude (London: Oxford University Press, 1937; reprinted 1961), 68–89.

W&P = *War and Peace,* trans. Ann Dunnigan (New York: Signet, 1968).

WIA? = *What Is Art?* trans. Aylmer Maude (New York: Bobbs-Merrill, 1980).

Dostoevsky

AWD = *A Writer's Diary,* vol. 2, 1877–1881, trans. Kenneth Lantz (Evanston: Northwestern University Press, 1994).

BK = *The Brothers Karamazov,* trans. Constance Garnett (New York: Modern Library, 1996).

C&P = *Crime and Punishment,* trans. Constance Garnett (New York: Modern Library, 1994).

NFU = Fyodor Dostoevsky, *"Notes from Underground" and "The Grand Inquisitor,"* ed. Ralph Matlaw (New York: Dutton, 1960).

Other Abbreviations

AoC = Albert R. Jonsen and Stephen E. Toulmin, *The Abuse of Casuistry: A History of Moral Reasoning* (Berkeley: University of California Press, 1988).

BoG = Gary Saul Morson, *The Boundaries of Genre: Dostoevsky's "Diary of a Writer" and the Traditions of Literary Utopia* (Austin: University of Texas Press, 1981).

Cos = Stephen Toulmin, *Cosmopolis: The Hidden Agenda of Modernity* (New York: Free Press, 1990).

DI = Mikhail Bakhtin, "Discourse in the Novel," in *The Dialogic Imagination: Four Essays by M. M. Bakhtin,* ed. Michael Holquist, trans. Caryl Emerson and Michael Holquist (Austin: University of Texas Press, 1981), 259–422.

EoL = *Merriam-Webster's Encyclopedia of Literature* (Springfield, Mass.: Merriam-Webster, 1995).

GT = *The Great Thoughts,* ed. George Seldes and David Laskin (New York: Ballantine, 1996).

G&P = *"Anna Karenina" on Page and Screen* (Studies in Slavic Cultures II), ed. Helena Goscilo and Petre Petrov (Pittsburgh: Department of Slavic Languages of the University of Pittsburgh, 2001).

ISG = *In the Shade of the Giant: Essays on Tolstoy,* ed. Hugh McLean (Berkeley: University of California Press, 1989).

K&M = *Approaches to Teaching Tolstoy's "Anna Karenina",* ed. Liza Knapp and Amy Mandelker (New York: Modern Language Association, 2003).

MBCP = Gary Saul Morson and Caryl Emerson, *Mikhail Bakhtin: Creation of a Prosaics* (Stanford: Stanford University Press, 1990).

MP = *Modern Poetry,* 2d ed., ed. Maynard Mack, Leonard Dean, and William Frost (Englewood Cliffs: Prentice-Hall, 1965).

N = the Norton Critical Edition of *Anna Karenina,* ed. George Gibian (New York: Norton, 1970).

N&F = Gary Saul Morson, *Narrative and Freedom: The Shadows of Time* (New Haven: Yale University Press, 1994).

PDP = Mikhail Bakhtin, *Problems of Dostoevsky's Poetics,* ed. Caryl Emerson (Minneapolis: University of Minnesota Press, 1984).

RtR = Stephen Toulmin, *Return to Reason* (Cambridge: Harvard University Press, 2001).

TCH = *Tolstoy: The Critical Heritage,* ed. A. V. Knowles (London: Routledge, 1978).

TSJ8 = *Tolstoy Studies Journal,* vol. 8 (1995–96), special issue on *Anna Karenina.*

WV = Allan Janik and Stephen Toulmin, *Wittgenstein's Vienna* (New York: Simon & Schuster, 1973).

Other References

Alexandrov, Vladimir E., *Limits to Interpretation: The Meanings of "Anna Karenina"* (Madison: University of Wisconsin Press, 2004).

Aristotle, *The Basic Works of Aristotle,* ed. Richard McKeon (New York: Random House, 1941).

Auden, Wystan Hugh, "Musée des Beaux Arts," in *Modern Poetry,* 2d ed., ed. Maynard Mack, Leonard Dean, and William Frost (Englewood Cliffs: Prentice-Hall, 1965), 198.

Babaev, E. G., *Lev Tolstoi i russkaia zhurnalistika ego epokhi* [Lev Tolstoy and Russian journalism of his epoch] (Moscow: Izdatel'svto Moskovskogo universiteta, 1978), cited in Orwin, *Tolstoy's Art and Thought,* 179, 244n26.

Bartlett, John, *Familiar Quotations: A Collection of Passages, Phrases and Proverbs Traced to Their Sources in Ancient and Modern Literature,* 15th ed., ed. Emily Morison Beck (Boston: Little, Brown, 1980).

Bayley, John, *Tolstoy and the Novel* (New York: Viking, 1966).

Bernstein, Michael André, *Foregone Conclusions: Against Apocalyptic History* (Berkeley: University of California Press, 1994).

Blake, William, "The Marriage of Heaven and Hell," in *English Romantic Poetry,* vol. 1, ed. Harold Bloom (New York: Anchor, 1963), 55–70.

Bloom, Allan, *Love and Friendship* (New York: Simon & Schuster, 1993).

Bloom, Harold, "Introduction," in *Leo Tolstoy's "Anna Karenina"*, ed. Harold Bloom (New York: Chelsea House, 1987), 1–6.

Blumberg, Edwina Jannie, "Tolstoy and the English Novel: A Note on *Middlemarch*," in *Slavic Review*, vol. 30, no. 3 (September 1971), 561–69.

Brewer's Famous Quotations, ed. Nigel Rees (London: Weidenfeld & Nicolson, 2006).

Browning, Gary L., "The Death of Anna Karenina: Anna's Share of the Blame," in *Slavic and East European Journal*, vol. 30, no. 3 (1986), 327–39.

Buckler, Julie A., "Reading Anna: Opera, Tragedy, Melodrama, Farce," in K&M, 131–36.

Clausewitz, Carl von, *On War*, ed. and trans. Michael Howard and Peter Paret (Princeton: Princeton University Press, 1984).

Edmundson, Helen, *"Anna Karenina" Adapted from Tolstoy* (London: Nick Hern Books, 1994).

Eikhenbaum, Boris, "The Puzzle of the Epigraph, N. Schopenhauer," in N, 815–21.

Eliot, George, *Middlemarch* (New York: Modern Library, 1984).

Ellis, John M., *The Theory of Literary Criticism: A Logical Analysis* (Berkeley: University of California Press, 1974).

Emerson, Caryl, "Prosaics in *Anna Karenina*, Pro and Con," in TSJ8, 150–76.

Evdokimova, Svetlana, "The Wedding Bell, the Death Knell, and Philosophy's Spell: Tolstoy's Sense of an Ending" in K&M, 137–43.

Feuer, Kathryn B., "Stiva," in *Russian Literature and Its American Critics*, ed. Kenneth N. Brostrom (Ann Arbor: University of Michigan Department of Slavic Languages, 1984), 347–56.

Gershenzon, Mikhail, "Creative Self-Consciousness," in *Signposts: A Collection of Articles on the Russian Intelligentsia*, trans. and ed. Marshall S. Shatz and Judith E. Zimmerman (Irvine: Schlacks, 1986), 51–69.

Goscilo, Helena, "Motif-Mesh as Matrix: Body, Sexuality, Adultery, and the Woman Question," in K&M, 83–89.

Gromeka, M. S., "The Epigraph and the Meaning of the Novel," in N, 801.

Grossman, Joan Delaney, "'Words, Idle Words': Discourse and Communication in *Anna Karenina*," in ISG, 115–29.

Gustafson, Richard F., *Leo Tolstoy, Resident and Stranger: A Study in Fiction and Theology* (Princeton: Princeton University Press, 1986).

Gutkin, Irina, "The Dichotomy Between Flesh and Spirit: Plato's *Symposium* in *Anna Karenina*," in ISG, 84–99.

Halévy, Elie, *The Growth of Philosophic Radicalism,* trans. Mary Morris (Boston: Beacon Press, 1955).

Hardy, Barbara, "Form and Freedom: Tolstoy's *Anna Karenina,*" in N, 877–99.

Holland, Kate, "The Opening of *Anna Karenina,*" in K&M, 144–49.

Holquist, Michael, "The Supernatural as Social Force in *Anna Karenina,*" in *The Supernatural in Slavic and Baltic Literature: Essays in Honor of Victor Terras,* ed. Amy Mandelker and Roberta Reeder (Columbus: Slavica, 1988), 176–90.

Hopkins, Gerard Manley, "Pied Beauty," in *Victorian Poetry: Clough to Kipling,* ed. Arthur J. Carr (New York: Holt, Rinehart and Winston, 1966), 240–41.

Howells, William Dean, "Editor's Study," in *Harper's Magazine* (1886), in TCH, 348–49.

Jackson, Robert Louis, "The Night Journey: Anna Karenina's Return to Saint Petersburg," in K&M, 150–60.

Jacobs, Jane, *The Death and Life of Great American Cities* (New York: Random House, 1992; originally published 1961).

Jahn, Gary, "The Image of the Railroad in *Anna Karenina,*" in *Slavic and East European Journal,* vol. 25, no. 2 (1981), 1–10.

Jones, Malcolm, "Problems of Communication in *Anna Karenina,*" in *New Essays on Tolstoy,* ed. Malcolm Jones (Cambridge, England: Cambridge University Press, 1978), 85–108.

Karpushina, Olga, "The Idea of the Family in Tolstoy's *Anna Karenina:* The Moral Hierarchy of Families," in G&P, 63–92.

Kashuba, Mary Helen, and Manucher Dareshuri, "Agrarian Issues in *Anna Karenina* as a 'Mirror of the Russian Revolution,'" in K&M, 90–94.

Kovarsky, Gina, "The Moral Education of the Reader," in K&M, 166–72.

Kropotkin, Peter, "'Superhuman Justice' or 'Society'?" in TCH, 366–70.

Lanoux, Andrea, "*Anna Karenina* through Film," in K&M, 180–86.

Lönnqvist, Barbara, "*Anna Karenina,*" in *The Cambridge Companion to Tolstoy,* ed. Donna Tussing Orwin (Cambridge, England: Cambridge University Press, 2002), 80–95.

Makoreeva, Irina, "Cinematic Adaptations of *Anna Karenina,*" in G&P, 111–34.

Mandelker, Amy, *Framing Anna Karenina: Tolstoy, the Woman Question, and the Victorian Novel* (Columbus: Ohio State University Press, 1993).

Merezhkovsky, D. S., "Tolstoy's Physical Descriptions," in N, 802–10.

Montaigne, Michel de, *The Complete Essays of Montaigne,* trans. Donald M. Frame (Stanford: Stanford University Press, 1965).

Murav, Harriet, "Law as Limit and Limits of the Law in *Anna Karenina,*" in K&M, 60–82.

Orwin, Donna Tussing, "Tolstoy's Antiphilosophical Philosophy in *Anna Karenina,*" in K&M, 95–103.

———, *Tolstoy's Art and Thought, 1847–1880* (Princeton: Princeton University Press, 1993).

Price, Martin, *Forms of Life: Character and Moral Imagination in the Novel* (New Haven: Yale University Press, 1983).

Rabinowitz, Peter J., *Before Reading: Narrative Conventions and the Politics of Interpretation* (Columbus: Ohio State University Press, 1998).

Rougemont, Denis de, *Love in the Western World,* rev. ed., trans. Montgomery Belgion (New York: Harper and Row, 1974).

Schultze, Sydney, *The Structure of "Anna Karenina"* (Ann Arbor: Arids, 1982).

Scott, James C., *Seeing Like a State: How Certain Schemes to Improve the Human Condition Have Failed* (New Haven: Yale University Press, 1998).

Shklovsky, Victor, "Art as Technique," in *Russian Formalist Criticism: Four Essays,* ed. Lee T. Lemon and Marion J. Reis (Lincoln: University of Nebraska Press, 1965), 3–24.

———, *Lev Tolstoy* (Moscow: Progress, 1978).

Silbajoris, Rimvydas, *Tolstoy's Aesthetics and His Art* (Columbus: Slavica, 1991).

Sloane, David A., "Anna Reading and Women Reading in Russian Literature," in K&M, 124–30.

Solzhenitsyn, Aleksandr I., *The Gulag Archipelago, 1918–1956: An Experiment in Literary Investigation,* vol. 3, trans. Harry Willetts (New York: Harper & Row, 1978).

Speirs, Logan, *Tolstoy and Chekhov* (Cambridge, England: Cambridge University Press, 1971).

Stankevich, A. V., "Stankevich on Anna, Vronsky and Karenin," TCH, 293–304.

Starr, G. A., *Defoe and Casuistry* (Princeton: Princeton University Press, 1971).

Tkachov, Peter, "Tkachov Attacks Tolstoy's Aristocratism" (1875), in TCH, 250–61.

Todd, William M., III, "Anna on the Installment Plan: Teaching *Anna Karenina* through the History of Its Serial Publication," in K&M, 53–69.

Trollope, Anthony, *Can You Forgive Her?* 2 vols. (Oxford: Oxford University Press, 1973).

Wachtel, Andrew, "Death and Resurrection in *Anna Karenina,*" in ISG, 100–114.

Wasiolek, Edward, *Tolstoy's Major Fiction* (Chicago: University of Chicago Press, 1978).

Weir, Justin, "Anna Incommunicada: Language and Consciousness in *Anna Karenina,*" in TSJ8, 99–111.

Wittgenstein, Ludwig, *Philosophical Investigations,* 3d ed., trans. G. E. M. Anscombe (New York: Macmillan, 1968).

———, *Tractatus Logico-Philosophicus,* trans. D. F. Pears and B. F. McGuiness (London: Routledge and Kegan Paul, 1961).

The Yale Book of Quotations, ed. Fred. R. Shapiro (New Haven: Yale University Press, 2006).

My Earlier Work

The present study draws on, and several of the critical works above refer to, work I have published on *Anna Karenina* over the past two and a half decades.

Articles include:

"Tolstoy's Absolute Language," in *Critical Inquiry,* vol. 7, no. 4 (Summer 1981), 667–87.

"Prosaics: An Approach to the Humanities," in *American Scholar* (Autumn 1988), 515–28.

"Prosaics and *Anna Karenina,*" in *Tolstoy Studies Journal,* vol. 1 (1988), 1–12.

"Prosaics, Criticism, and Ethics," in *Formations,* vol. 5, no. 2 (Summer–Fall 1989), 77–95.

"The Potentials and Hazards of Prosaics," in *Tolstoy Studies Journal,* vol. 2 (1989), 15–40.

"The Tolstoy Questions," in *Tolstoy Studies Journal,* vol. 4 (1991), 115–41.

"Anna Karenina's Omens," in *Freedom and Responsibility in Russian Literature,* ed. Gary Saul Morson and Elizabeth Allen (Evanston: Northwestern University Press and Yale Center for International and Area Studies, 1995), 134–52, 288–89.

"The Svijazhsky Enigma: Tolstoy and Brotherhood," in *Lev Tolstoy and the Concept of Brotherhood,* ed. Andrew Donskov and John Woodsworth (New York: Legas, 1996), 38–50.

"What Is Agriculture?" in *Russian Literature,* vol. 40 (1996), 481–90.

"Poetic Justice, False Listening, and Falling in Love, Or, Why Anna Refuses a Divorce," in *Tolstoy Studies Journal,* vol. 8 (1995–96; appeared 1997), 177–97; part of a "Critical Dialogue" on my reading of *Anna Karenina.*

"Tolstoy," in *The New Encyclopedia Britannica, Macropedia: Knowledge in Depth,* 15th ed., 1997, vol. 28, 687–91.

"Work and the Authentic Life in Tolstoy," in *Tolstoy Studies Journal,* vol. 9 (1997), 36–48.

"Tolstoi, Count Leo Nikolaevich," in *Routledge Encyclopedia of Philosophy,* ed. Edward Craig (London: Routledge, 1998), 435–40.

"Brooding Stiva: The Masterpiece Theatre *Anna Karenina,*" in *Tolstoy Studies Journal,* vol. 13 (2001), 49–58.

"The Daily Miracle: Teaching the Ideas of *Anna Karenina,*" in K&M, 27–32.

"Signs of Design" (on the Edmundson adaptation of Anna Karenina, forthcoming in *Tolstoy Studies Journal*).

There are also discussions of *Anna Karenina* in my earlier books:

Hidden in Plain View: Narrative and Creative Potentials in "War and Peace" (Stanford: Stanford University Press, 1987).

Mikhail Bakhtin: Creation of a Prosaics, co-authored with Caryl Emerson (Stanford: Stanford University Press, 1990).

Narrative and Freedom: The Shadows of Time (New Haven: Yale University Press, 1994).

Introduction

"Anna Karenina" in Our Time: Seeing More Wisely is the first of a series of studies demonstrating the relevance of Russian classics to our lives today. It envisages an audience of people interested in the issues Tolstoy's novel considers, from the nature of love and self-deception to the ways in which successful reforms must be implemented. This book addresses educated laypeople, students who want to make the book relevant to their lives, scholars of Russian literature, and specialists in other fields—in short, anyone interested in Tolstoy's wisdom. Several contemporary thinkers are already rediscovering Tolstoy. If this book achieves its goal, *Anna Karenina* will become a central part of current discussion.

I do not intend to situate Tolstoy's novel in its times. That kind of study can be important for understanding nineteenth-century Russian culture, but the present volume has been written to make the novel speak to our concerns today. When Tolstoy's book differs from the predominant beliefs of our time, I do not judge it morally or intellectually deficient. Rather, I ask whether Tolstoy might be more insightful than we.

Most of all, I avoid interpretations that think away the novel's concerns: for example, "If only Russian divorce laws had been different, Anna would have survived and lived happily ever after." Of course, the social conditions of her time affect Anna's life, but its central issues still pertain to our own time, sometimes even more strongly than to Tolstoy's.

To read the book as a mere historical document would be to muffle it. I treat it instead as a participant in a dialogue now taking shape.

There are two ways in which a book can speak to another age. Either its ideas may be especially relevant to that age or they may be relevant to any age. *Anna Karenina* speaks to us in both ways. Questions like "What accounts for the success or failure of different schemes to modernize a country?" press more strongly now than when the book was published. Other questions, such as the nature of honesty, ethical action, and a meaningful life will never cease to interest people.

I have tried to make this study readable for non-specialists. It would help

1

to have read *Anna Karenina* at some time, but no other special knowledge is needed. Scholarly apparatus is deliberately kept to a minimum and wherever possible comments on the scholarship are confined to the notes and refer to works available in English. In the text and notes, I have kept the use of Russian to a minimum. I aimed to make this book as brief as its purpose allows.

Readers the world over have typically regarded Tolstoy as the supreme realist. They have commonly expressed some variation on the thought that, if life could write directly, it would write like Tolstoy. Tolstoy's ideas shaped the way he wrote. The fact that *Anna Karenina* seems so true to human experience suggests that he must have gotten something right. His ideas are worth reconsidering so that, as Tolstoy intended, we learn to see the world, and our own lives, more wisely.

I know from reactions to my earlier work on Tolstoy that it is easy to misunderstand my intentions. I tend to write in a kind of novelistic free indirect discourse that enters the author's mind as I understand it, and so what I mean to be paraphrases of Tolstoy's ideas, with which I may or may not agree, can easily appear to be my own.

To be sure, I am broadly sympathetic to Tolstoy's viewpoint, but I hardly agree with him about everything. I do not concur that Shakespeare is not even a mediocre writer or that the work of historians is useless. I am neither a pacifist, a vegetarian, an anarchist, nor a defender of the Russian aristocracy. Even where my views overlap with Tolstoy's, they rarely coincide. Tolstoy tends to overstate, and he expresses even his hostility to melodrama melodramatically. For example, I agree that people tend to focus on dramatic and noticeable events when ordinary ones may be much more important than we allow. But I cannot accept, as Tolstoy asserts, that *only* ordinary events matter. Again, Tolstoy was right to question the role often assigned to history's "great men" and critical events; but surely he went much too far in asserting that great men and critical events have no effect at all. And although Tolstoy has a point in suggesting (as I argue he does in *Anna Karenina*) that negligence and inaction, rather than malice, cause much evil, he exaggerates in attributing *most* evil to negligence.

In paraphrasing Tolstoy's ideas, I try to present the strongest case for them so that readers can understand his way of thinking, particularly when it seems counterintuitive. I try to explicate in the spirit of the author. In my classes, I impersonate the author, explicating his ideas in the author's tone of voice and ethos. When I draw illustrations from our own culture, I do so in the way I imagine Tolstoy would, and express the implications of his views. I do so in order to create the sense of what it is to think like Tolstoy and see the world through his eyes. My purpose is not to get my listeners to agree with those views, which I often do not share myself, but to enable them to ask, when a difficult question arises, what a Tolstoyan response might be. Consciousness becomes richer when it can stage dialogues with great minds.

But I ask my readers not to assume that I therefore want to argue for whatever Tolstoy does. I want to make those ideas live, not as a set of dogmas, but as a vision worth considering and a philosophy worth arguing with. In this way, we can both understand and enrich our own perspective. My judgment of the novel's heroine, as well as its ideas, differs from his. I am less critical of Anna than I believe Tolstoy is. To be sure, if I had no sympathy with Tolstoy's perspective, I would probably not have written this book. But I do not recommend Tolstoy's views wholesale. Rather, I believe that Tolstoy's ideas, or some version of them, deserve more attention and can speak to us today.

At one point in this study, I present a debate between Tolstoy's and Dostoevsky's opinions on an ethical problem very much with us today. I have written as much about Dostoevsky as about Tolstoy, and am broadly sympathetic to some of his key ideas as well. The difference between the two authors on a lasting question allows for an illuminating dialogue. I hope I have presented each side so that one can see its force. I am not sure which is right or what a still more powerful third perspective would be. Even when I have no Dostoevsky to oppose to Tolstoy, I hope readers will, in examining Tolstoy's views, discover or construct a viable opponent. I want to present Tolstoy's ideas strongly, but I often leave it to the reader to construct counterarguments or add qualifications. That is where dialogue begins.

A colleague and friend, a specialist in medieval history, has expressed disagreement with my style of teaching, which, like the present study, endeavors to make great works of literature speak to us today. I avidly read studies that set literature in its period or use the period to illuminate the literature, and my admiration for Joseph Frank's multivolume biography of Dostoevsky, which does both and more, is boundless. But I prefer to use the works to create a dialogue with the present.

My friend contends that the proper goal of a scholar is to forget the present and immerse oneself in the culture of the time, not to take its works and treat them anachronistically as if they had just been written. I think this argument is a powerful one.

My answer is that this goal is always a good one but not the only good one. For one thing, it overlooks the difference between literary and nonliterary works. In an earlier book, I wrote that one way to define literature was by its "semiotic nature," by which I meant the appropriate process of arriving at its meanings: "to class a text as literary in this sense is to say that its semiotic interest is not limited for readers to its original context of communication and that the determination of its meaning is not equivalent to the reconstruction of the circumstances, causes, and effects of the original exchange between speaker and listener."[1] Thus, if one should read Gibbon's *Decline and Fall of the Roman Empire* to learn about Roman history, one would be reading it as a nonliterary document (and would have chosen a rather outdated source). But Gibbon's work survives the outdating of its scholarship because it can be read as a model of prose, of thought, or of narrative voice: that is, it can be read as literature.

Works of literature are characteristically written or read as both situated in and transcending their time. Great poets and novelists intend their works to be read long after the arguments of the day have ceased to be compelling. One does not have to be interested in Russian debates of the early 1860s to care about Turgenev's *Fathers and Children,* and readers who have little interest in Japanese or Arabian history read *The Tale of Genji* and *The Thousand and One Nights.* If writers intend their literary works to outlive the moment, then reading these works as mere documents of their time may be to misread even their original intention. Some documents were composed as more than mere documents, to be not just evidentiary but also exemplary. In short, I think that both approaches, that of my colleague and my own, have a place. Of course, they may also be combined.

The Russian literary theorist Mikhail Bakhtin distinguished three broad types of interpretation of literary works. To begin with, one may "enclose" the work in its time. Such a process may be a good first step, but if that is all one does, one destroys what makes the work great by misidentifying its nature. "'Enclosure within the epoch' . . . makes it impossible to understand the work's future life in subsequent centuries; this life appears as a kind of paradox" (MBCP, 286). A second type of interpretation, with which Bakhtin has little patience, is what he calls "modernization and distortion." One simply reads the work in terms of current interests and entirely loses its otherness. Enclosure within the epoch sees the author at the time of the work's creation but ignores later readers. "Modernization and distortion" does the opposite.

Bakhtin's preferred way of reading, which he calls "creative understanding," allows author and reader, the time of composition and the time of comprehension, to interact. One creates a dialogue by means of which their two voices produce something unforeseen. One lets Shakespeare, Goethe, or Tolstoy challenge us, and so, comprehending that challenge, struggles with it and offers tentative replies. The reason that such a dialogue is rewarding, or even possible, with great works is that they contain "potentials" for future dialogue. The author senses these potentials as a source of richness but he cannot specify their precise meanings because to do so would require knowing the context of future readers.

Great works therefore accumulate meanings—they live a "posthumous life"—for two reasons. They are "modernized and distorted" and have meanings foisted upon them; and their potentials are activated in a dialogue of creative understanding. Of course, it may be difficult to distinguish the two, especially with readings of one's own time.

Nevertheless, the very nature of great works is that they "outgrow what they were in the epoch of their creation. We can say that neither Shakespeare himself nor his contemporaries knew that 'great Shakespeare' whom we know now. There is no possibility of squeezing our Shakespeare into the Elizabethan epoch" (MBCP, 287), not just because modernizing distortions have added gratuitous encrustations but also because potentials really in Shakespeare's work have been activated. Bakhtin discovers wisdom in the old schoolboy joke that the ancient Greeks did not know the most important thing about themselves: they were *ancient* Greeks. In his notes, Bakhtin writes cryptically: "When Shakespeare became *Shakespeare*. Dostoevsky has still not become Dostoevsky, he is still becoming him" (MBCP, 287).

I hope to contribute to "Tolstoy becoming Tolstoy" by creating a dialogue between his ideas and some of our own. In that spirit, I draw "dotted lines" (to use Bakhtin's phrase) from his ideas to our own time. I do so not to endorse them but to allow them to enter into contemporary conversation. I mean to open debate, not to close it. My hope is that this dialogue with Tolstoy will yield new insights present neither to him nor to us. Out of genuine dialogue comes the new and surprising.

Even some types of intellectual history, which do not deal with literary works, create such dialogue. I have often had the occasion to look up a concept in both *The Encyclopedia of Philosophy* and *The Dictionary of the History of Ideas.* In the former, the main concern is typically: What position here is most likely to be correct? Historical alternatives are presented in logical order so as to show the terms of the debate, but not to show the chronological development of thought. By contrast, the latter work usually ignores the question of truth and shows how ideas developed from earlier ideas. In my view, these approaches complement each other and, taken together, allow one to reach a deeper understanding than with either by itself.

There exists a third approach, which, so far as I know, has no agreed-upon name. It combines historical and philosophical concerns, and so I like to think of it as "historiosophy." The historiosopher, for instance, may identify a time when Western thought took a mistaken turn. He explores why that turn would have seemed appealing, in terms of argument, intellectual currents, and so-cial needs of the time, and why it has continued to remain appealing even in changed conditions. He shows that the implications of this change have now led to an impasse and that it is time to explore the turn not taken. Such is the argument often constructed by Isaiah Berlin and Stephen Toulmin.

History needs to immerse itself in the perspective of the past if it is to be historical at all. But we tend to be interested in the past for a reason: Who are we and how did we get here? Did we make a mistake and could we correct it, or at least not repeat it? The present study is inspired by historiosophy and seeks "creative understanding."

Tolstoy and the Twenty-first Century

Tolstoy and the Twenty-first Century

Tolstoy Today

> Don't think, but look!
> —WITTGENSTEIN (*Philosophical Investigations,* paragraph 66)

Anna Karenina and *War and Peace* are typically considered to be among the finest, if not the very finest, novels ever written and Tolstoy ranks among the world's greatest authors. Students I teach express the vague but widely held belief that if they have read *War and Peace* they are educated. Perhaps no other literary work commands such respect.

Tolstoy has struck writers and readers for the unsurpassed realism of his two great novels. Arnold spoke for many when he declared that *Anna Karenina* is not so much a work of art as a piece of life, and Babel imagined that if the world could express itself directly, it would write like Tolstoy. We constantly read: consider the range of human experience he describes supremely well. Compared to Tolstoy, even Homer, Cervantes, George Eliot, and Dostoevsky seem like mere specialists in a few closely related aspects of life. Tolstoy equals each in his or her own preferred topics and alternates effortlessly among them. By common consent, he describes battle as no one from Homer to Stendhal ever has. Tolstoy once declared that, without false modesty, he could say that *War and Peace* resembles the *Iliad,* and its panorama of life and emotions exceeds even that book's epic sweep. With his supreme realism, Tolstoy makes all earlier descriptions seem as if they have been reproduced from the same template.

Of course, Tolstoy could also describe the usual subject matter of novels, including domestic life, romance, courtship, and adultery, with supreme mastery. We find moments of lyric ecstasy and tragic despair. The sensation of a young woman at her first ball, of a man lying in wait at a wolf hunt, or of guests at a wedding compete with descriptions of peasant life and the thrill of intellectual discussion. No one, except perhaps Dostoevsky, has ever made ideas so palpable.

Still more remarkable, Tolstoy could make ordinary people and everyday life interesting. Not just the heroic Prince Andrei, but also Nikolai Rostov, whom the author accurately describes as "mediocre," compels attention. Tolstoy makes us care when nothing special happens, as in scenes where children play and mothers watch over them. He fascinates with lengthy descriptions of events that contribute virtually nothing to the plot. Among his most memorable passages are the wolf hunt in *War and Peace* and the mowing scene in *Anna Karenina,* which could be omitted with no discernible effect on the plot and yet strike us as unique in world literature.

Tolstoy not only commands a wider range than other great writers, but also does what none of them ever could. Only twice in world literature has the experience of Christian love and a conversion to loving one's enemies been made psychologically convincing: once in *War and Peace* and a second time in *Anna Karenina.* Dostoevsky, a serious Christian and Tolstoy's only real rival as literature's best psychologist, tried again and again to accomplish this feat and never succeeded, as he well knew.

As Dostoevsky specializes in the unconscious, Tolstoy shows us the overlooked complexities of consciousness. Between two thoughts that apparently follow immediately one upon the other, Tolstoy sees several steps. He notices a series of almost instantaneous mistaken interpretations that we reject too fast to remember. He knows the tiniest moments of his characters' conscious processes better than the characters themselves ever could. He describes what takes place at the periphery of their attention, which, by definition, never comes into sufficient focus for conscious recollection. Tolstoy gives new meaning to authorial omniscience because, in a comparison often made, his resembles a god's.

Tolstoy cared most about what he called the innumerable "tiny alterations" of consciousness, where decisions we mistakenly attribute to a few critical moments are made. The need to include so many tiny alterations accounts in part for the great length of his works. Where others saw relative simplicity, he saw immense complexity. The closer we look at consciousness, and the smaller the interval we choose to examine, the less straightforward it seems and the more alternative outcomes we discern. Not surprisingly, Tolstoy wrote with withering sarcasm of all theories that view human experience, whether individual or social, as governed by relatively simple laws.

Tolstoy's contemporaries noted that he alone appreciated the way the body shapes the mind. In Tolstoy, thoughts and feelings follow not only from earlier ones and from our reaction to internal and external events, but also from the postures of the body. As one critic of his time observed, everyone knows that if one feels like praying one will assume a kneeling position, but Count Tolstoy understands that if by some chance one should find oneself in a kneeling position, one may very well feel like praying. The body has a mind of its own. It does not merely reflect our intentions and emotions but also manifests its own internal dynamic, no less than does the mind. It is a mistake to assume that each gesture derives from some mental process. Reading Tolstoy, we see that, but for our body's activity, our feelings and thoughts would be quite different.

In Tolstoy, and perhaps in Tolstoy alone, we find the author describing bodily actions that may mean absolutely nothing. In *War and Peace,* Pierre sees that his dying father, incapacitated by stroke and unable to speak, is looking straight at him. He and everyone else present wonder what that ineffable look could signify. Tolstoy comments: "When Pierre approached, the Count looked directly at him but with a gaze the intent and significance of which no man could have fathomed. Either it meant absolutely nothing more than that having eyes one must look somewhere, or it was charged with meaning" (W&P, 118).

In Tolstoy, both possibilities—significance and total insignificance—are always possible. Unlike other great novels, his do not allow us to assume that if an event is described it must mean something. He wants us to see that life is not like that and so he makes his novels not like that. Not everything in life has a "sufficient reason"; sometimes things happen just "for some reason," a favorite phrase of Tolstoy's. Between "sufficient reason" and "for some reason" lies a universe of difference. Others have thought that life was chancy, but writers from Aristotle on assumed that successful art has to exclude what does not fit the design of the work even if that exclusion makes art unlike life.

If an event happens in Dickens, we know it must lead to something or it would not be there, but in Tolstoy, as in life, events sometimes lead nowhere. With unparalleled power, Tolstoy argues that sheer contingency exists. He finds ways to make the unfitting fit our experience of life.

If one surveys the European novel, one may reflect that people do not seem to work very much. Who ever works in a Jane Austen novel? Some novelists describe work as hell. Only rarely does it define a life. *Adam Bede* impresses because George Eliot describes carpentry as creativity as well as drudgery. But only Tolstoy, so far as I know, gives us anything like the mowing scene in *Anna Karenina,* where we get, step by tiny step, the strain and pleasure, the merged mental and physical effort, the self-consciousness and loss of self, of a difficult job we are in the process of learning. Tolstoy understood what we have come to call "flow."

To many, the natural response to Tolstoy has been to gape with wonder. It was long thought that somehow Tolstoy's purely instinctive and natural gifts allowed him to describe the rhythms of life without thought or art. In the West, the myth of Russians as some sort of natural men more in touch with unrefined experience contributed to the idea that Tolstoy's unsurpassed realism happened without design. As a result, critics imagined there was no intention, no artistry, no meaning in Tolstoy beyond that of direct experience of life, and so he had nothing to teach us. We must appreciate his work, but can offer nothing by way of explication, because there is nothing to explicate. When I wrote my book on *War and Peace* (1987), I discovered shelves of studies explicating Dostoevsky's works and thoughts, but, apart from discussions of his life and works as a whole, almost no books in English about Tolstoy's fiction. The most notable exception, Isaiah Berlin's essay "The Hedgehog and the Fox," stood almost alone for its insight into Tolstoy's key concerns.

Nothing could be further from the truth than the idea that Tolstoy wrote without thought and without artistic devices. If one reads the stories written before the two great novels, one sees him experimenting with devices that cannot be missed, such as narration in the second person or by a horse. By the time he wrote *War and Peace* and *Anna Karenina,* Tolstoy had so internalized those devices that he could deploy them with a subtlety that concealed them. Many readers do not even notice the passages in *Anna Karenina* narrated from the perspective of Levin's dog Laska. These passages certainly do not feel artificial, as does Tolstoy's earlier story with an equine narrator. In the two great novels, he deployed devices so as to make narration appear totally without artifice and his world seem perfectly natural. How did he do so?

However strange it may sound, I think he accomplished this feat by close observation and philosophical reflection. If one really understands human experience, one can reproduce it such that devices used to do so will disappear. That was Tolstoy's credo and the belief of the artist he describes in *Anna Karenina.* One must first see what *is* there, not what convention, received opinion, or the histories of psychology, art, or philosophy tell us should be there. Subtract what everyone "knows," then look. The surprising appearance of previously unnoticed phenomena, the result of such unclouded looking, should lead one to wonder what the world must really be like. Such wonder begets Tolstoy's philosophy, which in turn shapes his writing.

By such looking, Tolstoy learned that the world differed radically from all usual accounts. His understanding of time shaped his plots and his descriptions of the stream of consciousness. As he watched social reforms fail or succeed, he reflected on the reasons, both in his novels and outside them. The fact that his novels have seemed so real—not just realistic—ought to suggest that his ideas were, in large measure, true. For if they had been false, his novels would have seemed so as well.

In his day, Tolstoy was known as a *nyetovshchik*—someone who says *nyet* (no) to all received ideas. Maintaining apparently perverse opinions, he was what Sergey Ivanovich in *Anna Karenina* calls the work's autobiographical hero, Konstantin Levin, a "paradoxicalist." Tolstoy questioned the fundamental premises of Western thought since the seventeenth century, premises that in his time appeared so obviously true that doubting them seemed like believing in a flat earth. The beliefs Tolstoy questioned remain with us today. Indeed, some predominate even more in our time than in his.

At the beginning of the twenty-first century, some thinkers have found our dominant paradigms wanting. We have, after all, just lived through the bloodiest century in human history. Perhaps we got something wrong?

Those who have felt that current received truths might not be true after all have sometimes seen in Tolstoy the greatest exponent of ideas that have been alive for centuries. This tradition, or countertradition, includes thinkers as diverse as Alexis de Tocqueville, Edmund Burke, Carl von Clausewitz, Jane Jacobs, Sir Isaiah Berlin, Ludwig Wittgenstein, Stephen Toulmin, Stephen Jay Gould, and Freeman Dyson. In a sense, it also includes the implicit wisdom of a genre, the realist novel. The last five thinkers I have listed explicitly cite Tolstoy as an influence. He was, indeed, Wittgenstein's favorite author. Because Tolstoy not only questioned the dominant view but also offered an alternative, he should have much to teach us today.

What he has to teach us, and how *Anna Karenina* teaches it, is the theme of the present book. A great deal is at stake. If we are to avoid the horrors of the twentieth century, we may need to think differently. Perhaps Tolstoy's insights with their inspiring prescience will help us. They may also help people to live their individual lives more fully and with greater self-awareness. Even where they are overstated, mistaken, or simply perverse they may initiate a dialogue in which something vital may be said.

So iconoclastic is *Anna Karenina* that some of its challenges to common opinion have not even been noticed. When a belief is *too* iconoclastic, it may remain invisible. We cannot even imagine that someone could think that way, no matter how explicit he may be. In explicating this novel, I try to make the paradoxical sensible and the invisible perceptible.

Let us begin by considering the paradigms that Tolstoy rejected.

Theoretical and Practical Knowledge

Two stories describe the origin of the rationalist paradigm created in the seventeenth century. Narrating one of them, Stephen Toulmin argues that the religious wars between Protestants and Catholics—especially the Thirty Years War from 1618 to 1648—proved so horrific that philosophers sought ways of thinking that might settle disputes without bloodshed. They sought a court above both sides—the court of pure, abstract reason. For reason is neither Catholic nor Protestant, old or new, aristocratic or bourgeois, but universal, general, and timeless. Like the axioms and theorems of Euclid, or Plato's idea of the timeless forms, reason so conceived pays no respect to persons, special histories, or partisan traditions. The aspiration to create such a rational system inspired Descartes, Leibniz, Spinoza, and others who have come to be known as the seventeenth-century rationalists and their heirs. They provided a model of what real knowledge should be, and therefore marked a decisive break with previous thinking. (See Cos.)

In contrast to philosophy from Aristotle to Montaigne, this conception of rationality favored argument by abstract principles over consideration of particular cases. In the *Nichomachean Ethics,* Aristotle maintained the opposite, that some cases cannot be encompassed by any conceivable principles: "The Good has no universal form, regardless of the subject matter or situation: sound moral judgment always respects the detailed circumstances of particular cases" (Cos, 31–32). Precisely because principles are general, they cannot anticipate the oddities of special cases.

By contrast, in the 1650s, Henry More and the Cambridge Platonists established ethical reasoning as a matter of abstract theory. From that point on, reasoning by cases appeared unphilosophic, if not evasive or dishonest. The very term "casuistry"—reasoning by cases—came to be pejorative, as it usually is today. At best, reasoning by cases could be considered a place-holder until a true theory could be developed.

From the rationalist perspective, successful theories apply to particular cases as surely as the Pythagorean theorem applies to all right triangles. As we shall see, Tolstoy regarded ethics in exactly the opposite way. Agreeing with Montaigne, he saw, with his keen eye for particularities, all the ways in which generalizations oversimplify.

Abstract rationality favors deduction from axioms or the discovery of abstract laws allowing us to do away with appeals to experience. Once those laws are known and applied, nothing is "left over." In *War and Peace,* the wise general Kutuzov asserts the opposite. Prince Andrei comes to learn Kutuzov's lesson that good judgment, which cannot be formalized, surpasses theoretical knowledge not only in battle but also in all other human affairs. Indeed, one could tell Prince Andrei's story as the journey from theory to experience, from mere rationality to wisdom. We do not recognize a wise person, capable of making ethical decisions, by that person's knowledge of the right theory. Rather, he or she has reflected with sensitivity on countless cases. The process of doing so never ends and, unlike Euclidian geometry, cannot guarantee the right answer. In his belief that the quest for certainty deludes, Tolstoy is one of the great skeptics.[1] (See Orwin, "Antiphilosophical Philosophy.")

Aristotle contended that Euclidian reasoning cannot serve as a model for all knowledge, because in some fields—like ethics, medicine, or navigation—what is right on one occasion is wrong on another. Anyone who reads Aristotle may notice how often he uses the phrase, "on the whole and for the most part." Such a phrase, as he pointed out, has no place in geometrical reasoning or the sort of thinking Plato recommended as truly philosophical. Anyone who said that, on the whole and for the most part, the angles of a triangle total two right angles would not just be making a mistake but would be demonstrating he did not understand what mathematics is. But for Aristotle the reverse also applies: anyone who treats ethics as a matter of mathematical certainty displays a mistaken conception of the very nature of ethical choice.

When Levin argues with his half-brother, Sergey Ivanovich, the latter appeals to chains of reasoning while Levin appeals to his experiences. But Levin's experiences do not tend in the same direction. He has no idea how to characterize "the peasants," with whom he lives and works, any more than he can generalize about people as a whole. As a result, Levin "was readily convicted of contradicting himself. In Sergey Ivanovich's eyes his younger brother was a splendid fellow . . . with a mind which, though fairly quick, was too much influenced by the impressions of the moment, and consequently filled with contradictions" (252–53). We sense Tolstoy's palpable irony: Levin cares about what is really there, which is never simple, constantly varies and changes, and so does not lend itself to generalization. He cannot arrive at the sort of abstractions that would help in intellectual argument precisely because he respects the complexity of life.

The fact that Levin loses arguments convicts not the way he thinks, but rather, the way intellectuals think. Because circumstances differ from place to place and time to time, for Levin answers must be specific and timely. Levin can arrive at no abstract truths about peasants and no single remedy for social problems.

Tolstoy utterly rejected the intellectuals' ideal of rational thought. Kutuzov and Bagration, the best generals in *War and Peace,* conspicuously disregard abstract theory and the absurd idea of a science of battle. For them, a good general knows how to take advantage of unforeseen opportunities and regards his soldiers as real people with emotions and moral feelings, neither of which can be formalized. In short, they cultivate not theoretical reasoning but practical reasoning.

In *Anna Karenina,* which deals primarily with domestic life, Dolly and Kitty play the roles of Kutuzov and Bagration. In a fit of pique, Levin disapproves of how Dolly makes her children ask her questions in French so as to teach them the language in preparation for examinations. For Levin, this technique teaches "insincerity." His judgment is not so much wrong as too general. In fact, Tolstoy tells us, Dolly has considered this objection but has decided that, in her circumstances and with the alternatives available to her, the trade-off is worth it. Here, as in all other instances where someone disagrees with her, Dolly is right, although she cannot provide general arguments for her position.

When his brother Nikolai is dying, Levin finds that for all his reading of the great philosophers, he can only gape in horror at his brother's condition and the terrible mystery of death. He makes the situation worse. But Kitty and the servant Agafya Mikhailovna constantly observe Nikolai, note his needs, and listen to his voice, so that even when he groans something unintelligible, they understand and know how to make him more comfortable. Helping Nikolai, "Kitty showed that alertness, that swiftness of reflection which comes out in a man before a battle," a comment that makes the connection between the two novels clear (522). Levin at last realizes that his wife, who is no intellectual, and who cannot even follow abstract arguments, knows more about death than he does.

> "Thou has hid these things from the wise and prudent, and hast revealed them unto babes." So Levin thought about his wife as he talked to her that night.
>
> Levin thought of the text, not because he considered himself "wise and prudent." He did not so consider himself, but he could not help knowing that he was more intelligent than his wife and Agafya Mikhailovna. . . . Different as these two women were. . . . both knew, without a shade of doubt, what sort of thing life was and what death was. . . . though neither of them could have answered, even have understood, the questions that presented themselves to Levin. . . . The proof that they knew for a certainty the nature of death lay in the fact that they knew without a second of hesitation how to deal with the dying. (521)

Their knowledge is practical. Learning from them, Levin comes to regard that kind of knowledge as not only valid but also superior to theoretical knowledge. He recognizes as well that their knowledge is "not instinctive, animal, irrational," but conscious, considered, and thoughtful, although by standards of thoughtfulness differing from those taught at the university (522).

Astronomy and Utopia

The other story of modernity traces the origin of the rationalist paradigm not to religious wars but to the great discoveries of Sir Isaac Newton. Pope's lines are usually cited: "Nature and nature's laws lay hid in night./ God said, Let Newton be! and all was light." The significance of Newton's work went far beyond mathematics and astronomy.

Newton's discoveries impressed for a variety of reasons. For one thing, they showed that the same laws applied throughout the universe, to the heavens as well as to the earth. Because laws are universal, worlds do not differ. For another, they gave decisive formulation to a belief Galileo had held: the language of nature is mathematics and any true science must ultimately be quantitative. Finally, and most importantly, they demonstrated that a vast number of phenomena could be explained by very few laws — three laws of motion and the law of universal gravitation. What had seemed complex for so many centuries was, once understood, extremely simple. That standard of simplicity has governed the evaluation of theories in many fields ever since.

Behind the vast multiplicity of the world a few simple laws operate. This simplicity intimated a sort of scientific aesthetic: nature tends to the economical, the optimal, and the symmetrical. Theories should do the same, and when they do, they are "beautiful." They should reflect not the chaos, complexity, and asymmetry that first strike us but the purity and perfection that *must* lie beneath.

Contrast this set of beliefs with Aristotle's:

> Our discussion will be adequate if it has as much clearness as the subject-matter admits of, for precision is not to be sought for alike in all discussions, any more than in all the products of the crafts. . . . We must be content, then, in speaking of such subjects and with such premises to indicate the truth roughly and in outline, and in speaking about things which are only for the most part true and with premises of the same kind to reach conclusions that are no better. In the same spirit, therefore, should each type of statement be received; for it is the mark of an educated man to look for precision in each class of things just so far as the nature of the subject admits; and it is evidently equally foolish to accept probable reasoning from a mathematician and to demand from a rhetorician scientific proofs. (Aristotle, 936)

Plato, Spinoza, and many others have taken Euclid's geometry as the exemplar of knowledge, and I have often thought that our high schools, in teaching Euclidian geometry, fail to convey its pervasive influence as the model to which many disciplines aspire. Aristotle totally rejected the view of a single model of knowledge. He contended repeatedly that some disciplines cannot be approached in a Euclidian way, and not because they are only just beginning but because of the nature of their subject matter. Medicine, navigation, and ethics can hope for maxims that hold only "on the whole and for the most part."

In the passage just cited, Aristotle's term "rhetoric" refers to disciplines where Euclidian proof is not possible. The fact that "rhetoric," like "casuistry," has now become pejorative ("mere rhetoric") testifies to the triumph of the Platonic view.

So amazingly successful was Newton at explaining problems that had bedeviled the best minds since antiquity that his *Principia,* even for those who did not read it, came to occupy the same position that Euclid's *Elements* had for

Plato. Astronomy soon served as the model for what any good discipline should look like. Indeed, theoreticians often presume that only a science can provide true knowledge and that a discipline may be judged to be scientific to the extent that it resembles physics and astronomy.

Why couldn't such an approach apply to the social realm as well? Surely, many thinkers reasoned, what Newton did for astronomy can be done for all subjects: for psychology, politics, history, ethics, and what we have come to call economics, sociology, and anthropology. Elie Halévy has famously named this idea "moral Newtonianism" (Halévy, 6). For three centuries now moral Newtonianism has seemed self-evidently true, to the point where if one should say that a given discipline cannot be scientific one is taken to mean it can offer no useful knowledge. Aristotle based his *Ethics* on the contrary assumption, and it is obvious that in daily life we constantly depend on all sorts of knowledge that cannot be demonstrated scientifically. We could not function without such purely experiential knowledge. In practice, we cannot but rely on practical reasoning. Our loyalty to theory remains largely theoretical.

Many have regarded it as obvious that everything must be amenable to a scientific approach, with astronomy and physics serving as models of science. Does not everything have a cause and is not causal determinism the only coherent view? For what would an uncaused event be? Are we not products of nature and therefore subject to natural laws, no less than the planets? In *The Brothers Karamazov*, Dmitri paraphrases the physiologist Claude Bernard's view that all our so-called free choices are really the result of neurons with little tails. With a slight change of language, the same idea is often repeated today. Nothing happens by chance, there can be no freedom, and contingency simply marks the present limits of knowledge: as knowledge advances, we recognize how the apparently contingent is law-governed. "Science does not permit exceptions," as Bernard famously wrote (GT, 45).

The founder of anthropology as a serious discipline, Bronislaw Malinowski, insisted that anthropology teaches that nothing social can ever be contingent or a mere holdover from the past because such a view would be "unscientific." With perfect circularity, he also maintained that anthropology is a science because it denies the contingent. Malinowski asserted as well that anthropology would soon be capable of prediction. These views were shared by his great successor, Claude Lévi-Strauss. Differing schools of psychology, from Locke to Freud, have also claimed scientific status. The founder of modern sociology (and the inventor of the term "sociology") originally called his new field "social physics." Cournot thought of economics and physics as branches of "rational mechanics" and Walras thought of economic equilibrium as an analogue to the stability of the solar system (See RtR, chapter 4). Today, economics claims to be the queen of the social sciences because it most closely resembles a hard science, and many political scientists have therefore adopted its assumptions and methods. They have attempted to mathematicize their discipline as if, because physics is mathematicized, anything mathematicized is a sort of physics.

The age of reason is also the age of utopias. Utopianism has gone hand in hand with the belief in social science (in the hard sense). From Locke on, thinkers have assumed that since one can know the laws governing human behavior, one can use those laws to redesign individuals or groups. Social engineering for perfection, or at least optimality, would then be applied social science, much as technology is (it is assumed) applied physics and chemistry. One need only discover the laws! As Tolstoy pointed out, the rewards for having discovered them would be so great that wishful thinking insures the belief they have been discovered. Counterevidence is ignored, explained away, or described as simply a problem yet unsolved. The failure of so many attempts to achieve scientific status has not proven cautionary. Like a loan from the World Bank, the promissory note of "science" can always be refinanced to avoid default.

If we reflect on the twentieth century, we can see the colossal havoc utopianism based on a supposed science has wrought. The most sensational example, of course, is Marxism-Leninism—or, as it called itself, scientific socialism—with its claim to have discovered the laws of economics, society, and history. For a long time, anyone who opposed scientific socialism risked designation, or self-designation, as a person "on the wrong side of history"—a devastatingly effective argument to many—or, still worse, as a traitor or madman. For if, as the Soviets claimed, the laws of history are known as surely as the laws of physics, then denying them is like denying the law of gravity. Locking dissidents up in a madhouse was not so much an exercise in sadism as the natural consequence of such beliefs. When things did not work out as predicted, that failure could not refute the science but only confirm a supposition of sabotage and justify more violence to combat it.

Utopianism so conceived allows no more for legitimate difference of values or opinion than for dissent about the Pythagorean theorem and the law of inertia. Opposition, even potential opposition, must be suppressed. Solzhenitsyn once asked why Macbeth killed only a few people whereas Lenin and Stalin killed tens of millions. He answered that Macbeth did not have an ideology, or, as we might say, a utopianism based on a supposed science.

As we shall see in chapter four, even in societies where utopians do not enjoy a monopoly of force, pseudo–social sciences have produced a variety of destructive effects. As a result, opposition to moral Newtonianism has come from diverse sources. Some, like Jane Jacobs in her study of cities or James Scott in his work on agriculture, have responded to the failure of utopianism by rethinking key assumptions of their discipline. Others have pointed out that the model of a science employed by social sciences derives from nineteenth-century physics but does not square with twentieth-century physics. Or perhaps Walras and other founders of modern theoretical economics, who took physics and astronomy as models, even misunderstood what Newtonian physics had accomplished. They appealed to a "physics that never was," as Poincaré and Toulmin have thought (RtR, 47). Indeed, why choose physics as a model at all? After all, some sciences, such as geology and evolutionary biology, allow for contingent events, and human life clearly has more to do with biology than with astronomy.

Darwin never thought his theory could do away with contingency, a hope he considered essentially theological. Nor did he think his theory any the worse because it was not quantitative: there are no tables or formulae in *The Origin of Species*. More recently, Stephen Jay Gould has insisted that evolution allows for many different paths depending on haphazard events that happen constantly. Perhaps the determinism of simple laws appeals because it makes us, as the end of the evolutionary process, inevitable. Gould recognized Tolstoy as the great proponent of contingency.

God Substitutes

As Aristotle defined the term, a contingent event is one that can either be or not be—one that, as we would say today, might just as well not have happened. Nothing in the nature of things insures its occurrence. If such events exist, then the possibility of certain prediction goes by the board. But the nascent social sciences assumed that certain prediction must be attainable: that could be known a priori. Tolstoy encountered a consensus that contingency in Aristotle's sense does not, indeed cannot, exist.

The seventeenth-century rationalists created a sort of bridge between traditional theological and modern scientific denials of contingency. Notwithstanding the change in language, the two lead to the same consequences. For Leibniz, contingency in Aristotle's sense is inconceivable because, if events could either be or not be, and if subsequent events depend on prior events, then the world would become an endlessly ramifying set of possibilities, any of which could happen. If that were the case, then God could not foresee the future and so would not be omniscient.

For much the same reason, Leibniz also argued that miracles, in the usual sense of divine interventions suspending the laws of nature, could not exist. He regarded the Bible's apparent endorsement of miracles as a mere concession to the ignorance of a primitive tribe. For if God had to supersede His own laws, then He could not have made them perfectly in the first place: He would be, as Leibniz liked to say, "an inferior watchmaker." Divine intervention would also signify that God had not foreseen the results of His laws from the outset.

Miracles in the usual sense therefore imply a God *within* time reacting to events *as* they unfold, but a truly omniscient and omnipotent creator would have to exist outside of time. He would be totally unaffected by events and never act in response to them.

Because the denial of "miracles" and "contingency" was theologically and philosophically unwise, Leibniz resorted to a technique that has appealed to many: he *redefined* the terms. In his metaphysics, a "contingent event" no longer means one that might or might not take place, but one which, if it happened, would imply no logical contradiction. Contingent events so defined still cannot happen, because God chose a chain of events that did not include them. Leibniz's definition allows contingency without allowing for real possibilities that have not but might have happened.

Leibniz insisted that, at any moment, one and only one event can take place because there must be a "sufficient reason" for everything—or, as we might say, a unique causation insured by natural laws. As for miracles, Leibniz described them not as suspensions of the natural laws (as we might suppose if we thought of the sun stopped at Jericho, the parting of the Red Sea, or the raising of Lazarus) but as laws of nature whose operation we see rarely, like snow in the Sahara.

In short, God, existing outside of time, created natural laws that operate seamlessly. When He created the world, He knew everything, down to the last detail, that would ever take place. Since the set of events He chose is necessarily the best (or He would have chosen a better set), any intervention on His part could only worsen the world overall. The world tends to optimality.

The entire tradition of natural theology that followed presumed that one could understand God and His perfection by studying nature and its laws. God wrote two books, the Bible and creation, and in studying either we are piously examining God's mind. Nevertheless, it should be apparent how readily one could, when temperaments changed, just eliminate God from this model. Spinoza had already spoken of "God or nature" as if the two were the same thing. As one often-quoted anecdote goes: Laplace once explained astronomy to a puzzled Napoleon. When the emperor wondered why God was not mentioned, Laplace answered: "I have no need for that hypothesis" ("Je n'avais pas besoin de cette hypothèse").

For Laplace and many others, the laws of nature allow for prediction in principle. Laplace asserted that if some intelligence could understand all the laws of nature and the positions of all particles at a given moment, then to that intelligence "nothing would be uncertain, and the future as the past would be present to his eyes" (Bartlett, 397).

God was eliminated, but otherwise the model and the world remained the same as in Leibniz and natural theology. In this sense, we have *not* really broken with the dominant theological tradition. So far as the openness of time is concerned, it hardly matters whether we say the future is already known to God or the future is knowable "in principle." Instead of divine omniscience, it is mechanistic determinism that eliminates contingency. Not divine perfection but natural order assures simplicity, symmetry, and optimality. We have surrendered God only to replace Him with *God substitutes* that, without God, do what God would do.

So powerful has this way of thinking proven that great thinkers who challenged it have been made retrospectively to fit it. As political opponents may be neutralized, thinkers too important to disregard are *Leibnizized*.

When social scientists speak of a process as "Darwinian," they usually mean that competition, like Darwinian natural selection, insures an optimal result because anything less than optimal would be driven out of existence. To argue this way is not just to exaggerate Darwin's ideas but to get them exactly wrong. Darwin above all wanted to demonstrate that species resulted from a historical process, and optimality or perfect design easily testifies to creation by a single intelligence at a single moment. The proof of a long process of historical evolution lies in the fact that organisms are *im*perfectly designed, as anything responding to contingent events and unforeseeable circumstances would be. Animals possess organs and other anatomical features that do not contribute to, or perhaps even impede, survival. Such organs testify not to perfect fit with present circumstances but to an earlier stage of the species' history.

Among other examples, Darwin cited a certain species of mole that lives its whole life underground and yet has eyes. A thick membrane covers these eyes, so they would be useless even above ground. Like any organ, these blind eyes require energy to support. Since they do not pay their way with a compensating advantage, they decrease optimality. They probably constitute a mere survival from some earlier stage when the mole's ancestors lived above ground. Organisms are palimpsests, with layer upon layer of adaptive and merely inherited features from different epochs. Their suboptimal anatomy testifies not to a single moment of intelligent design but to a contingent historical process consisting of multiple uncoordinated forces.

In short, social scientists have treated natural selection as if it were the equivalent of Adam Smith's "invisible hand," which allegedly insures optimality by economic competition. But anyone who actually reads Smith will see that he, too, has been Leibnizized. Far from saying that optimality always obtains, or that people always make rational choices, Smith's book *The Wealth of Nations* contains long historical sections attributing economic change to "human folly." Rather than a utopia, Smith's book, like Gibbon's *Decline and Fall*, resembles those satires on human nature so common in the eighteenth century. *The Ori-*

gin of Species also displays a satiric edge when Darwin parodies idyllic views of a beneficent nature.

Darwin meant natural selection and Smith the invisible hand to be loose regulating principles operating along with other forces that do not drive toward optimality. Neither thinker regarded his key ideas as allowing for reliable prediction. Textbooks reflect how their followers saved them from these embarrassing lapses by making them fit the dominant model that seemed so much more scientific.

The fact that thinkers have recently become aware that Darwin, Smith, Clausewitz, and others contradict the textbooks invoking them suggests that the age of God substitutes may be ebbing. We may at last be ready to move beyond God and the world as each is described by the dominant theological tradition and its heirs. Some theologians have embraced a God who exists within time and reacts to events. We may now be ready to do away with substitutes for the traditional God as well. Either way, we would understand the world differently by admitting the contingency on which Tolstoy's two great novels insist.

Contingency and Presentness

Anna Karenina continues and deepens the ideas of *War and Peace.* In the earlier work, Tolstoy groped his way to his new vision of experience. In *Anna,* written about a decade later, he handled that vision with assurance as he refined and extended it to new areas of life.

As *War and Peace* begins, Prince Andrei believes, as most generals do, in a science of warfare. He imagines that success in battle, as in all activities, depends on unclouded reason and determined will. Andrei possesses plenty of both. He fantasizes about solving strategic puzzles that bedevil others and putting his solutions into practice when the less valiant hesitate. He comes at last to learn that epic bravery counts less than ordinary courage and that there can never be a science of warfare or of anything else in the social world.

Tolstoy intends the book's several councils of war to be metaphors for decision-making in general. The purported science of battle represents any purported social science. General Pfühl plans campaigns on the basis of "science, that is, the supposed knowledge of absolute truth" (W&P, 770). His "science" is

> the theory of oblique movements deduced by him from the history of Frederick the Great's wars—and everything he came across in the histories of more recent wars seemed to him absurd and barbarous, crude struggles in

which so many blunders were committed on both sides that these conflicts could not be called wars; they did not conform to a theory, and therefore could not serve as material for science. (W&P, 771)

Pfühl cannot be refuted, because even when he loses a battle, he contends that defeat resulted not from his plan but from the failure to execute his orders precisely. Since battle orders can never be executed precisely, his "science" insures itself against contrary evidence. Here and in other passages, Tolstoy examines the ways in which a supposed science is based on sheer faith.

The commander-in-chief Kutuzov knows that all "scientific" talk of "oblique movements" and the like is nonsense, a mere professional jargon concealing ignorance, but he is wise enough not to say so. By the end of the book, Prince Andrei realizes that Kutuzov has been right all along. Listening to General Pfühl, Andrei concludes at last that "there was not and could not be a science of war" (W&P, 775). "What theory or science is possible," he reflects, "when the conditions and circumstances are unknown and cannot be determined, and especially when the strength of the active forces cannot be ascertained?" (W&P, 775). Purely contingent factors—such as a single man shouting "Hurrah!" instead of "We are cut off!"—can dramatically affect the strength of a regiment. No science can ever predict the moral state of each soldier as it changes moment by moment in response to perceptions too various to be named. A centimeter of difference in the trajectory of a bullet can determine whether a given soldier is killed, and that soldier's moral influence on those around him may have substantial and concatenating effects. No science can ever predict the path of each bullet.

In short, battle, like practical life generally, is significantly shaped by sheer contingency. "What science can there be," Prince Andrei asks himself, "in a matter in which, as in every practical matter, nothing can be determined and everything depends on innumerable conditions, the significance of which becomes manifest at a particular moment and no one can tell when that moment will come?" (W&P, 775). "As in every practical matter": Tolstoy indicates that his skepticism of a science of warfare applies to the whole social world.

Just before the battle of Borodino, the novel's other main hero, Pierre, visits Andrei and mouths the common belief in military science. A skilled commander, Pierre repeats, can "foresee all contingencies" (W&P, 929), an assertion that Andrei regards as ridiculous. "You talk about position: the left flank weak, the right flank extended," he tells Pierre. "That's all nonsense, doesn't mean a thing. But what are we facing tomorrow? A hundred million diverse chances, which will be decided on the instant by whether we run or they run, whether this man or that man is killed" (W&P, 930).

"Manifest at a particular moment," "decided on the instant": Prince Andrei stresses the importance of *presentness*. If there could be a hard science of battle or anything else in the social world, then each moment would be a mere derivative of earlier moments, calculable in advance, the way one can calculate the position of Mars at any time. But if contingency reigns, then the present moment may contain influential features that could not have been predicted in advance, even—to use the words of the most common fudge factor—"in principle."

If one's model is Newtonian astronomy, one mark of a hard science is that it can eliminate narrative explanation. Of course, one *could* describe the orbit of Mars as a story—first Mars was here, then it followed its orbit to that place, and now it is over there—but such a story would be entirely superfluous, because the formulae already give Mars's location at any moment. Specific stories can at best *illustrate* general laws, but cannot add to them. This consideration explains why doctoral training in economics, which once required courses in economic history, has now almost entirely dispensed with them in favor of more work in mathematical modeling. In this view, narrative begins where knowledge ends.

By contrast, to the extent that contingency governs, particular moments matter. When more than one path is possible, narrative becomes essential. Let us define the term "narrativeness" to mean the indispensability of narrative explanation in a given situation. We may then phrase Tolstoy's question this way: Does the world display narrativeness, presentness, and surprisingness? Or are all those apparent features of experience mere illusions, like belief in occult forces, to be explained away as science advances?

Decisions in a World of Uncertainty

The novel's most effective soldier, Nikolai Rostov, is neither especially intelligent nor particularly brave, but he is alert to the opportunities of the moment. Watching the French climb a hill, he guesses, on the basis not of theory but of his experience as a hunter and a soldier, that "if his hussars were to charge the French dragoons now, the latter would not be able to withstand them, but that it would have to be done at once, instantly, or it would be too late" (W&P, 786). *Now, at once, instantly:* presentness matters. No theory could have predicted this brief opportunity. Alert line officers make all the difference. So do their analogues—decision-makers close to the flux of events—in every social activity.

Tolstoy's point concerns decision-making in general. In situations where predictability is possible, advance planning is worth the effort. But to the extent that situations are uncertain, alertness matters more than planning. If we are to be effective, we need to distinguish which situation is which. Kutuzov actually falls asleep at the council of war before Austerlitz and at last calls a halt to the proceedings: "'Gentlemen, the disposition for tomorrow—or rather, for today, for it is past midnight—cannot be altered now. . . . You have heard it, and we shall all do our duty. And before a battle, there is nothing more important . . .' he paused, 'than a good night's sleep'" (W&P, 323). A good night's sleep is more important than planning because in a world of radical uncertainty, a world where presentness counts, alertness matters most of all. Before Borodino, Andrei also concludes his talk with Pierre by stressing the importance of "a good night's sleep"(W&P, 933).

Complexity and Impurity

Nature has designed amazingly complex structures—think of the liver— but it has never designed an animal with wheels, even though wheels are a lot simpler than livers.[2] Why not? The answer is that the world is not paved. Wheels convey great advantage when we can count on regularity—when we know that the smooth surface of a highway continues even where we cannot see it over the next hill. No one who could drive from Chicago to San Francisco would walk. The fact that we nevertheless do not have wheels testifies to the unpredictability and variability of terrain. Imagine an animal with wheels trying to get by a fallen tree; it would rapidly be devoured by enemies. Legs, though less efficient in a smooth and predictable world, work better in an uncertain one because they are more flexible and so more useful in facing the unforeseeable. Our very bodies signify the world's unpredictability.

Moral Newtonianism depends on a faith that behind the vast complexity of the world, a few simple laws govern events. If we trace phenomena back to their causes, and those causes to earlier causes, moral Newtonians presume that the causes simplify. But why could it not be the case in the social world that the very opposite is true: that the more we trace events to their causes, the more complexity we detect? For Tolstoy, things do not simplify, they ramify. We have no guarantee that laws are *few*. The assumption that they must be is based either on an unjustified analogy from astronomy or on sheer faith in simplicity and symmetry. It is ultimately not scientific but aesthetic.

For the sake of argument, let us allow that determinism is true. Tolstoy contended that determinism would make no difference if the laws governing events were as numerous as the events themselves. Instead of an unmanageably large series of contingent events, we would have an unmanageably large series of ad hoc laws. Insofar as prediction is concerned, the social universe, whether governed by determinism or not, behaves indeterministically. Determinism or indeterminism is therefore the wrong question for Tolstoy: the right one is whether the world is fundamentally simple or not.

For Tolstoy, the natural state of the world is mess. That is why, if we leave things to themselves, they always get more chaotic, never more orderly. Order requires work. Situations of even relative predictability require enormous effort and represent the achievement of ages. Purity is not be thought of. If Tolstoy were writing today, he might counter the appeal to Newtonian mechanics with the analogy of entropy.

Montaigne, who wrote just before the seventeenth-century rationalist enterprise, and whom Tolstoy loved, composed an essay entitled "We Taste Nothing Pure." "Man, in all things and throughout, is but patchwork and motley," Montaigne asserts. "Profound joy has more seriousness than gaiety about it; extreme and full contentment, more soberness than sprightliness. *Even felicity, unless it tempers itself, overwhelms* [Seneca]. Happiness racks us" (Montaigne, 510). Tolstoy echoes these lines in one of the absolute statements of *War and Peace:* "But pure and perfect sorrow is as impossible as pure and perfect joy" (W&P, 1286).

Symmetry and homogeneity in a model betray that it rests upon error. Utopias therefore deny the very nature of things. In *War and Peace,* Pierre's utopian dreams are shaken when he gives a speech to his fellow Masons. Not disagreement but agreement most disturbs him, because each of those who concur understands Pierre in a different way.

> At this meeting Pierre for the first time was struck by the endless variety of men's minds, which prevents a truth from ever appearing the same to any two persons. Even those members who seemed to be on his side understood him in their own way, with stipulations and modifications he could not agree to, since what he chiefly wanted was to convey his thought to others exactly as he understood it. (W&P, 528)

If perceptions and values cannot be exactly shared by any two persons, and if variety is so ineluctable, then how could a society based on a single idea ever exist? Montaigne would have reminded Pierre that he differs not only from others but also from himself. Over time, and in different moods, each person is sure to understand his own ideas variously. "Those who make a practice of comparing human actions are never so perplexed as when they try to see them as a whole and in the same light. . . . we change like that animal which takes the color of the place you set it on. . . . We float between different states of mind" (Montaigne, 239–40).

Tolstoy and the Realist Novel of Ideas

Hostility to oversimplifying theories characterizes the realist novel in general. Whereas utopian fiction tells the story of a hero who discovers that the world is much simpler than he supposed, realist novels of ideas tell the opposite story. Lydgate in *Middlemarch,* Raskolnikov in *Crime and Punishment,* and

Bazarov in *Fathers and Children* all undergo experiences showing that the world, and they themselves, display more complexity than they ever imagined. The genre in which these characters appear subjects their beliefs to an irony of outcomes, as life refutes theory. The key plot of the realist novel of ideas is the gradual discovery and appreciation of complexity.

As theory came to dominate the intellectual world, opposing insights took refuge in the novel. The history of nineteenth-century Russian thought could be told as the battle between an intelligentsia addicted to salvationist grand theories and the great writers who insisted on the messy particularities of life. The critic Mikhail Gershenzon observed in 1909 that "in Russia an almost infallible gauge of the strength of an artist's genius is the extent of his hatred for the intelligentsia" (Gershenzon, 60). If we think of Tolstoy, Dostoevsky, and Chekhov, this judgment is largely true.

Realist novels everywhere offered a counterview to predominant assumptions. Russian writers developed that counterview with special power. In Russia, everything intellectual tended to a theoretical extreme: to paraphrase an observation of Dostoevsky, a Russian intellectual is someone who can read Darwin and promptly become a pickpocket. Answering a fanatic faith in theory, the Russian novel of ideas therefore became especially explicit, elaborate, and uncompromising in developing its antitheoretical critique. Fighting theory with countertheory, Tolstoy and Dostoevsky sometimes seem fanatic in their anti-fanaticism.

War and Peace and *Anna Karenina* make explicit the usually tacit presuppositions of the realist novel.

The Prosaic Novel

Tolstoy extends the insights of a particular kind of realist novel, which I like to call the prosaic novel. All realist works, by definition, contain many particularities and ordinary events; prosaic novels regard such events as the locus of value. For these novels, grand drama and ecstatic moments do not make a life good. Life is an everyday affair, and the sum total of unremarkable, daily happenings defines its quality. Like good, evil affects us most strongly in countless small ways, each of which is barely visible.

In the prosaic novel, heroes and heroines who live for extreme moments misunderstand what life is. Such characters embody the unprosaic values of other genres, such as the romance, the epic, the lyric poem, or the utopia. Prosaic novels often express their own values by subjecting these antithetical genres to scrutiny. In Trollope and Jane Austen, characters who cite romantic lyrics often do so to deceive themselves or others. As *War and Peace* begins, Prince

Andrei tries to live the life of an epic hero in a novelistic world. He is, so to speak, a *genre expatriate* from the epic, and must learn novelistic lessons. Imagining that she is a romantic heroine, Anna Karenina is a genre expatriate from romance in the world of the prosaic novel.

Middlemarch famously begins and ends in explicit dialogue with other genres. Eliot's heroine Dorothea tries to live the life of a saint and of an epic hero in an everyday world. Like Saint Theresa, she strives for meaningfulness through grand actions, but she, no less than we ourselves, lives in an everyday world remote from the faith that would underwrite such saintliness. "Many Theresas have been born who found for themselves no epic life wherein there was a constant unfolding of far-resonant action; perhaps only a life of mistakes, the offspring of a certain spiritual grandeur ill-matched with the meanness of opportunity; perhaps a tragic failure which found no sacred poet and sank unwept into oblivion" (Eliot, 7). Like Prince Andrei, Dorothea gradually learns that meaningful actions are small and prosaic. Taken together, such actions lend themselves to no gripping story but they may do considerable good, as grand actions usually cannot.

Prosaic novels *redefine* heroism as the right kind of ordinary living and sainthood as small acts of thoughtfulness that are barely perceived. Many can perform heroic actions in the sight of all, but few possess the courage to do small things right without recognition. Dorothea at last achieves this kind of prosaic heroism. *Middlemarch* concludes:

> Her finely-touched spirit had still its fine issues, though they were not widely visible. Her full nature, like that of the river of which Cyrus broke the strength, spent itself in channels which had no great name on the earth. But the effect of her being on those around her was incalculably diffusive: for the growing good of the world is partly dependent on unhistoric acts; and that things are not so ill with you and me as they might have been, is half owing to the number who lived faithfully a hidden life, and rest in unvisited tombs. (Eliot, 795)

A similar perspective informs the works of Jane Austen, Anthony Trollope, Chekhov, and others in the prosaic tradition. Tolstoy takes these insights the furthest. In *War and Peace,* prosaic actions account for the historical process, including all its most dramatic incidents. Whereas received histories and philosophies of history stress grand events and major figures, history is really made by "the elemental life of the swarm"—by countless small acts never intended to be "historic," performed by people who do not usually appear in documents. This Tolstoyan insight has influenced historians in our time, who have tried to find some way to tell history from the perspective of the "unhistoric."

Fallacies of Perception and Plot

Tolstoy asks: why do historians attribute the burning of Moscow, which so devastated the French, to the decision of some significant historical figure, like Moscow's mayor Rostopchin? They do so because of unexamined assumptions. Not used to thinking in prosaic terms, they tend to regard the result of a hundred thousand small actions as if it were accomplished at a stroke, and so look for some figure who accomplished it. To illustrate the fallacy involved in such thinking, Tolstoy asks us to imagine a group of men hauling a log, each pulling in his own direction. Because the log is bound to go in the direction one of them is pulling, we may easily but mistakenly conclude that the person pulling in that direction commanded the result. Elsewhere Tolstoy defines a related fallacy of perception, which he calls "the law of reciprocity." Forgetting that he has made similar blunders all along, someone who has lost a game of chess attributes his defeat to a particular move. The move he identifies as "decisive" is no worse than his other moves; it is simply the one his opponent exploited. *War and Peace* identifies several fallacies of perception that lead us to magnify the significance of apparently "decisive" actions while overlooking the efficacy of the ordinary.

What is truly "historic" is the unhistoric. No one decided to set fire to Moscow. It burned because almost all Muscovites abandoned it, and a city of wood, where small fires are always starting, is likely to burn down when deprived of its inhabitants. Each person left Moscow with no thought of saving the fatherland but for selfish reasons more effective than overtly patriotic ones. This form of "latent patriotism," Tolstoy concludes, "expresses itself not in words, not in sacrificing one's children to save the fatherland, or any other such unnatural deeds, but simply, unobtrusively, organically and therefore in a way that invariably produces the most powerful results" (W&P, 998).

Historians typically favor a given type of story that their temperament, school, or period makes plausible. But often enough, history, shaped by countless prosaic events tending in no single direction, is not story-like at all. Still less often is it made by "heroic" action.

We who were not living in those days, when half of Russia had been conquered . . . tend to imagine that all Russians, from the least to the greatest, were engaged solely in sacrificing themselves, in saving the fatherland or weeping over its ruin. . . . But in reality it was not like that. It appears so to us because we see only the general historical issues of the period and do not see all the personal human interests of the people of the day. (W&P, 1126)

Tolstoy observes that because novels deal primarily with the personal interests of individual people, they may, despite their fictionality, offer a more accurate account of *how* things happen than nonfictional histories.

Rather paradoxically, Tolstoy offers a sort of inverse law of effectiveness: those who "endeavored to understand the general course of events, and hoped by self-sacrifice and heroism to take part in it, were the most useless members of society; they saw everything upside down, and all they did for the common good turned out to be futile and absurd" (W&P, 1126). Conversely, "the more closely a man was engaged in the course of events . . . the less perceptible was their significance to him" (W&P, 1127). Society women may have lamented the fate of the fatherland, but in the army "no one swore vengeance on the French; they were all thinking about their pay, their next quarters, Matryoshka the canteen woman, and the like" (W&P, 1127).

Tolstoy offers us one of his negative absolutes, a statement about what cannot be understood: "The law forbidding us to taste of the fruit of the tree of knowledge is particularly manifested in historical events. Only unconscious action bears fruit, and a man who plays a part in a historical event never understands its significance. If he tries to understand it, he becomes ineffectual" (W&P, 1127). Critical moments only appear decisive because we forget that they are the product of a hundred thousand small moments creating them. Here we see Tolstoy, whose temperament was anything but understated, taking his prosaic insight to an epic extreme. After all, one may grant the importance of the ordinary without asserting that *only* the ordinary can be important.

Prosaics

In an essay published while *War and Peace* was being serialized, Tolstoy gives us his most memorable account of a perceptual fallacy, the fallacy of "the treetops." Looking back on history, we see only grand events and readily conclude that they predominated or were, at least, the most significant. But such a conclusion "would be just as incorrect as for a person, seeing nothing but treetops beyond a hill, to conclude there was nothing but trees in that locality" (Jub, 16:8).

In our own lives, as well, we tend mistakenly to focus on noticeable and conventionally "significant" events, rather than on the tenor of ordinary events. *Anna Karenina* tries to redirect our attention to aspects of everyday living: love and the family, moral decisions, the process of self-improvement, and, ultimately, all that makes a life feel meaningful or leads us to contemplate suicide.

I call the complex of views that Tolstoy developed *prosaics*. At the minimum, prosaics insists on the fact of contingency and the importance of the ordinary.

It tries to revive practical and case-based reasoning and teaches suspicion of theory.[3] For prosaics, theory's proper role is essentially mnemonic: it serves as a series of tentative generalizations from practice that must not dictate to practice. *Anna Karenina* illustrates why we would be wise to proceed from experience up. Developing prosaics in unforeseen directions, it offers ways of comprehending not only individual lives but also general issues of social reform. Those insights apply to today's world with special force.

To speak in the spirit of this novel we may say: We need to see what is openly camouflaged right before our eyes. Throw away the telescope and attend to the ever-changing world around us. Learn to focus on the tiny alterations. To achieve prosaic wisdom, we must remove blinders and educate our vision.

CHAPTER TWO

Dolly and Stiva:
Prosaic Good and Evil

Dolly and Stiva:
Prosaic Good and Evil

Happiness

Anna Karenina begins with one of the most widely quoted sentences in world literature: "All happy families resemble each other; each unhappy family is unhappy in its own way." The meaning of this aphorism, apart from introducing the theme of happy and unhappy families, has remained obscure.

In Tolstoy's diaries and letters of the period, in *War and Peace,* and in a variant of *Anna Karenina,* he mentions a French proverb quite similar to this sentence: "Happy people have no history." (See Orwin, *Art and Thought,* 179, 244n26; Babaev, 133; Shklovsky, *Tolstoy,* 483; Bayley, 203). They have no history because what makes a history is eventful difficulty. Allegedly, an old Yiddish curse goes: "May you live in interesting times!" This idea was, in fact, commonly expressed by writers Tolstoy knew.[1]

I believe Tolstoy's thought is: Unhappy families, like unhappy lives, are dramatic. They have a *story* and each story is different. But happy lives are undramatic. Critical events do not characterize happy families. There is no story to tell about them. It is in this sense that they all resemble each other.

The more story, the less happiness. Where there is history there is misery.

Two Bad Lives

What makes a life good or bad is how the ordinary moments are lived. If we live only for critical moments and regard ordinary ones as mere intervals, we are sure to live badly. But even an ordinary life without high drama may be bad if it is lived wrongly day to day. So there are two mistaken ways to live: by regarding prosaic experience as a mere preparation for real life and by indulging in prosaic badness that ruins ordinary moments. In Chekhov's plays and stories life is ruined in both of these ways, an insight probably derived from *Anna Karenina.*

Anna herself exemplifies one mistaken view, as she lives a life based on extremes and the melodramatic. Her brother Stiva lives undramatically and contentedly but wrongly moment to moment. This family illustrates how not to live. Anna's choices lead naturally to dramatic miseries and a destructive end, Stiva's to a hedonistic emptiness and thoughtless harm. His evil, hidden in everyday charm, spreads more widely and so proves even more destructive. But he escapes the pain he visits on others. There is no poetic justice.

Overcoming the Bias of the Artifact

Tolstoy's opening aphorism suggests an aesthetic problem. How does one tell a story showing that good lives and happy families lack a story? After all, what can one say, they did not quarrel again today? Or: once again, nothing special happened? Novels require a plot, but plot, in this view, is what happy lives do not have. Plot may be an index of error, but it is also the source of interest.

William Blake asserted that "the reason Milton wrote in fetters when he wrote of Angels & God, and at liberty when of Devils & Hell, is because he was a true Poet and of the Devil's party without knowing it" (Blake, 58). A moment's reflection might suggest a rather different reason that Milton made Satan more interesting than God. Change cannot happen to a perfect Being, Who neither acts nor suffers. Experiencing no uncertainty, He cannot strive or doubt. But Satan, who is neither perfect nor omniscient, constantly strives and responds to events whose outcome he cannot foresee. The author's sympathies aside, it is virtually impossible to make such a God more interesting than such a devil.

Utopian fiction illustrates the same point. Not only does its didacticism irritate readers, but its lack of story bores them. Utopias must lack incidents because by definition, no problems can arise in a perfect world. Once a visitor from our society reaches the ideal one, nothing can happen. Instead, the hero simply tours the new world and learns the perfect solution to a previously perplexing problem. Drama can exist in utopian fiction only in the journeys to and from the perfect society or in sections dealing with the present world. By contrast, anti-utopias have an inbuilt advantage. They can hardly help being more interesting than utopias. Even when they are set in a spuriously perfect world, like *We, Brave New World,* or *Nineteen Eighty-Four,* a hero discovers the falsehood and rebels against it. Where there is imperfection, there can be plot.

One reason evil is interesting is that plot is interesting; and vice versa.

Tolstoy's aesthetic problem, then, is a more general one. To be interesting, novels require drama, but Tolstoyan happiness excludes it. The central idea of *Anna Karenina* runs counter to its genre. Tolstoy needed to find a way to overcome the implicit prejudices of the genre, what I like to call *the bias of the artifact.*

Tolstoy found an intriguing solution. He placed the dramatic characters, especially Anna, in the foreground of the story, which exemplifies mistaken values. Dolly, who understands life correctly, remains largely in the background. The novel therefore has an interesting plot while also showing that what really matters in life exists beyond plot.

Retraining Perception

This method also allowed Tolstoy to illustrate his key lesson about perception. I refer to his simile of a person viewing a distant region where only trees are visible and concluding that the region contains only trees. We often misperceive because we focus on the dramatic and miss the significance, or the very existence, of the undramatic. *Anna Karenina* tries to teach us to overcome this perceptual fallacy.

In addition to placing the embodiment of goodness in the background, Tolstoy used a technique that might be called *open camouflage*. He places essential information right before our eyes, but in a context where our attention turns to something apparently more important. Key facts appear in the middle of long paragraphs dealing with something else, or in subordinate clauses of lengthy sentences with a different point. We read these facts but overlook their significance and easily forget them. Only if we learn to overcome our perceptual biases and to redirect our attention can we understand events correctly. We must learn to see what is right before our eyes but hidden in plain view.

Tolstoy's method entails risks. Readers rarely notice that they have not noticed something. Overlooking the openly hidden facts, they fail to correct their ways of perceiving. In the process, they misread the novel as a book celebrating high drama and grand romance.

When readers make this mistake, they may *understand the story as Anna herself might have told it.* Like the Greta Garbo film, they get the book *exactly* wrong: the Garbo version unwittingly but precisely conveys the set of values the novel tries to discredit. Tolstoy's method of discrediting those values makes misinterpretation easy.

Think of the work's title. Like *Middlemarch, Anna Karenina* tells three stories, but unlike George Eliot's novel, it is named after one of them. It is almost as if Tolstoy were anticipating the many dramatizations of the book that focus entirely on Anna.[2] Tolstoy has significantly "misnamed" his book. Like noticeable events, the title is a decoy. It is the title that Anna herself would have chosen. Following Tolstoy's lead, Chekhov was to do something similar in *Uncle Vanya,* a title that overtly names the melodramatic hero and only intimates the prosaic heroine, Sonya. Just as the characters in the play underestimate Sonya, so readers, viewers, and directors have usually missed that the title tacitly names her as well, since only she could call Voinitsky "Uncle Vanya." Sonya is the openly camouflaged heroine.

Most critical interpretations and popular renditions present Anna as a tragic heroine and Dolly as insignificant. Open camouflage has proved a strategy that readily goes awry. Perceptual biases have often overcome the attempt to correct perceptual biases.

The Third Story

The story of Anna, Vronsky, and Karenin occupies roughly forty per cent of the book. In Part Eight, it barely appears. The Levin story takes up about the same number of pages. The remainder of the book concerns Dolly and Stiva. This third story is the one readers most often overlook.

And yet the book begins with this third story. Critics typically analyze this beginning in purely technical terms. They explain that Dolly and Stiva serve as a bridge between the other two stories because Dolly is Kitty's sister and Stiva is Anna's brother as well as Levin's friend. Tolstoy thereby makes it possible to shift between the Anna and Levin stories seamlessly through the intermediary account of Stiva and Dolly.

This explanation has merit, but it ultimately fails to satisfy. For one thing, Tolstoy often switches directly between the Anna and Levin stories. More importantly, a great writer, especially one so overtly philosophical as Tolstoy, avoids using a device that is *only* technical without also advancing his themes.

The novel begins with Dolly and Stiva because they define themes essential to the work's meaning.

The Prosaic Hero

If by the hero of a work we mean not the character who occupies the dramatic foreground but the one who most closely embodies the author's values, then the hero of *Anna Karenina* is Dolly.[3] When other characters disagree with her, they err, as we see when Levin understandably but mistakenly objects to the way she teaches her children French. She lives a life focused on the everyday and on that most ordinary of institutions, the family. She is a good mother. She smoothes over quarrels within her family when Kitty falls ill. And she values most highly the moments that, from Tolstoy's perspective, make a life most meaningful.[4]

In Part Three, Stiva leaves Dolly and the children in the country to save money. The money in question is largely hers. Stiva is always selling some forest of hers so he can spend money on what he thinks life is really for, his pleasures and his lovers. Dolly has begged Stiva to make sure the house in which she and the children will be staying is in good repair, but he has merely improved its appearance, as he would for a mistress. Tolstoy describes his psychology: "In spite of Stepan Arkadyevich's efforts to be an attentive father and husband, he never could keep in his mind that he had a wife and children" (274–75). The roof leaks, the cows provide no milk, no horse is available for driving, a bull threatens the children, the few cupboards that exist do not close, and Dolly can discover no pots, pans, or ironing board.

As usual in Tolstoy, help comes not from someone dramatic but from "one inconspicuous but most valuable and useful person, Matryona Filimonovna," who borrows or jury-rigs what Dolly minimally requires (276). This scene is so remote from the main plots concerning Anna and Levin that, if omitted, it would hardly be missed. But right after Matryona Filimonovna solves Dolly's problems, one of the book's key passages occurs:

> Darya Aleksandrovna [at last] began to realize, if only in part, her expectations, if not of a peaceful, at least of a comfortable, life in the country. Peaceful with six children Darya Aleksandrovna could not be. One would fall ill, another might easily become so, a third would be without something necessary, a fourth would show symptoms of a bad disposition, and so on. Rare indeed were the brief periods of peace. But these cares and anxieties were for Darya Aleksandrovna the sole happiness possible. Had it not been for them, she would have been left alone to brood over her husband who did not love her. And besides, hard though it was for the mother to bear the dread of illness, the illnesses themselves, and the grief of seeing signs of evil propensities in her children—the children themselves were even now repaying her in small joys for her sufferings. Those joys were so small that they passed unnoticed, like gold in sand, and at bad moments she could see nothing but the pain, nothing but sand; but there were good moments too when she saw nothing but the joy, nothing but gold. (276–77)

Unlike her husband's pleasures or Anna's dramatic encounters, these small and unplotworthy activities exemplify what life is really about. In this novel nothing is more important than raising children.

Real joys do not fit a plot. It is easy to overlook them or, if noticed, to forget them. It would be impossible to tell an interesting story about them. Nevertheless, it is moments like these that make a life meaningful. They may pass unnoticed, like gold in sand, but they are nonetheless golden.

Dolly experiences the book's most meaningful moments, but they are openly camouflaged. I know no interpretation that mentions the importance of this passage. An important scene occurs soon after. Dolly's son Grisha has disobeyed the English governess, who has punished him by forbidding him pie for dessert. Though saddened, Dolly upholds the governess's authority. Not much later, she happens to catch sight of a scene that deeply moves her. Her daughter Tanya, under pretext of taking some pie to one of her dolls, has secretly taken it to her brother.

> While still weeping over the injustice of his punishment, he was eating the pie, and kept saying through his sobs, "Eat yourself; let's eat it together . . . together."
>
> Tanya had at first been under the influence of her pity for Grisha, then of a sense of her noble action, and tears were standing in her eyes too: but she did not refuse, and ate her share. (279)

The kindness of Tanya's subterfuge, her willingness to risk punishment to help her brother, Grisha's unselfish insistence on sharing, and Tanya's readiness to forgo a sense of superiority by sharing with her brother: all these signs of good character and love become for Dolly one of those golden moments. In the bustle of constant activity, she may never remember this scene and most readers entirely forget it. Much as incidents like this do not advance the novel's overall plot, so the best moments of our lives rarely fit the life-stories we tell ourselves.

When Dolly takes her children bathing, a group of peasant women admire them, and Dolly discusses weaning and child-rearing with them. She finds that her interests are not merely similar but identical to theirs; she becomes utterly engrossed in the conversation, and she deeply appreciates their admiration of her children. The novel contains several brief scenes like these, and each is openly camouflaged. What really matters is so prosaic, so ordinary, that we overlook it. The novel tries to teach us to see what we usually miss and so to correct a perceptual error that reflects mistaken values.[5]

Dolly's Quandary

Because of Stiva's infidelity, Dolly suffers, and so her story does have a plot. The novel begins with the dramatic moment when she first discovers one of Stiva's affairs. Most of this story is told from Stiva's and then from Anna's perspective, as if Dolly's hurt feelings were simply a difficulty to be fixed as quickly as possible so that others can get on with their lives. Even the servants, though they know Stiva is in the wrong, side with him, because it is Dolly's reaction that has disrupted their daily routine.

Dolly realizes that her feelings do not matter to anyone. She is simply handy for running the household as cheaply as possible, for keeping the children from being a bother, and for providing some property that her husband can sell. All the more, then, does the injury she suffers hurt her pride.

It is not until chapter 4 of Part One that we switch from Stiva's point of view to Dolly's. We find her pretending to herself that she will leave him, but she knows that she cannot. For one thing, she still loves her husband, and, for another, "she realized that if even here in her own house she could hardly manage to look after her five children properly, they would be still worse off where she was going with them all" (13). In the three days since the discovery, one child has already fallen ill from eating spoiled soup and the others have almost gone without dinner. Matryona Filimonovna has posed urgent questions about the children. Two of Dolly's children have died. She fears the possible consequences of disrupting a routine. Moreover, as a passage occurring at the beginning of Part Two apparently indicates, she is pregnant at this time, and so has yet another impediment to leaving. She is torn. "She was conscious that it was impossible to go away; but, deceiving herself, she went on all the same, sorting her things and pretending she was going away"(13).

She can neither leave nor return to her old routine as if nothing has happened. With his amazing social skills and ability to empathize momentarily with anyone, Stiva would be able to solve Dolly's quandary if he were not himself the culprit. But it is Anna who succeeds in resolving the problem. Anna possesses all Stiva's abilities but can speak with seeming disinterest. Since Dolly herself knows she must find some way to return to her activities as a mother, she readily accepts the solution Anna offers: as a Christian, Dolly forgives her apparently repentant husband and so earns a measure of self-esteem. Later, she will advise Karenin to embrace the same answer.

Dolly begins the novel entirely innocent—she has always imagined her husband was pure when they married—but she is no fool. Over the next few hundred pages, she comes to learn that Stiva's affair with the governess is not just a momentary slip. She comes to regard her husband's life as pitiful. She habitually addresses him with a "faint note of irony" (597) indicating impotent contempt.

Habits

In Part Six, Stiva suggests that Dolly visit Anna and Vronsky in the country, and she does. Her visit to Anna occupies nine chapters and some forty pages. These chapters indicate a good deal about Anna and Vronsky, but, even more importantly, they represent the culmination of Dolly's story. Virtually the entire visit is narrated through Dolly's eyes.

The journey breaks Dolly's habitual activities. Because ordinary moments define a life, habits assume supreme importance in *Anna Karenina*. A life is lived well or ill largely because of good or bad habits. One reason that child-rearing is so important is that people acquire most habits in childhood. Breaking or acquiring even a single one demands immense effort. Even the realization that a habit should be broken depends on other habits of perception and self-evaluation that we usually learn in childhood. Dolly is correct to worry about whether her children are developing good dispositions, her words for habits of living and feeling.

Because habits shape lives, people become especially vulnerable when routines are interrupted. In this novel, characters are more likely to make significant mistaken choices, or to experience true or false revelations, when they cannot rely on habits to guide most of what they do. Anna's journey to Moscow in Part One separates her from her son for the first time. That break in daily habits partially explains her susceptibility to Vronsky's advances, especially after she shares a train compartment with Vronsky's mother, whose life has been filled with affairs and who describes her son in enticing ways. Later in the novel, Levin's routine is broken when he brings Kitty to Moscow for her confinement, has no work to do, and comes to share Oblonsky's social interests. Stiva plays the role of Vronsky's mother and brings Levin to Anna, who tries to captivate him. She succeeds as much as possible in one encounter with an honest man, as Kitty understands quite well.

Arriving at a Question (Part Six, Chapter 16)

Interruptions of routine may provoke reflection on the course of one's life. Anna rethinks her affair and her attitude to Karenin when she suffers from fever after giving birth. As Dolly travels to Anna's, Tolstoy describes, step by small step, how her thoughts change. This remarkable chapter, which another writer might have summarized in a sentence, illustrates Tolstoy's approach to consciousness as a series of tiny alterations.

Dolly's thoughts begin with concerns about the children in her absence, then move to decisions she needs to make in the near future, all of which Tolstoy describes in detail. Next Dolly wonders whether she is pregnant again and worries about how she will manage if she is. Her last baby died, and that memory recalls a conversation she had with a young woman at the inn who expressed a sense of liberation at the death of her baby. Dolly finds that sentiment repulsive, but she now reflects that there is a grain of truth in it. During her fifteen years of marriage, her frequent pregnancies have meant agony, dullness of mind, anxiety, and, above all, disfigurement. They have left her repulsive to her husband and so, it seems, have led to his affairs.

Dolly now meditates on how hard it is when children are infants. She shudders at the recollection of how sore her nipples become. Then there is the trouble of raising children, educating them, teaching them Latin, worrying about their illnesses, and, several times, the pain of seeing them die. She remembers the funeral of her last child: "the callous indifference of all at the little pink coffin, and her own torn heart, and her lonely anguish at the sight of the pale little brow fringed with curls, and the open, surprised little mouth seen in the coffin when it was being covered with the little pink lid with a cross braided on it" (634). Dolly suffered her grief alone, just as she does in the novel's opening scene when no one else appreciates her injury.

She asks herself: "And all this, what's it for? . . . That I'm wasting my life, never having a moment's peace, either with child or nursing a child, forever irritable, peevish, wretched myself and worrying others, repulsive to my husband, while the children are growing up unhappy, badly educated, and poor" (635). She dwells on her financial difficulties, her parents' inability to help her, and her humiliation at having to accept help from the Levins, however tactful they may be. And the most she can hope for, she reflects, is that the children will not die and will be simply decent people, all at a tremendous cost that no one appreciates: "what agonies, what toil! . . . one's whole life ruined!" (635). The one person who does appreciate her efforts is the author, for whom motherhood is more important than any other occupation.

So perhaps that woman at the inn was right, she asks? Catching herself in such an immoral and frightening thought, Dolly checks it by inquiring of the coachmen how far they are from Anna's. Next she sees some peasant women, whom she imagines are happy while she is as if in prison. She has taken another step in her reflections, as her memories of troubles lead her to consider how else she might have lived. "They all live, those peasant women and my sister Natalie and Varenka and Anna, whom I am going to see—but not I" (635).

At this thought of Anna, Dolly finds herself coming to Anna's defense because Anna now represents for her the life she might have lived. If Dolly is to evaluate her life, she must grasp the alternative, and to do that, she must enter empathetically into the life of the person who embodies it. "She wants to live. God has put that in our hearts. Very likely I should have done the same. Even to this day I don't feel sure I did right in listening to her at that terrible time when she came to me in Moscow. I ought to have cast off my husband and been loved the real way" (635). The question posed by the novel's opening scene now returns, with all the consequences of the choice she made present to Dolly's eyes. Her thought has taken another small step, as she begins to imagine more concretely what else she might have done.

To be loved the real way: that is what she gave up and Anna (she imagines) embraced. But such love requires attractiveness, and Dolly wonders if she has any left. She considers taking the traveling mirror out of her bag. In a brilliant touch, Tolstoy has her refrain from doing so out of embarrassment before the coachman and office clerk traveling with her. We are not told but invited to consider the nature of this embarrassment: perhaps Dolly fears she will seem vain to them, or worse, ridiculous as an unattractive woman trying to fool herself, or still worse, they may guess her thoughts and catch her in immoral reflections. When Tolstoy traces the course of a character's thoughts and feelings step by tiny step, he often invites us to fill in still more steps in just this way, by imagining what one or another character may be feeling.

In this novel, mirrors recall Anna, who frequently looks at herself, and so Dolly's checked action suggests both her attraction to and repulsion from Anna's choice. Dolly does not look in the mirror but instead reflects on men who admire her, including Stiva's good-natured friend Turovtsyn, "who had helped her nurse her children through scarlet fever, and was in love with her" (636). Stiva has mentioned as a joke a quite young man who thought her more beautiful than her sisters, and we can sense both how this comment aids her in imagining an alternative life and how it must have hurt that Stiva would find it humorous that anyone could think her beautiful. Now the alternative has become vivid, as she has particular men in mind, and "the most passionate and impossible romances rose before Darya Aleksandrovna's imagination" (646). As she reflects again on Anna's love affair, Dolly constructs an almost identical one for herself. When she picture's Stiva's amazement upon discovering that she, too, has a lover, we see that the injury to her self esteem has never healed.

The question of whether Dolly has lived right has been implicit all along. It would have been easy to use a single memory or incident, or the very fact that she is going to see Anna, to make that question sufficiently believable. But Tolstoy shows us how consciousness actually works, how even an obvious thought does not arise immediately but develops through many small steps.

Dolly's question shapes all her perceptions of Anna. Whatever she observes at Anna's implicitly addresses that question. Because Tolstoy has described Dolly's thoughts during the journey in such detail, we can see how each observation during the visit resonates with one or another thought or feeling that, for Dolly, are part of the question of her life.

Looking Is an Action

The chapters devoted to Dolly's visit also describe, step by tiny step, the changes in Dolly's consciousness, either explicitly or by implicitly asking us to imagine her reactions. Space does not permit me to do more than indicate the basic pattern of Dolly's observations.

Tolstoy tells us that Dolly is an especially keen observer. Anna, who is no less perceptive, detects Dolly's "intense look of inquiry" and watches how Dolly watches things. Dolly soon begins to wonder not only about what she sees but also about her own reactions: why, for instance, she "surprised herself that she should respond so coldly [to Anna's question] about her children" (643).

Because Dolly knows that she is viewing Anna's life as an alternative to her own, she attends to her own emotional responses to everything she sees of that life. They betray her immediate feelings before she can judge or apologize for them. Dolly's reactions also matter for Anna since Dolly represents the best possible, because least hostile, observer of her situation. That is why, immediately upon her arrival, both Anna and Vronsky tell Dolly, with special emphasis, how much importance they attach to her visit. The entire sequence of chapters becomes a drama of mutual observation.

As is so often the case with Tolstoy, *looking is an action*. Indeed, it is often the most important one we perform. His point is the opposite of that old proverb, "a cat may look at a king," which suggests that looking either is passive or carries no moral weight. On the contrary, it matters greatly where we focus our attention, how we train ourselves to observe and listen, and whether we view people charitably or not. If ordinary actions count most, then it must make a difference how we choose to pay attention. We make that choice constantly. The choices made at each infinitesimally small moment shape the habits of perception we acquire.

As we shall see, this theme—that looking is an action—recurs throughout this novel. It pertains to ethical problems and to the drama of self-deception. Without grasping this theme, one cannot understand the Anna story. It explains how Tolstoy narrates several of the novel's best-known passages, such as the horse race and the visit to Mikhailov's studio. In these scenes, as in Dolly's visit, we watch people looking at how others look at how they are looking, while we, as readers, may ask ourselves about our own ways of seeing and paying attention. The drama of looking implicates the action of reading. If we learn to watch our own reactions as Dolly attends to hers, we may begin to notice much about ourselves that we usually miss.

Work

Why does Dolly reply so coldly to Anna's question about her children? To see Anna, Dolly has had to defy the Levins, who do not approve of her visit, and to expose her children to the risk of connection with a scandalous person. But so important is it to show that her feeling for Anna has not changed, and to repay Anna for her past kindness, that she endangers what matters most to her. That is one reason she reacts coldly when Anna asks about her children. Dolly may also recall Anna's assuming an interest in the children so as to win Dolly's good will and smooth over her quarrel with Stiva. Dolly already wonders about Anna's choice to leave her son and the way in which she cares for her daughter. Dolly reflects that the way Anna galloped up when she first caught sight of Dolly in the carriage did not indicate a woman who devotes herself to her child.

Anna rapidly poses the question that she expects Dolly to answer:

You haven't told me yet how and what you think about me, and I keep wanting to know. But I'm glad you will see me as I am. Above all, I don't want
you to think I want to prove anything; I merely want to live, to do no one
harm but myself. I have the right to that, haven't I? (643–44)

Characteristically, Anna regards the visit as all about herself, not her guest. Anna
has already described herself to Dolly as "inexcusably happy" (640), but her
intense desire to prove that she does not want to prove anything betrays her
doubts. A hint of suicide lurks in her comment that she wants to harm no one
"but myself."

After asking her question, Anna defers any possible discussion of it: she
keeps saying that they will "talk about it later." Dolly notices that Anna has developed a new habit, dropping her eyes "as if not to see things." Using opium,
Anna blanks her mind as well. Could it be that her whole life now consists of an
attempt not to see it?

The novel's theme of work now takes on special significance. Dolly has just
regretted that she does nothing but work, but she has no doubt that the work
genuinely contributes to her children's welfare. It is not make-work. Although it
helps her to avoid brooding about her husband, her activity is not invented primarily for that purpose. She did the same before discovering Stiva's infidelity.

"With her experienced housewife's eye" (644), Dolly surveys her room, the
less luxurious one in which she has been placed so as to be closer to Anna. With
everything new, expensive, and imported, it displays "luxury of which she had
only read in English novels" (644). Dolly chooses everything for use rather than
show and is now ashamed of her own patched bed-jacket. As she soon sees,
everything at Anna's has been chosen for the sake of appearance. This house is
dedicated to showing itself off.

Dolly attaches the greatest significance to the nursery, but here, too, she
encounters expensive substitutes for parenting.

There were little carts ordered from England, and appliances for teaching
babies to walk, and a sofa after the fashion of a billiard table, purposely
constructed for crawling, and swings and baths, all of a special pattern, and
modern. They were all English, solid, and of good make, and obviously very
expensive. (646)

Dolly meets several nurses, one of whom is evidently so disreputable that she
wonders how Anna, "with her insight into people" (646) could have hired her;
but the nurse, like the furniture, is English. Despite the nurses, no one takes
care of little Annie. It is clear that Anna's visit to the nursery is exceptional.
Dolly wonders that Anna does not know how many teeth the baby has. What-

ever Anna is doing, it is not tending to her child. Dolly soon discovers that not Anna but Vronsky manages the house.

Vronsky, who is bored, looks for occupation. He tells Dolly, a bit too strenuously, that he has really found something to do and that what he does is not "*un pis-aller,*" a last resort. He has built a hospital for the peasants and equipped it, as he has the nursery, with modern English contraptions. Not only his insistence on his hobby's meaningfulness but also his evident need for others to admire what he has done betray his anxiety that it is fake. Dolly learns that he decided to build the hundred-thousand-ruble hospital not to cure people but in order to show Anna that he is not miserly. (We have just been told that twenty rubles to hire horses is a serious matter for Dolly.) He has chosen a hospital, rather than some other kind of philanthropy, because hospitals are now in fashion.

Anna and Vronsky must have guests to entertain. They provide games for the guests to play, but the play is as fake as the work. The hosts play only to amuse the guests and the guests play to show the hosts they are amused. The falsity of the play derives from the falsity of the work. Just as someone retired or unemployed cannot take a vacation from work, so those who do not know how to work cannot really play.

Dolly does not enjoy the game of lawn tennis and is struck by "the unnaturalness of grownups, all alone without children, playing at a child's game" (663). To Dolly, it is all show, and "all that day it seemed to her as though she was acting in a theater with actors cleverer than she, and that her bad acting was spoiling the whole performance" (663). Now the maternal cares and worries Dolly had so hated on her journey "struck her in quite another light, and tempted her back to them" (663). However arduous, they mean something.

Dolly at last answers the riddle of what occupies Anna's time. She discovers that what Anna does is look beautiful and act seductive. Anna is constantly changing her dresses, even more often than before, and she "devoted just as much care to her appearance when they had no visitors" (671). She pretends an interest in Vronsky's projects. Dolly's distaste at how Anna spends her time explains her reaction to Anna's use of birth control. Dolly has never heard of birth control. For Dolly, the possibility of preventing pregnancy, which has caused her such pain, "is so immense that all one feels for the first instant is that it is impossible to take it all in, and that one will have to reflect a great, great deal upon it" (666). Birth control could be the answer to her most pressing problem, and yet, when she considers why Anna uses it, it seems wrong. Anna explains that birth control insures that her looks will not be destroyed by repeated pregnancies. For Dolly, that reason renders Anna's love and family life as fake as the estate's nursery and work substitutes. Anna's use of birth control, Dolly thinks, "is too simple a solution to too complicated a problem" (666).[6]

In a life well-lived, one never has to look for work to do. As both Levin and Dolly know, time is always too short to do all that is necessary. Anna's and Vronsky's need to fill time betrays the essential emptiness of their existence. When Dolly returns home, she defends Anna and Vronsky, but the questions that occurred to her on the journey, the questions that have been raised by her whole life, have been answered. The way Dolly lives is truly meaningful. She sees the alternative is fake. Dolly has now accepted the value of her life. As she does so, the novel's story about her is resolved.

Stiva and the Russian Idea of Evil

> Oblonsky is one of the sweetest characters in all of Tolstoy. . . . He brings life and goodwill wherever he goes.
> —ALLAN BLOOM (237)

As Dolly represents good, Stiva represents evil. And the first thing to notice about evil is that it is not grand, Satanic, or alien, but friendly, charming, and ordinary. If a supernatural being incarnated this sort of evil, he would be socially adept. Everyone would know him. Dostoevsky did in fact represent the devil in just this way, and his ordinary demon is one of his greatest creations. Chekhov, too, saw evil in terms of prosaic failures we see all around us. Indeed, I think we can speak of the idea of "evil as ordinary" as a distinctively Russian insight. In the twentieth century, of course, Hannah Arendt's *Eichmann in Jerusalem* would argue a related point about the banality of evil.

I believe that Dostoevsky's devil, whom he created within a few years of reading *Anna Karenina,* was in fact modeled on Stiva. Dostoevsky wrote extensively about this novel in his *Writer's Diary* and viewed Stiva pretty much as I do, as the incarnation of evil. "Yes, the Stivas would get very angry if the Kingdom of Heaven were to arrive," Dostoevsky describes the enemies of his Christian ideals (AWD, 884). Both Stiva and Ivan Karamazov's devil prefer the pleasures and opportunities of the world as it is.

According to Dostoevsky, the Stivas are "regarded as innocent and genial good fellows, affable egotists who do no one any harm, witty, and enjoying their pleasures to the full" (AWD, 872). They "love refinement and art and love to converse on all subjects" (AWD, 872). They may have children, but "they give them little thought" (AWD, 872), a characteristic of great significance in *Karamazov,* which deals so much with the neglect of children. As one of these Stivas, the devil in *Karamazov* resembles those society gentlemen who find it unseemly to mention their children and neglect them. "They gradually lose sight of their children altogether" (BK, 724). Evil as symbolized by neglect of children: this theme in both novels marks the similar importance each attaches to the family.

Though the incarnation of evil, Dostoevsky's devil, like Stiva, hardly appears evil and is in fact generally well liked. After all, he has a "companionable and accommodating disposition" and is "ready to assume any amiable expression as the occasion might arise" (BK, 724), a line that recalls Stiva's amazing amiability and talent for reading people. By assuming exactly the right tone or impression "as the occasion might arise," Stiva can win anyone over.[7] Both Stiva and the devil are chameleons.

Evil conquers by redirecting our attention from what we should do. It tempts us to negligence.

Evil is ordinary, and Stiva its incarnation, neither because the *worst* evil is ordinary nor because the cruelest people resemble Stiva. That is obviously not the case. If we think of evil as committed by Torquemada, Hitler, Stalin, or Pol Pot, we will never be able to imagine how Dostoevsky's devil or Stiva could be its incarnation. And that is the whole point. We are almost helpless against evil because we think only of a part of it that is unrepresentative of the whole and largely the result of the rest. As with the trees on a distant hill, we notice the noticeable and imagine that is all there is.

In this view, the Stivas commit not the worst evil but the *most* evil. Life is made up primarily of ordinary moments and even what happens at extraordinary ones is largely their product. If we think of evil as grand, Satanic, and alien, we will miss its presence in ourselves. We will also miss how we contribute to the possibility of the more noticeable evil. From this perspective one might say: no ordinary neglect and petty selfishness, no Lenin. We have met the enemy and he is us.

Like good, evil is right here and right now. We like it, and do not even see the harm in it, which is one reason there is so much of it.

If the cause of most evil were primarily something extraordinary and extreme, evil would be comparatively easy to get rid of, once and for all. Just defeat Hitler, or the class enemies, or the Elders of Zion, and you will be done with it, as countless utopians have dreamed. Utopianism, indeed, depends on seeing the cause of all evil as singular (or small in number) and so easily eradicable. But if the causes of evil are ordinary and everywhere, one cannot find and execute them. We must, among other things, seek them in ourselves, which is much less pleasant than attributing evil to something alien.

Negligence and Negative Events

Tolstoy's idea of evil differs from Dostoevsky's in one important respect. For Dostoevsky, evil is ordinary primarily because we all frequently entertain evil wishes. Taken together, those wishes shape the field of possible actions and so insure that, one way or another, evil will take place. Like Ivan Karamazov, we all want to "kill our fathers" even though we would not act out that wish. But in

Tolstoy, evil is first of all what the novel refers to as a "negative event." It does not require even evil wishes, just forgetting, the way Stiva never can remember he has a wife and children. Evil is an absence, which is why, like so many important things, it is camouflaged and sought in the wrong places. Rather than an action, even an interior action like wishing, it more closely resembles criminal negligence.

To illustrate that evil does not require malice, Tolstoy gives Stiva no malice at all. In fact, Stiva, an evil character who intends nobody any harm, stands as one of Tolstoy's boldest and most original creations, all the more so because Stiva's psychology is entirely convincing. The fact that so many readers have liked Stiva illustrates Tolstoy's point all the more.

Even if we could eliminate all malice, we would not have touched the main source of evil.

Stiva likes and is liked by everyone, and, Tolstoy remarks, his acquaintances from the extreme ends of the social ladder would be surprised to know that they had something in common, their friendship with Stiva. Stiva "was the familiar friend of everyone with whom he took a glass of champagne, and he took a glass of champagne with everyone" (20). He not only enjoys himself but has also thought a great deal about pleasure and the state of mind it requires. He is quite brilliant on the topic, both theoretically and practically. With his keen intelligence, he is no simple hedonist.

Stiva has learned how to create the right state of mind in himself and others, and we catch him doing so with Levin at a restaurant, with the several guests at his dinner party, and elsewhere. Almost everyone experiences delight when encountering him even if nothing particularly delightful happens. Because "the distributors of earthly blessings" were all his friends, his success in the service depends entirely on what he does *not* do: "He had only not to refuse things, not to show jealousy, not to be quarrelsome or take offense, all of which from his characteristic good nature he never did" (17). His "complete indifference" to his job means that "he was never carried away, and never made mistakes" (18).

The Forgettory

Tolstoy describes Stiva's complex of qualities as "the liberalism of the blood," the sign of which is his default expression, a good-natured smile. When Dolly confronts him with the letter proving his infidelity, he is at first so nonplussed that "his face utterly involuntarily (reflex action of the brain, reflected Stepan Arkadyevich, who was fond of physiology)—utterly involuntarily assumed its habitual, good-humored, and therefore foolish smile" (5). For all its evident absurdity, there is nevertheless a grain of truth in his idea that not the affair but his smile is to blame for his present troubles. Dolly was evidently attracted to Stiva in part for his good nature, but when, caught red-handed, he smiles in that characteristic way, she realizes what that good nature means in practice: "And that disgusting good nature of his, which everyone likes him for and praises—I hate that good nature of his" (13).

Stiva knows that pleasure depends on oneself even more than on one's amusements. He therefore makes sure that inopportune memories never diminish his pleasure in the moment and so manages to forget what one would think were the most obvious facts. Within a few pages, he encourages both Vronsky and Levin in their pursuit of Kitty and even quotes the same verses to each. If one does not understand Stiva, one might think he must be lying to at least one of them. But if by lying we mean consciously telling a falsehood, he is not lying, and would pass a lie detector test. At the moment he is with either of the men interested in Kitty, he genuinely sympathizes and simply does not call to mind the hopes he may have expressed for the other. His talent for this kind of immersion in the moment partially explains how he can be the perfect chameleon. It is not quite correct to say he has a bad memory; rather, he has an excellent "forgettory."

Honesty

As a book about infidelity, *Anna Karenina* is also a book about the nature of honesty and truthfulness. Stiva's dishonest honesty indicates from the very beginning that honesty is not an obvious concept. As Tolstoy paraphrases Stiva's thought in Stiva's language, we hear repeatedly, and with mounting irony, that the perpetually unfaithful Stiva considers himself a "truthful" and "honest" person. Stiva means that he would much prefer to have his pleasure without lying about it, since lying is itself unpleasant.

Tolstoy's point is that honesty requires a lot more than not telling a conscious falsehood. It requires work, the work of actively searching one's memory for anything that might contradict what one is saying or convict one of hypocrisy. Levin is always stopping in mid-sentence when he recalls such a contrary fact. In preaching sexual purity and Platonic love to Stiva, Levin suddenly ceases abruptly as he recalls his own indiscretions. Levin's sudden changes resulting from a search for disconfirming evidence characterize him as a truly honest person who has, through considerable effort, made a habit of self-reflection.

When Stiva sees Dolly's misery, he feels genuine pity for her, and it would be a mistake to think this sympathy is feigned. He really feels it, but only while in her presence. The moment he leaves, he immediately forgets his sympathy, which will not change his actions in the slightest. The trainman's death truly shocks Stiva, but by the time he prepares to leave the station he is already in an animated conversation about a new singer. Most horribly, in Part Eight, after his sister Anna's suicide, someone mentions to Stiva that Vronsky is nearby. The name Vronsky brings Anna to Stiva's mind. "For an instant Stepan Arkadyevich's face looked sad, but a minute later, when, smoothing his whiskers and with a spring in his walk, he went into the hall where Vronsky was, he had completely forgotten his own despairing sobs over his sister's corpse, and he saw in Vronsky only a [war] hero and an old friend" (806–7).

In everyday life we sometimes encounter a person who asserts something flatly contradicting something else he knows and yet is genuinely convinced of his truthfulness. Or we may be disturbed by someone who excuses a broken promise by mentioning an obstacle that was entirely foreseeable. Each of these people would be sincerely offended if accused of falsehood because neither intended to deceive. But they are still being false because to assert something seriously includes, at the minimum, checking one's assertion against obvious objections. To promise something means one has already considered easily foreseeable obstacles. Since some sort of obstacles impede all actions, promises would mean nothing if they did not bind one to fulfilling them nevertheless.

Fatalism and Blame

Stiva awakes: that is the novel's first action. He recalls his exceedingly pleasant dream of a dinner party. Glass tables sang, appropriately enough for Stiva, Don Giovanni's serenade from Mozart's *Don Giovanni* (or perhaps "something better"!). On the table were little decanters "and they were women, too," he ponders as his eyes twinkle gaily (4).

Anna will later tell Dolly that Stiva is racked with guilt, but we see from the start that he is not. Stiva does not even remember the infidelity or the quarrel that keeps Dolly awake until he "cheerfully" feels for slippers and his hand by habit reaches for his dressing gown. Only when he does not find the dressing gown does Stiva realize that he is not sleeping in the usual place because of the quarrel. His body, not the current of his dreams or thoughts, brings the new situation to mind.

Now he reflects on the incident, only to excuse himself in a characteristically Oblonsky-like way: "And the most awful thing is that it's all my fault—all my fault, though I'm not to blame. That's the whole point of the situation" (4).

This paradoxical reflection poses a delicious riddle, because one might think that being at fault and being to blame were the same thing. In Russian they come from the same root (*vina* and *vinovat*) and so another translator renders the paradox, "I'm the guilty one in it all—guilty but not guilty" (P&V, 2). What Stiva means is that, while the action was committed by him, and is in that sense his fault, it happened inevitably, as if by a force of nature acting through him. What else could a susceptible man of thirty-four married to an unappealing wife do? He is not to blame because the action could not *not* have happened.

Fatalism as an excuse appeals because it is always applicable. It denies one's blameworthiness by denying responsibility altogether.

It is often observed that Tolstoy, unlike other novelists, creates families that are not just collections of individuals but also have a distinctive culture all their own. Outsiders often cannot appreciate what is going on. The Rostovs, Bolkonskys, and Kuragins in *War and Peace,* the Shcherbatskys and Levin brothers in *Anna Karenina:* each family displays its own feel of life, its own ways of seeing and acting. To understand the individual one needs to understand the family, and each member can shed light on the others. So it is with Anna and Stiva. The first thing one needs to know about Anna is that she is the former Anna Oblonskaya, Stiva's sister, and so it is not surprising that she, too, resorts to fatalism when justifying her actions to Dolly: "But I was not to blame. And who is to blame? What's the meaning of being to blame? Could it have happened otherwise? What do you think? Could it possibly have happened that you didn't become the wife of Stiva?" (664). Both Anna and Stiva use this excuse but, as we shall see, for different reasons. It thereby marks both their family resemblance and their individual differences.

He Had Never Clearly Thought Out the Subject

At the beginning of Part One, chapter 2, we eavesdrop on Stiva's thoughts to the accompaniment of the author's irony:

> Stepan Arkadyevich was a truthful man with himself. He was incapable of deceiving himself and persuading himself that he repented of his conduct. He could not at this date feel repentant that he, a handsome, women-prone man of thirty-four, was not in love with his wife, the mother of five living and two dead children, and only a year younger than himself. All he was sorry for was that he had not succeeded better in hiding it from his wife. . . . Possibly he might have managed to conceal his sins better from his wife if he had anticipated the effect on her should she discover them. He had never clearly thought out the subject, but he had vaguely conceived that his wife must long ago have suspected him of being unfaithful to her, and shut her eyes to the fact. He had even supposed that she, a worn-out woman no longer young or good-looking, and in no way remarkable or interesting, merely a good mother, ought from a sense of fairness to take an indulgent view. It had turned out quite the other way. (5–6)

The point of view and sequence of thoughts here is Stiva's, as are some phrases ("truthful man," "incapable of deceiving himself"): we are supposed to hear him saying, "I am a truthful man, I am incapable of deceiving myself," and so on. But we also hear another voice, the author's, who adds a word here or there and intones Stiva's words rather differently. This "double-voicing," as Mikhail Bakhtin called this common technique of realism, becomes especially apparent in the last sentence. The fact that it had "turned out quite the other way" surprises Stiva, not the ironic narrator, and the difference between the two voices speaking the same words leads to the humor.

The author's irony is easy to catch. More difficult, but no less important, is his implicit invitation to hear what Stiva says from the point of view of the one Stiva describes, Dolly. As so often in this novel, we will miss a great deal if we do not ask: But how would the other person respond to these thoughts if he or she could hear them?

To Stiva, those two dead children are insignificant enough to be placed in the middle of a long sentence that is mainly about something else. But we are to learn, and here can already imagine, the agonies Dolly suffers at the death of a child. Stiva therefore does not even consider what is obvious to Dolly, that if two children could die, so might any of the others. He does not even suspect her constant worry and frequent alarm. For Stiva, those two dead children signify little more than two more pregnancies that have left Dolly even less attractive. When Anna uses birth control, she hopes to forestall precisely this sort of reaction on Vronsky's part.

In Stiva's reflection that he has never clearly thought through what his wife's reaction would be, we see a kind of cruelty by neglect. How could he not consider her feelings? The absurdity of her taking an indulgent view out of simple fairness exemplifies his failure to think about his behavior from her perspective at all. This absence of thinking is the sort of negative evil event (or non-event) Tolstoy wants us to grasp.

Stiva's whole attitude here is horrible as well as funny. Dolly will later come to speak of Stiva with an irony resembling the author's in this passage.

We see the difference between Stiva's and the author's perspective most starkly in Stiva's characterization of his wife as "only" a good mother. As neglect is evil, so Dolly's attentiveness to her children exemplifies the book's idea of goodness.

It is easy to miss Tolstoy's invitation to consider Stiva's thoughts from Dolly's point of view, much as it is easy to miss similar invitations elsewhere. For Tolstoy, goodness and evil are always right before our eyes, camouflaged but visible to those who learn to see them.[8]

CHAPTER THREE

Anna

Introduction to a Contrary Reading

When I was about thirty, I discussed *Anna Karenina* with a friend. I presented the novel as I then understood it and as I assumed it pretty much had to be understood. Anna undergoes great suffering, and we are expected to sympathize intensely with her. The society that condemns her is utterly hypocritical: the very people who have countless affairs, like Betsy Tverskaya, condemn her because she actually loves and acts on her passion. She loves not wisely but too well, and her tragedy results from the impossibility of transcending a culture of lies.[1]

I thought: Anna is married to a much older man before she knows what love is. Tolstoy indicates that her marriage to Karenin has been erotically unsatisfying. It would be hard for anyone to be married to Karenin, much as it would be hard to be married to Casaubon in George Eliot's *Middlemarch*. Late in the book, Karenin reveals himself to be a moral monster, and I assumed that Anna, who has claimed to understand him better than others, has detected that moral monstrosity from the novel's beginning. If her husband had any human feeling, would he not care more about her infidelity than about observing the proprieties?

When Anna at last leaves Karenin, she must abandon her son to do so and then endure the pain of separation. The scene where she must sneak in to visit Seryozha on his birthday moved me deeply, both for her and for him. A true tragic heroine, Anna has had to choose between two terrible alternatives, abandoning her lover or her son. Either choice would have been unendurable. Vronsky's incapacity to understand her contributes to the despair that leads her to take her life, an outcome that Tolstoy has foreshadowed in Part One with the "the evil omen" of the trainman's death. The allegory of the horse race, in which Vronsky makes an "unpardonable mistake" and breaks the horse's back, also foreshadows Anna's end.

In short, I had adopted what might be called the "majority reading" of the novel.[2] I knew that Tolstoy himself had suggested a reading critical of Anna, but then Tolstoy was always saying perverse things. A writer does not always understand his own work. As some critics would say, the author *of* the work, the biographical author, does not necessarily coincide with the author *in* the work, the implied author.

I knew as well that a minority critical tradition held a negative view of Anna, often on religious grounds. In subsequent years, Richard Gustafson was to extend this reading with considerable power. But I did not see the need for a religious (or otherwise moralistic) reading, which seemed to rely on considerations outside the work itself.[3] It seemed not implausible, but nevertheless untrue to my experience of reading the book.

My friend, who had recently read the novel, asked me: "how old were you when you last read *Anna Karenina?*" "Twenty-one," I answered. "I see," she replied, "perhaps you should read it again."

I did not give the novel a serious rereading until I had finished my study of *War and Peace.* In that study, I offered an unconventional reading of Tolstoy's book. I coined the term "prosaics" for the belief, expressed by Tolstoy, that the most important events in history and individual lives are the small, prosaic ones we barely notice and may not even remember. In the view of prosaics and Tolstoy, melodrama misleads and romanticism obscures. I now asked myself: Does Tolstoy develop or reject this view in his next major work of fiction, *Anna Karenina?* For there is no reason that an author could not change his mind, and, indeed, *Anna* was written while Tolstoy was going through the crisis that would soon lead to the rejection of many of his views. I certainly remembered the book as romantic, not prosaic.

I tried to suspend my earlier reading and see the work as if for the first time. To do so, I also had to try to think away the history of the work's interpretation. The fact is, I reflected, no one comes to a classic without expectations. In my first book, I had stressed the generic conventions that shape our perceptions and interpretations of a work from the outset. A good deal happens "before reading," as Peter Rabinowitz has put the point (Rabinowitz, *Before Reading*). For many, the Garbo film, endless other versions, jacket blurbs, and common opinion predispose readers to see the work romantically. Romances sell. For scholars, the history of interpretation exerts added effect. Indeed, it most likely shaped their reading even as students, before they had read any criticism, because the classes in which they first studied the novel were shaped by prevailing critical opinion.

The Russian critic Victor Shklovsky famously asserted that the defining quality of literature lies in its "defamiliarizing" the world. Shklovsky cites a passage from Tolstoy's diaries:

> I was cleaning a room, and meandering about, approached the divan and could not remember whether or not I had dusted it. Since these movements

are habitual and unconscious, I could not remember and felt it was impossible to remember—so that if I had dusted it and forgot—that is, had acted
unconsciously, then it was the same as if I had not. If some conscious person had been watching, then the fact could be established. If however, no
one was looking, or looking on unconsciously, if the whole complex lives of
many people go on unconsciously, then such lives are as if they had never
been. (Shklovsky, "Art as Technique," 12)

Shklovsky comments:

And so life is reckoned as nothing. Habitualization devours works, clothes,
furniture, one's wife, and the fear of war. "If the whole complex lives of
many people go on unconsciously, then such lives are as if they had never
been." And art exists that one may recover the sensation of life, to make the
stone *stony*. The purpose of art is to impart the sensation of things as they are
perceived and not as they are known. The technique of art is to make objects
"unfamiliar" . . . (Shklovsky, "Art as Technique," 12)

I wanted to grasp the sensation of *Anna Karenina* as it is perceived, not as already known. My idea was: criticism should periodically make works unfamiliar by reading them as if for the first time. Of course, as I would now say, one
cannot just think away the history of reception. But to say that such a direct
experience is impossible is not to say that we cannot suspend some knowledge
long enough to see the work in a new, if not wholly innocent, way.

In this way, I arrived at an interpretation at odds with much (though by
no means all) of my earlier one, and at odds with some key aspects of both the
majority and minority traditions. I came to see Tolstoy as highly critical of Anna
for a variety of reasons. It is not just that her romantic view and belief in omens
contradict Tolstoy's sense of the ordinary and his belief in contingency. Even
more important, Anna teaches herself to misperceive others and herself. She
does so primarily from a sense of guilt, and so her studied misperceptions demonstrate that she has a conscience, as others, like Betsy and her brother Stiva, do
not.[4]

By stressing Tolstoy's criticism of Anna, my interpretation differs from the
majority view. Nevertheless, I still believe Tolstoy makes it clear that Anna's marriage to Karenin is not satisfying and does not engage her soul deeply. Karenin
does end as a moral monster. I do not doubt Karenin's weak eroticism, the hypocrisy of the society that condemns Anna, and the deep pathos of her visit to
her son. Above all, I not only believe in Anna's intense suffering but think that
the suffering of her last moments has been underappreciated.

I realized that even though I now saw Tolstoy's view of Anna as critical, I was still more sympathetic to her than he was. But I thought it important to distinguish the two reactions.

My interpretation differs from those of the minority view that invoke religion and the morality usually derived from it.[5] Odd as it may seem, Tolstoy seems to disapprove not so much of Anna's adultery as of her self-deception. To use Bakhtin's term, Anna does not "sign" her actions: rather than take responsibility for her choices, she chooses to misperceive her own actions and those of others.

Why, then, have so many of the best readers read the work "romantically"? And am I so sure they are wrong? No, I am not sure, and perhaps I shall change my mind again, or find a way to combine more aspects of opposing readings. After all, critics I particularly respect—almost all American Slavists, Russians as insightful as Boris Eichenbaum, and non-Slavists as sensitive as Barbara Hardy—have seen the work as sympathetic to Anna.

I do not have a fully adequate explanation for why the work has been so frequently misinterpreted in this way. My own experience suggests a few possibilities:

(1) We come across the work already read. Received opinion and scholarly instruction shape what we see. I already knew the Garbo film and still remember the jacket back of the edition I first read.[6] As I know from experience, it is extremely difficult and time-consuming to identify, much less suspend, earlier opinion.

(2) As I argue below, Tolstoy was taking on the ideology of romantic love. So pervasive is that ideology, arguably even stronger today than in Tolstoy's time, that readers do not recognize it *as* an ideology. Romantic love is just what love is. It is therefore hard to entertain the possibility that the author could be criticizing it.

(3) If Tolstoy were critical of Anna, he would have to be more sympathetic to Karenin. And he would have to be questioning a rebellion against social hypocrisy. We do not easily investigate these possibilities.

(4) We have come to accept implicitly that truth lies in the extreme, that life is lived most fully when it is lived most intensely (see Bernstein). That ideology has become so widespread that advertisers routinely rely on it. Detecting and questioning it is not impossible, but, again, these are not our first reactions. Tolstoy's prosaic philosophy, like his making Dolly the novel's moral compass, comes as a shock.

(5) We first see Anna at the train station brimming over with suppressed vitality. Her eroticism seems to embody the force of life. Harold Bloom voices a truism when he writes: "Anna, vital and attractive in every way, is

someone with whom most male readers of the novel fall in love, and Tolstoy clearly loves her almost obsessively" (Bloom, 1). Bloom explains that "what matters most about Anna, at least to the reader, is her intensity, her will to live" (Bloom, 3). Criticizing Anna may therefore resemble criticizing life itself.

(6) Perhaps most important: Anna suffers, and we vicariously share her suffering. Tolstoy presents events that happen to her primarily through her eyes. As we read, we identify and, identifying, sympathize. To criticize her is to deny our experience of identification. It almost feels as if we were adding to her suffering or coming to resemble the social world that condemns her so cruelly.

(7) We have all engaged in self-deception, as Anna has, either to rationalize our behavior or to assuage our guilt. Perhaps we do it daily. Over time, we look back on our lives and detect earlier self-deceptions that once seemed so convincing. How are we to criticize her for what we all do?[7] That would be too much like faulting ourselves.

I have also come to see that Tolstoy employed strategies that risked, almost invited, misreading. He uses open camouflage: he places key information in subordinate clauses or buries it in long paragraphs primarily about something else. I think Tolstoy does so to illustrate his ideas of perception and memory. The problem is, it is easy to overlook passages that rely for their point on being easy to overlook.

Tolstoy relies heavily on a "free indirect discourse" narration of Anna's experience. He weaves in and out of her consciousness and presents in the third person perceptions and evaluations that are Anna's, not the author's. Perhaps recognizing that it is easy to mistake these perceptions as belonging to the author, he sometimes interrupts to tell us that Anna was deliberately teaching herself to misperceive, that she was enjoying the very practice of falsehood, or that she was not considering the other person's point of view. Such explicit statements, which I cite below, carry less force than the emotional experience with which we identify. Perhaps if Tolstoy had gone as far as he did in *War and Peace* and included lengthy essays about his points, he would have run less of a risk of misunderstanding—at the possible expense of harming his work in other ways.

I mean this interpretation of Anna to open debate, not close it. In paraphrasing what I take to be Tolstoy's views I am not enunciating my own.

Anna and the Kinds of Love

Now my idea is clear to me. In order for a work to be good, one must love its main basic idea, as in *Anna Karenina* I love the idea of a family.
— TOLSTOY (N, 751)

Murder an Infant (a Tolstoyan Meditation)

The road of excess leads to the palace of wisdom. He who desires but acts not, breeds pestilence. Sooner murder an infant in its cradle than nurse unacted desires. Originally intended to be shocking, these three of Blake's "proverbs of Hell" now read like cinematic (or therapeutic) clichés. To criticize their point seems stodgy, repressed, or positively quaint. In the extreme is truth: this idea has afflicted Western thought at least since the Romantics.

So deep is the cult of extremes that we tacitly equate intensity of experience with real life. The most hackneyed advertisements promise such intensity. What does not thrill, jolt, or shock seems, almost by definition, boring. In politics, too, revolution, utopianism, and the radical sexiness of primitivism have attracted even the gentlest souls. Ideologies seduce by the lure of fanaticism. Che Guevara images have become a commercial glut, and box office hits pretend, in a protected setting, that madmen are the truly sane and revolutionaries are more humane than shopkeepers.

Intellectuals have proven especially susceptible to belief systems that equate liberation with extremism of one sort or another. "The will to destroy is also a creative will," as the anarchist Mikhail Bakunin wrote.

Chekhov defiantly advocated traditional virtues — self-mastery, cleanliness, politeness, care for one's family, paying one's debts, and other "bourgeois" tenets — and observed that if those who advocate extremism should ever gain power, the result would be worse than the Spanish Inquisition. Too often, morals sound benighted or out-of-date and provoke not as much critique as eye-rolling. Only hypocrites advocate moderation, while rage signifies sincerity. Prisons are built with stones of law, brothels with bricks of religion.

Under the spell of extremism, we routinely equate misdeeds to the Holocaust. Or we may hear: any morality that would not help one survive Auschwitz must be faulty. A moment's reflection would lead to the conclusion that a morality good for Auschwitz would be disastrous in ordinary life. (See Bernstein.)

Moderates did not build the Gulag, plan the Holocaust, or create the Cambodian killing fields. These emblems of the twentieth century resulted from apocalyptic appeals to total liquidation or a final solution for designated incarnations of evil. Intellectuals safely abroad endorsed such appeals. Horror fascinates and totalism titillates.

As bad money drives out good, so extremist concepts drive out accurate descriptions. Like "fascism" in another era, "genocide" is now often used to name anything evoking great disapproval. The cases that really are extreme or genocidal lose their distinctiveness. When every sinner is a devil, the real devil can work openly.

Fatality

Our ideas of love also tend to an extreme. Tolstoy would largely have agreed with the central argument of Denis de Rougemont's classic study, *Love in the Western World.* De Rougemont regards our civilization's idea of love as a myth, a set of images and beliefs we accept so totally that we do not even entertain the possibility of alternatives. To us, romantic, passionate love simply *is* love. From popular culture to high romance, and from teenage infatuations to great literature, it is what we mean by "true love." Everyone understands the phrase "true love" this way. De Rougemont wants to make us conscious of this myth *as* a myth so that we may recognize the possibility of a different kind of love.

As Bakhtin would say, de Rougemont wants to resituate us from a Ptolemaic to a Copernican universe. Much as Copernicus showed the earth is not the center but just one planet among many, so romantic love must be seen as just one kind of love. It cannot then be accepted unthinkingly but must be justified. It becomes, as Bakhtin also liked to say, contesting, contestable, and contested; or, as we may say more simply, it becomes a choice. De Rougemont states his purpose: "And what I aim at is to bring the reader to the point of declaring frankly, either that 'That is what I wanted!' or else 'God forbid!'" (de Rougemont, 25).

Like other questioners of received myths, de Rougemont locates an origin (twelfth-century Provençal) and traces a history of romantic love in order to demonstrate that what we accept as natural and universal is in fact contingent and local. Romantic love is an ideology. It did not always exist and has not flourished everywhere, so we can choose either to keep or to abandon it. De Rougemont ascribes the extremism at the heart of this conception of love to its origins in Manicheanism and the Albigensian heresy. Romantic love derives from mysticism and in our time, has become a sort of secular religion. In the absence of God, romantic passion substitutes as a source of meaning, and so its domination of our culture grows.

> Love and death, a fatal love—in these phrases is summed up, if not the whole of poetry, at least whatever is popular, whatever is universally moving in European literature. . . . Happy love has no history. Romance only comes into existence where love is fatal, frowned upon and doomed by life itself. What stirs lyric poets to their finest flights is neither the delight of the senses nor the fruitful contentment of the settled couple; not the satisfaction of love, but its *passion*. (de Rougemont, 15)

Romantic love is passion in the full sense of the word. It is not an action but a passion; like Christ's passion, it is something we suffer. We do not leap into love, we fall in love. In the Tristan story and elsewhere, this sense of passion was figured by a love potion that possesses us against our will. In our own time, we speak not of a love potion, but, let us say, of psychological factors that overwhelm our will.

We cannot resist passion. We do not choose it, and so we are not responsible for our actions under its spell. This love transcends good and evil, goes beyond pleasure and pain, and therefore neither moral nor consequential arguments apply. So often have readers taken *Anna Karenina* to be an expression rather than a critique of romantic love that moral concerns about Anna's behavior have seemed either philistine or beside the point.[8]

Under the spell of the romantic myth, many readers apologize for Anna's abandonment of one child and neglect of another, her failure to care at all about Karenin's feelings, or her willingness to revenge herself on Vronsky by committing suicide. Anna herself knows it gives her an alibi. In this reading, Anna could not help what she did. The passion to which she succumbs represents an unstoppable overflow of sheer vitality that makes right and wrong irrelevant. Such readings entirely embrace Anna's explicitly stated views and the complex of romantic beliefs she accepts.

In this interpretation, Anna lives more fully, more intensely, and more radically than others, and so she is bound to come into conflict with society, which subsists by hidebound rules and norms. Either from conservatism, hypocrisy, or both, society must persecute the true lover as it does the true genius. The myths of love and of genius are in fact quite closely allied. Anna and these readers imagine her to be an exceptional person, and this alleged exceptionality connects the novel with another Tolstoy admired, *Crime and Punishment*. The hero of that novel, Raskolnikov, divides people into extraordinary people, like Napoleon or Lycurgus, to whom the moral law does not apply, and ordinary ones who are, as Katavasov states in *Anna Karenina,* mere breeders. Katavasov may represent Tolstoy's tacit nod to Dostoevsky.

Romantic love is fatal in both senses of the word.[9] It is preordained, both in its flaring up and in its end, which is death. Anna accepts these ideas without reservation. She believes herself to be what Liza Merkalova has called her, "a genuine heroine of a romance" [or: of a novel] (315. See Sloane, 125 and Orwin, *Art and Thought,* 171–80). She teaches Vronsky to speak the language of romance instead of the language of dissolute officers he is used to.

Anna believes in omens, as we first learn when, after the trainman is run over, she pronounces the event "an evil omen." She believes as well in prophetic dreams. One of her dreams of the hideous peasant opens into another where Korney interprets the first as an omen that she will die in childbirth. Anna accepts this interpretation. She fends off questions about the future with statements that she will have no future after giving birth. As we have seen, Anna's family culture already inclines her to fatalism as an excuse, but she adds to this self-interested fatalism a romantic one, which her brother Stiva would never accept. This romantic fatalism absolves her from guilt by subjecting her to forces leading to suffering and death. Stiva feels no guilt and would never embrace suffering. He is a hedonist, but Anna is a romantic for whom suffering and death confer meaning and glory.[10]

Narcissism

> Anna is a marvelous creation. It is difficult from the outset not to love her.
> . . . She is a good wife and above all a passionately dedicated mother.
> —ALLAN BLOOM (238)

Fatality feeds narcissism. It is heady to have been chosen, among all others, to act out the myth of love even, or especially, if one has to suffer and die for it. Such a death is a form of election, and the tragic end, no less than the intense life that leads to it, marks one's superiority to everything ordinary. Recall that when Anna declares the trainman's death to be "an evil omen," she means an omen about her and only her. Why of the many people at the station should the death be about her? The narcissism of this interpretation should leave us unsurprised by Tolstoy's countless other indications of Anna's narcissism. We constantly catch her changing clothes or dealing with her dressmaker. During her visit to Anna's, Dolly is amazed at how often Anna changes clothes and the attention she gives to her dresses. The day she commits suicide she spends two hours at her dressmaker's.

It would be tedious to list all the references to Anna's energetic care of her appearance. We repeatedly detect her before the mirror. She titillates men, even Levin, with the amazing portrait she places strategically so that they see it before she appears. Her servant is Annushka, her daughter is Annie, and when she takes an English girl under her protection, we learn that the girl's name is—Hannah: everywhere around Anna we find Anna. Tolstoy could hardly signal her narcissism more clearly.

Consider once more the title of the novel. Given the book's dual (or triple) plot, why not call it something that would embrace both? Why did Tolstoy reject *Two Families?* Tolstoy could easily have picked a title that, like *Middlemarch, Can You Forgive Her?,* or, for that matter, *War and Peace,* could have applied to more than one story. If we consider Anna's narcissism, a reason for the title suggests itself: it is what Anna herself would call the novel. It is not exactly Anna's inner speech, but given her desire to be the heroine of a novel, it might be called potential inner speech. The Garbo version of the novel, which almost entirely leaves out the Levin story, is eerily true not to the novel but to how Anna herself would tell it: Anna's *Anna.*

The love Anna feels for Vronsky is, though real, also a form of narcissism. More than Vronsky she loves love itself and the act of loving. What most appeals to her about Vronsky is that puppy-dog look of submission on the face of this strong officer—an expression of "bewilderment and submissiveness, like the expression of an intelligent dog when it has done wrong" (88). The powerful man loves yielding to her power. When both people embrace this kind of love, it becomes, as de Rougemont aptly puts it, "a twin narcissism."

Since Vronsky must be taught the language of romantic love, he does not always get it quite right. "All is over, I have nothing but you," she tells him in the consummation scene. When he refers in response to his "happiness," she teaches him that such love is not about happiness but something more terrible, more dangerous, and more significant. Indeed, it is precisely danger, which marks one's exceptionality, that feeds this kind of love. At the end of Part Four, when they are about to run off together, Vronsky runs into her room so that "his passion overwhelmed her" (456).

> "Yes, you have conquered me, and I am yours," she said at last pressing his hands to her bosom.
>
> "So it had to be," he said. "So long as we live, it must be so. I know it now."
>
> "That's true," she said, getting whiter and whiter, and putting her arms around his head. "Still there is something terrible in it after all that has happened."
>
> "It will all pass, it will all pass; we shall be so happy. Our love, if it *could* be stronger, will be strengthened, because there is something terrible in it," he said . . . (456)

If this tissue of clichés, which might appear in a mass-market romance, were offered without authorial irony, then Tolstoy would be a mediocre writer. Or else this would be the worst passage in the book. But the language here belongs not to Tolstoy but to Anna, who imagines herself the heroine of a romantic novel, and to Vronsky, who has (not entirely perfectly) learned it from her. "So it had to be": fatalism in this book is repudiated by the author but embraced by Anna. Love as stronger and more vibrant because there is "something terrible" about it: contrast this set of beliefs, as the author implicitly does, with the love of Kitty and Levin. The very awfulness (in the evaluative sense) of Anna's and Vronsky's exchange marks the distance between author and characters.

To Anna's increasing annoyance, Vronsky does not keep to the script. When Dolly visits the couple, she sees that Vronsky has come to love her as a wife. He wants to marry her and it is he, not she, who wants her to get a divorce so they can marry. As she says later, she prefers to be a mistress.[11] Anna has evidently refused to listen to Vronsky's requests, and so he has asked Dolly to persuade her, as if the avatar of romance would heed the embodiment of laborious domesticity. He wants children and worries that, like Annie, the ones to come will be legally Karenin's. Clearly, Anna has not told him that she is using birth control, and she tells Dolly, not him, that there will be no more children.

Vronsky's desire for children later becomes a point of contention between them. He wants a normal, conventional marriage and family, but she regards such a desire as an indication he no longer loves her. Marriage binds one legally, but she wants love not out of duty, as she puts it, but out of total devotion leaving room for no other desires. Children would not only diminish her allure but would also compromise her status as the sole object of love. Marriage would turn the grand romance into a boring routine.

Anna's love for her son Seryozha reflects the same kind of thinking. Readers often wonder, as Dolly does, why Anna so idealizes Seryozha, who is Karenin's child, and neglects Annie, the child of the man she loves. One reason is that, as Stiva is for obvious reasons more interested in his daughter, so Anna is more interested in her son. But a more important reason is that she can easily idealize Seryozha. She can readily love him with romantic longing and nostalgia precisely because he is absent. It is not the real Seryozha she loves, but the idealized four-year-old boy of her pictures. Before she abandons him, she thinks not of how her affair will affect him, but "of his future attitude toward his mother, who had abandoned his father" (201). At another moment, she "felt with joy that in the plight in which she found herself she had a support, quite apart from her relation to her husband or to Vronsky. This support was her son" (306). Seryozha exists for her sake.[12]

Even before leaving Karenin, she idealizes Seryozha rather than wonder about his real needs. Such idealization reflects the narcissism of romance. With Vronsky, too, "she was, every time she saw him, comparing the picture she painted of him in her imagination (incomparably superior, impossible in reality) with him as he really was" (377).

Anna cannot love her daughter that way, because Annie is always right there, with her illnesses, her need to be changed, and other prosaic demands. Annie plays virtually no role in her mother's inner thoughts as Tolstoy allows us to eavesdrop on them. This absence, if we detect it, is one of the novel's most horrible examples of negative evil, and it derives directly from Anna's romantic narcissism.

Marrying Romeo

> For Iseult is always a stranger, the very essence of what is strange in woman and of all that is eternally fugitive, vanishing.
> — DE ROUGEMONT (284)

As Anna understands, and as de Rougemont argues, passionate love is incompatible with marriage. For romance depends on mystery, which the very propinquity of married couples makes impossible. That is why Anna, when living with Vronsky, expends so much effort on preserving her romantic allure. What mystery is possible when one knows all the least romantic facts about one's lover's bodily processes, defects, and signs of aging? Tolstoy hints at this question when he shows the romantic hero Vronsky beginning to bald.

Imagine that the Capulets and Montagues should relent and let Romeo and Juliet marry. The very absurdity of this supposition already marks the gap between romance and marriage. Four years later, we catch the couple at the breakfast table, Romeo unshaven, with his face buried in the sports pages, and Juliet ill-tempered in her robe. Both are wondering: where has *love* gone? They may suppose that they have simply chosen the wrong partner, but not doubt that love is passion. How could they think otherwise? We see why adultery plays such a large part in European literature.[13]

Love and Work

Marriage depends on a different kind of love, which (in a Tolstoyan spirit) we might call prosaic love. Prosaic love thrives not on mystery but on intimacy. It consists in loving the other person, not love itself, and loving all the more the better the other is known. It seeks daily opportunities to learn about each other, manage the details of life, and raise a family. It involves work.

Levin originally fell in love not with Kitty but with the whole Shcherbatsky family and "he was so far from conceiving of love for a woman apart from marriage that he actually pictured to himself first the family, and only secondarily the woman who would give him a family" (101). He is evidently well suited for prosaic love. He nevertheless does not fully grasp it and Kitty has to teach it to him.

Levin has imagined married love neither as romance nor as prosaic intimacy but as a sort of idyll, an idealization that leaves out the crucial component of work:

> Levin had been married three months. He was happy, but not at all in the way he had expected to be. At every step he found his former dreams disappointed, and new unexpected surprises of happiness. He was happy; but on entering upon family life, he saw at every step that it was utterly different from what he had imagined. At every step he experienced what a man would experience who, after admiring the smooth happy course of a little boat on a lake, should get himself into that little boat. He saw that it was not all sitting still, floating smoothly; that one had to think too, not for an instant to forget where one was floating; and that there was water under one, and that one must row; and that his unaccustomed hands would be sore; and that it was only to look at it that was easy; but that doing it, though very delightful, was very difficult. (504)

In this passage, Tolstoy teaches us about happiness by offering an analogy concerning perception. Like his simile about the distant hill, the simile of the boat contrasts the distant image with the immediate experience, the view of a boat from afar with the experience of rowing it. Prosaic love differs from its outward appearance. One cannot know the work without doing it. Levin's dreams are disappointed, and we expect to hear that he is unhappy, but we learn instead that this disappointment leads to a different happiness. Prosaic love, he finds, is "difficult delight," a paradox that captures the novel's sense that meaningfulness always comes from hard work.

Why They Quarrel

Levin has imagined married life "to consist merely in the enjoyment of love, which nothing must hinder and from which no petty cares must distract" (504). "Petty cares," Kitty's concern for the "pettiest details" of setting up a household, "her trivial cares and anxieties": all these phrases are Levin's and express his lack of understanding that life is all about the details. Only from a mistaken perspective can they seem petty or trivial. Levin "by tradition" has expected much from their honeymoon, but it remains for both as one of their most painful memories (507). He is hurt that Kitty has declined a tour abroad. But she knows what he has to learn, that it is daily life and not a conventional separation from it that really matters. In going to Italy with Vronsky, of course, Anna imagines the opposite.

Contrary to what both an idyllic and a romantic view would predict, the Levins' first months prove the most difficult. Romantic love flares up and is then exhausted by routine and familiarity, but prosaic love depends on intimacy, and it is only with time that husband and wife can know each other well. At first, Levin and Kitty quarrel frequently and sometimes cannot even remember the cause, but these quarrels arise, Tolstoy tells us, "from the fact that they did not yet know what was of importance to each other" (507).

Levin discovers a new sensation in their quarrels. At first, he is hurt by her and he feels "an agonizing sense of division." He wants to defend himself, but cannot, because "she was himself":

> He felt for the first moment as a man feels when, having suddenly received a violent blow from behind, turns around, angry and eager to avenge himself, to look for the antagonist, and finds that it is he himself who has accidentally struck himself, that there is no one to be angry with, and that he must put up with and try to soothe the pain. (506)

This simile, too, points to a change in perspective that is part of achieving prosaic love. One looks around and is surprised to discover that the antagonist is a part of oneself. Because prosaic love thrives on closeness, one suffers the very pain one inflicts.

Broderie Anglaise

Levin does not understand how Kitty could, instead of indulging intellectual interests, spend her time beautifying the house with her *broderie anglaise*. We may recall that when Stiva wakes up at the beginning of the novel, he drops his feet into slippers that, as a birthday present, Dolly "has embroidered for him . . . on gold-colored morocco" (4). Embroidery in this novel signifies the value of ordinary life through the effort to beautify it with one's work. Tolstoy's wife wrote in her diary:

> L. N. was just saying to me how the ideas for his novel came to him: "I was sitting downstairs in my study and observing a very beautiful silk line on the sleeve of my robe. I was thinking about how people get the idea in their heads to invent all these patterns and ornaments of embroidery, and that there exists a whole world of woman's work, fashions, ideas, by which women live. . . . I understood that women could love this and occupy themselves with it. And, of course, at once my ideas moved to Anna. . . . Anna is deprived of all these joys of occupying herself with the woman's side of

life because she is all alone. All women have turned away from her, and she has nobody to talk with about all that which composes the everyday, purely feminine occupations." (N, 761)

When Kitty insists on going with him to his dying brother Nikolai, Levin imagines that she is simply afraid to be alone. But for her, sharing such an experience is essential to the partnership of marriage, which is not an alliance for amusement or pleasure. Precisely because she understands everything prosaically, she proves of great help both to Levin and to Nikolai by attending to "the petty details":

> It never entered his [Levin's] head to analyze the details of the sick man's situation, to consider how that body was lying under the blanket, how those emaciated legs and thighs and spine were lying huddled up, and whether they could not be made more comfortable. . . . It made his blood run cold when be began to think of all these details. . . .
>
> But Kitty thought, and felt, and acted quite differently. On seeing the sick man, she pitied him. And pity in her womanly heart did not arouse at all that feeling of horror and loathing that it aroused in her husband, but a desire to act, to find out the details of his condition, and to remedy them. . . . The very details, the mere thought of which reduced her husband to terror, immediately engaged her attention. (518)

The word "details" (*podrobnosti*) appears four times in this passage because the experience of death, no less than of life, is a matter of details. Kitty cares for, as she lives by, the small gestures of life. She improves the situation by making Nikolai's room cleaner and more orderly, by attending to every detail of his surroundings, until, at last, we see on the table her *broderie anglaise*. Levin acknowledges the correctness of her idea of love and marriage.

Eroticism and Dialogue

Tolstoy presents several portraits of Kitty and Levin together. He indicates, as clearly as the conventions of the time allow, that their intimate love is highly erotic. At the end of Part Six, chapter 5, we catch them in a deep kiss. Their eroticism derives from knowing each other's body and emotions well enough to reach heights otherwise impossible. Familiarity can produce a sexuality so intense that mysterious first encounters seem to be primarily about something else. In contrast to Levin and Kitty, Anna and Vronsky must constantly provoke desire in the face of declining mystery.

Along with their eroticism, Levin and Kitty experience other kinds of intimate bliss that Levin has never suspected. When the pregnant Kitty leans on his arm and presses it closely to her, Levin "felt, now that the thought of her approaching motherhood was never for a moment absent from his mind, a new and delicious bliss, quite free from sensuality, in being near the woman he loved" (585). The fact that he is surprised at a bliss without sensuality indicates how sexual their love usually is.

Their closeness allows for a form of communication not possible for Anna and Vronsky. They watch each other so attentively, and they think so much about what the other is thinking, that they can readily understand each other. Each rapidly grasps what the other wants to say from words too abbreviated for any outsider to decipher. Levin "knew that his wife, in such moments of loving tenderness as now, could understand what he meant to say from a hint, and she did understand him" (585). When they are talking this way, their dialogues approach inner speech. Love based on intimacy offers the joys of understanding and being deeply understood.

Although de Rougemont stressed the incompatibility of romance and marriage, he could not show another kind of love that would be better and he could not defend marriage positively. De Rougemont asks for fidelity to "a troth that is observed *by virtue of the absurd*—that is to say, simply because it has been pledged—and by virtue of an absolute which will uphold husband and wife as persons" (de Rougemont, 307). Such love becomes a kind of religious testing, another simile de Rougemont invokes. This, I suppose, is the marriage of two existentialists, whose love is mediated by philosophy.

It is hard to see how marriage based on the absurd could be any more stable than marriage based on pure romance.

In contrast to de Rougemont, Tolstoy describes what intimacy can really offer in the way of happiness and, no less important, of self-knowledge possible only through dialogue with another.

Intimate love is above all a way of paying attention.

The Prosaic Sublime

Tolstoy narrates the sequence in which Levin's son is born almost entirely from Levin's point of view. To everyone but Levin, the event seems, as it is, utterly commonplace, just one of the facts of life. The comedy of the scene derives from Levin's unfeigned surprise that others do not find labor and child-birth unusual, as he does. Levin cannot comprehend how the doctor can drink his coffee and the pharmacist can meticulously prepare the package of opium. As so often in Tolstoy, the naïve or comic figure turns out to be right, because, in fact, the most significant dramas of life are the ordinary ones.

I know of nowhere else in world literature where a husband's feelings at such a time are described with such care. Tolstoy is at the height of his powers here as he traces Levin's tiny alterations of consciousness. This brief event, lasting only hours, occupies three chapters (some fifteen pages) and so time slows down for the reader much as it does for Levin. "Three minutes passed; it seemed to Levin that more than an hour had gone by" (739).

We see, as Levin reacts to Kitty's first terrible scream, that his mind does not immediately draw the obvious conclusions that it is she screaming and that she is screaming from labor pains. He briefly asks himself "Whose scream was it?" (744). Between a fact and an obvious deduction a *process* takes place, and the steps of that process may become visible when they briefly take a wrong turn.

When Kitty begins to suffer, "for the first minute, from habit, it seemed to him that he was to blame" (737), and even though Levin knows he is not to blame, the irrational feeling keeps returning whenever she screams. However common childbirth may be, and however essential to the human condition it must have always been, reason proves entirely inadequate when one lives through one's own wife's agony.

His reason suspended out of an intense empathy, Levin, an unbeliever on rational grounds, finds himself praying, and "not only with his lips" (738). Why he, an atheist, prays sincerely at this moment becomes for him a riddle touching on life's essential meaning. Desperate to do something but with nothing to do, Levin has simply to endure, a state that (as we shall see with Karenin) provokes the soul torn from its habitual responses to experience the sublime.

By taking us through Levin's consciousness in small steps, Tolstoy makes the experience of the sublime palpable and entirely believable. Realism by definition excludes the mystical and supernatural, but Tolstoy often describes unearthly experiences as genuine without embracing a mystical or supernatural explanation. They lift the soul to heights it has never experienced and lead to perceptions impossible at any other time, and yet they result from the same ordinary processes that govern everything else. For Tolstoy, transcendence is not a departure from but an aspect of the ordinary.

Precisely because Levin has grown so used to sharing Kitty's feelings in everyday life, he suffers an especially intense agony of empathy. That empathy, when combined with the feeling that he must help but cannot help, takes him bit by bit into a world "where nothing could strike Levin as strange" (744). In his helplessness, Levin feels that what is happening closely resembles his experience at his brother's deathbed, but with joy taking the place of grief. "Yet that grief and this joy were alike beyond the ordinary conditions of life; they were openings, as it were, in that ordinary life through which there came glimpses of something sublime . . . while reason lagged behind, unable to keep up with it" (742).

So intense is Levin's empathy and his fear of Kitty's death when hearing her screams, that at last, just before the birth, he realizes that "he had long ago ceased to wish for the child. He did not even wish for her life now, all he longed for was the end of this awful anguish" (744). Except Tolstoy, perhaps only Dostoevsky could have understood that Levin would cease even to wish for Kitty's life.

When Kitty's screams cease, and before he precisely realizes why, Levin "felt himself all in an instant borne back to the everyday world" (745), but an everyday world now radiant with unbearable happiness. In his confused way, he realizes a Tolstoyan truth: "The whole world of woman, which had taken for him since his marriage a new value he had never suspected before, was now so exalted he could not take it in in his imagination" (746). Whoever may think that intense feelings require strange events simply does not understand the immense depth, complexity, even sublimity of the ordinary.

It was once commonly said that realist novels can no longer be written because their subject matter has been exhausted and a changed world has left them behind. Tolstoy would reply: only someone who does not understand daily life could think its subject matter could ever be exhausted. We can no more leave behind problems of birth, work, child-rearing, love, and death that we can cease to be human.

Much as he expected marriage to be an idyll, Levin has expected to feel fatherly pride and elation at the sight of his son. This conventional expectation proves as false as most other conventional expectations in the light of Tolstoyan realism. Levin "made strenuous efforts to discover in his heart some traces of fatherly feeling" (747), but he finds nothing of the kind. Instead, "he felt nothing but disgust" and then, when he sees the baby, whose big toe differs from the rest, he experiences above all intense pity. He is disappointed, above all with himself, that "this splendid baby excited in him no feeling but disgust and compassion. It was not at all the feeling he had looked forward to" (747). But disgust and compassion are what real, prosaic love feels like at such a moment. Levin has expected a storybook emotion but, as in his marriage, finds something much deeper. He now begins to experience actual love for an infant.

Kitty's Mistake

No matter how good one's upbringing, and no matter how much implicit wisdom one's habits and approach to life may contain, one can still be misled by abstract ideas or social myths. After making a mistake, one may reflect on how the misleading idea or myth runs counter to all one feels most strongly. In so doing, one can become conscious of one's deepest beliefs.

What one sincerely professes is not necessarily what one truly believes. For Levin, Dolly, Anna, and the rest of us, it often takes a conflict between one's professions and one's beliefs to reveal the difference. Once one understands the conflict, one can choose to learn one's deepest beliefs more clearly and to live according to them or not.

Kitty's story begins with a mistake that reveals to her what she really values, and thereafter she chooses to live accordingly. Because she has been swayed by the wrong view of love, she first rejects Levin's proposal and hopes to marry Vronsky. After Vronsky abandons her without a thought, she falls ill and comes to reflect on what she really wants. Realizing her error, she not only decides to accept Levin should he propose again, but also understands how to conduct a marriage in the right way.

Crises

Kitty regards the evening when she eagerly expects something decisive from Vronsky, and knows that Levin will surely offer his hand, as the "turning point" of her life. In Tolstoy's two great novels, such a feeling almost always represents a misperception arising from the mind's attempt to find easily narratable plots featuring critical moments. The people gathered around Nikolai Levin's sickbed, knowing that he cannot last more than a few hours, repeatedly imagine that the critical moment has come. At one point, the priest interrupts his reading, puts the cross to the cold forehead, and, at last, solemnly declares "he is gone" (530). The priest "was about to move away when suddenly there was a faint stir in the clammy mustaches of the dead man and quite distinctly through the stillness they heard from the depths of his chest the sharply distinct sounds: 'Not yet . . . soon'" (530). The dead man speaks. Perhaps only Tolstoy would risk a comic note in such a scene. He does so to redirect our thoughts away from stories with critical moments.

We tend to regard as critical moments conventionally regarded as such. In the sequence leading to her suicide, Anna constantly manufactures signs that her relationship with Vronsky has reached a turning point, that he is about to leave her, and that things cannot go on a moment longer. The Garbo film creates crises not present in the novel: for example, in the film, Vronsky is about to desert her in order to fight in the Eastern War. But in the novel she kills herself not because of an actual crisis but because, thinking in terms of crises, she believes she is in the midst of one.

Proposals, of course, may easily be experienced as "now or never" moments. Both Varenka and Sergey Ivanovich believe that if he does not propose on that very walk, he will never do so. When stray interruptions deflect him, both assume their marriage was just not meant to be. Each feels: "Now or never it must be said." But apart from their belief that the possibility exists only for one intense moment, there is no reason on earth why he cannot propose the next day. Ironically enough, the fact that they sense the scene in such a similar way shows how well suited for each other they might be.

The Word Love

As she awaits her suitors, Kitty meditates. She knows that she should marry the one she "loves," and so the meaning of that *word* takes on crucial significance. If she could understand the author's point that there are different kinds of love, she could make a choice on the merits. But like almost everyone, she tacitly accepts romantic love as the only kind. The meaning her culture has assigned to a word forecloses consideration of what she really wants and which man would make the better husband. She really loves Levin, but her feeling does not match the myth of "love." Vronsky more closely fits the myth, so her decision is a foregone conclusion.

Kitty is continually picturing both men.

> When she mused on the past, she dwelled with pleasure, with tenderness, on the memories of her relations with Levin. The memories of childhood and of Levin's friendship with her dead brother gave a special poetic charm to her relations with him. His love for her, of which she felt certain, was flattering and delightful to her; and it was pleasant for her to think of Levin. In her memories of Vronsky there always entered a certain degree of awkwardness, though he was in the highest degree well bred and poised, as though there were some false note—not in Vronsky, he was very simple and nice, but in herself, while with Levin she felt perfectly at ease. But, on the other hand, as soon as she thought of the future with Vronsky there arose before her a perspective of brilliant happiness; with Levin the future seemed misty. (52)

The choice of words and sequence of thoughts in this passage belong to Kitty. She, not the author, recalls her awkwardness with Vronsky and immediately tells herself: he is simple and nice, the problem is in me. She may love Vronsky or she may not. If she does, mysterious brilliance attracts her. Though not fully romantic, this feeling resembles romance more closely than her feeling for Levin does. Her sense of closeness to Levin depends not on anything brilliant or mysterious, but, quite the contrary, on lifelong acquaintance, on an intimacy too close for strangeness, and on a friendship that has, in a sense, existed before she was born. A relationship with Levin would be prosaic, and, given how the word "love" is used, she does not recognize that feeling *as* love. So she refuses him.

Love that is not called love may not seem like love at all.

The Second Proposal and How It Works

Kitty soon realizes her mistake, falls ill, and, until she does become engaged to Levin, frequently broods on the scene with regret, guilt, and humiliation. Even more humiliated, Levin also broods. Her words of refusal "it cannot be" (*etogo ne mozhet byt'*) burn in each one's thoughts. It would be entirely incorrect to read the second proposal scene, in which Kitty guesses Levin's words when he writes only the first letter of each, as signifying the romantic and mystical connection of two souls destined for each other. As always, Tolstoy shows how such a conclusion might understandably be drawn but also why it is mistaken.

A person who wins the lottery may easily imagine that fate has chosen him or her. But since the lottery must be won by someone, it requires no supernatural explanation to see that someone will feel chosen by fate.

Kitty and Levin understand each other not because of some mysterious or supernatural "call," like the one in *Jane Eyre,* nor because fate unites true lovers, but because they have meditated on the same words of refusal. They both have often and intensely wished to repeat the proposal with a different ending, and they both have remembered with pain the exact words of Kitty's response. So when the first letters of those words appear, and in a context where another proposal is possible, their meaning is obvious. Once guessed, these words provide the clue to the others. This kind of understanding, based on constant thought and focus on details, looks forward to the kind of intimate conversations that will characterize their marriage.

Tiny Alterations

Anna Karenina constantly, if implicitly, invites us to contrast the two kinds of love on which its two major plots are based. If we do, we may, as de Rougemont urges, choose between these kinds of love. For Tolstoy, one kind represents a mistaken view of life as a whole. It is as mistaken as Pierre's numerology in *War and Peace,* as the romanticization of war, and all forms of extremist thinking.

For Tolstoy, true love and true life are experienced at moments that are barely noticeable at all. In one of his essays, Tolstoy tells the story of the painter Bryullov, who corrected a student's sketch. The student remarks: "Why, you only touched it a tiny bit, but it is quite another thing," Bryullov answers: "Art begins where the tiny bit begins." Tolstoy explicates:

> That saying is strikingly true not only of art but of all life. One may say that true life begins where the tiny bit begins—where what seem to us minute and infinitely small alterations take place. True life is not lived where

great external changes take place—where people move about, clash, fight, and slay one another—it is lived only where these tiny, tiny, infinitesimally small changes occur. (R&E, 81)

Tolstoy is the artist of tiny alterations. In *Anna Karenina,* the key mistake is to equate intensity with truth. Such an equation spells disaster.

If we reflect on our own lives, and on the history of the twentieth century, we may recognize that Tolstoy's prosaic view, which runs counter to our most common assumptions, may have something to offer. If we do, we may learn to see the world and ourselves more wisely.

Anna and the Drama of Looking

Honesty, continued

One can lie by looking and practice falsehood in silence.

Most critics read the Anna story under the sway of the romantic myth. Such readings not only miss the novel's point but almost exactly invert it. Just as thinkers who accepted contingency have been Leibnizized into the opposite view, so *Anna Karenina,* with its critique of the romantic and the extreme, has been repeatedly Garbo-ized.

I should like to retell Anna's story as I think the novel presents it. Anna makes her destiny. It derives not only from her belief in romance and extremism, but also from the way in which she teaches herself to misperceive. For Tolstoy, looking is an action, one that, like speaking, can be done truly or falsely. The Anna story is a drama of perception and misperception, listening and deliberately mistaken listening, looking and false looking. It develops the novel's lessons about honesty.

Fake Simplicity

Kitty's lasting hatred of Anna derives not from her loss of Vronsky, which she soon ceases to regard as a misfortune, but from Anna's falsity. The key moment occurs at the ball. Characteristically, almost nothing happens.

Kitty comes to the ball in "an elaborate tulle dress" with "rosettes and lace" (83) and she expects Anna to be dressed, in a similar spirit, in lilac. Instead, she finds Anna in a "simple," low-cut, black gown, "showing her full shoulders and bosom that looked as though carved of old ivory, and her rounded arms, with tiny, slender wrists" (85). Kitty understands that Anna has dressed so that her dress would not be conspicuous on her. She intends it to be the barely noticed frame from which she—"simple, natural, elegant"—stands out. Anna has chosen her clothes with an eye to their erotic effect, which is all the stronger for being apparently unintentional.

That "simple" dress, and Anna as "simple" and "natural" — these, we learn, are Oblonsky characteristics. Visiting Anna and Vronsky, Dolly notices Anna's incredibly expensive "simple" dresses that are, of course, anything but simple. The Oblonskys understand the magnetic power of fake simplicity. When Stiva brings his friend Vasenka Veslovsky to hunt at the Levins', Vasenka, a fop, dresses in brand-new English attire, with a brand-new English gun and a Scotch cap with ribbons, but Stiva outdoes him by being "simple" and "natural." Stiva "was dressed in rough leggings . . . torn trousers, and a short coat. On his head there was a wreck of a hat of indefinite form . . . and his game bag and cartridge belt, though worn, were of the best quality" (602). So struck is Vasenka by the impression of "Stiva in his rags" that he realizes it can be truly "chic to be in tatters, but to have a shooting outfit of the best quality." Vasenka makes up his mind to dress the same way in the future (602).

Studied spontaneity, fake simplicity, and assumed sincerity: these skills characterize the Oblonskys, Anna and Stiva. At the ball, Anna's hair is perfectly arranged except for "little willful tendrils of her curly hair that would always break free around her neck and temples" (85). So entranced have readers been by Anna that they have taken these willful tendrils as an unconscious expression of suppressed vitality. Given how frequently we see Anna arranging her dress and staring in the mirror, and given the family characteristic of contrived naturalness, is it not more likely that she has made sure those tendrils would assert themselves "against her will"? Of course Anna has genuine vitality, but she also knows how to imitate herself for effect.

We watch the ball through Kitty's eyes. She soon sees on Anna's face the thrill of being admired and then, to her horror, detects that it is Vronsky's look that thrills her:

> They were speaking of common acquaintances, keeping up the most trivial conversation, but to Kitty it seemed that every word they said was determining their fate and hers. And strange it was that they were actually talking of how absurd Ivan Ivanovich was with his French, and how the Eletsky girl might have made a better match, yet these words were important for them, and they felt just as Kitty did. (87)

If one encountered these two sentences out of context, one would guess they were by Chekhov. They typify Chekhov's sense that what really matters in life takes place when nothing special happens: all that is heard is the sound of chewing and cutlery, and yet lives are being smashed. It almost seems as if Chekhov had influenced Tolstoy. But Tolstoy wrote these lines when Chekhov was too young to have published a word, and they testify instead to the debt Chekhov's prosaics owes to Tolstoy's.

Just as Dolly has come to hate Stiva's good nature, so Kitty comes to detect the falsity in Anna's simplicity. Watching Anna, Kitty feels that "she was enchanting in her simple black dress, enchanting were her round arms with their bracelets . . . fascinating the straying curls of her loose hair . . . but there was something terrible and cruel about her charm" (89). When Kitty comes near Anna, she gazes at her in dismay, evidently asking Anna what she thinks she is doing. Anna answers by smiling and pressing Kitty's hand, as if to assure her of her friendship and devotion. Kitty does not believe her and responds to Anna's smile with a look of "despair and amazement" (89). When her reassurance fails, Anna simply "turned away from her, and began talking to the other lady" (89).

When Kitty detects her in a falsehood, Anna cuts her. It is this incident that Kitty can never forgive. Anna not only has betrayed her, but has also tried to deceive her, and, failing, has cut her in public. Kitty can only think of Anna as immoral, not because of her affair (there is as yet no affair), but because of her falsehood. The fake simplicity of her dress, like Stiva's smile, betrays for Kitty who Anna really is. Anna knows it and hates Kitty, too.

What Touches Dolly the Most

We first encounter Anna in Part One when she arrives in answer to Stiva's summons to help pacify Dolly. It is hard to evaluate Anna's character from these chapters because, although she uses dishonest methods, the result saves Dolly's pride. Because of Anna's intervention, Dolly can, without further humiliation, do what she has to do anyway, return to her daily routine.

Falsehood characterizes Anna's mission from the beginning. Dolly is unaware that Anna has not just happened to be passing by but has deliberately come as her brother's agent. If Dolly knew why Anna was visiting, she could not, upon first seeing her, look into Anna's face "to find out whether she knew" (73). Anna immediately wins Dolly's heart by charming her children and remembering everything about them. When her mission is accomplished, Anna takes no more interest in the children, and they sense it. Does she change because her mind is on Vronsky, or because her initial interest reflects her Oblonsky, chameleon-like ability to win Dolly over? Or is it both?

We may question Anna's apparent sincerity when she tells Dolly that Stiva is "weighed down by remorse" (74). We have just seen Stiva, in the novel's opening, waking up and going about his day without a shred of remorse, and it is clear that Anna knows her brother very well. Does she speak of Stiva's remorse just to extenuate his behavior?

Dolly astutely replies: "Is he capable of remorse?" (74). Anyone who doubts Dolly's perspicuity might pause on this comment, which is exactly right. Stiva is capable of momentary empathy but, living entirely in the moment, and cultivating an ability to forget anything that might disturb his pleasure, he is indeed incapable of remorse. He makes sure to be incapable. Anna replies to Dolly's question:

> "Yes. I know him. I could not look at him without feeling sorry for him. We both know him. He's good-hearted, but he's proud, and now he's so humiliated. What touched me most . . ." (and here Anna guessed what would touch Dolly most) "he's tortured by two things: that he's ashamed for the children's sake and that loving you—yes, yes, loving you beyond everything on earth," she hurriedly interrupted Dolly, who would have answered—"he has hurt you, pierced you to the heart." (74; ellipsis in original)

"And here Anna guessed what would touch Dolly most": Anna is saying whatever will work, whether true or false. She reflects on what will touch Dolly most (it is, of course, the children first of all) and so her deceptiveness and manipulation are clearly deliberate. Critics sympathetic to Anna overlook this authorial comment, as they also miss several other explicit comments about Anna's lying or manipulation.

The Stiva we have seen is anything but humiliated, just inconvenienced. Stiva has not even thought of the children, and he has long ceased to love his wife "beyond everything on earth." Anna next tells Dolly that the infidelity is a single lapse and cannot be repeated, which is technically true if we are thinking only of that lover. But the comment is nevertheless deceptive. If Anna "knows him," and knows the world as well as she says, she must also at least suspect that the infidelity has been and will be repeated. If she does not know this, it is because she has not bothered to find out. Saying whatever will touch Dolly the most, she is not interested in what is true.

Relativity

On the train ride home, in the shaking compartment with its rapid transitions from hot to cold, Anna, fighting sleep, tries to read an English novel. "But it was distasteful to her to read, that is, to follow the reflection of other people's lives. She had too great a desire to live herself" (106). Is this how a narcissist reacts to fiction?[14] As Anna leaves off reading, we follow her thoughts from within. Just as she is longing to go with the novel's hero to his estate,

> she suddenly felt that *he* ought to feel ashamed, and that she was ashamed of the same thing. But what had he to be ashamed of? "What have I to be ashamed of?" she asked herself in injured surprise. She laid down the book and sank against the back of the chair, tightly gripping the paper cutter in both hands. There was nothing. (107)

The fact that the referent of "he" (Vronsky) need not be explained indicates that we are tracing her dialogue with herself. Although the narration is still technically in the third person, we must therefore hear her asking herself: What had he to be ashamed of? The next sentence is in quotation marks, but so imperceptibly do we slide from paraphrase of her thoughts to her actual words that the quotation marks could have been supplied before or after. She is telling herself "there was nothing," but her very shame, and her need to tell herself there was nothing, indicates that her reassurance is false.

Anna reviews the ball, and Vronsky's look of "slavish adoration," to assure herself "there was nothing shameful." All the same, "the feeling of shame was intensified, as though some inner voice, just at the point when she thought of Vronsky, were saying to her, 'Warm, very warm, hot'" (107)—a reference both to the children's game and to how the train's temperature becomes integrated with her thoughts. It may also suggest erotic heat. Now Anna indulges the thought of Vronsky without reserve. "She passed the paper knife over the windowpane, then laid its smooth, cool surface to her cheek, almost laughed aloud at the feeling of delight that all at once without cause [*bezprichinno*] came over her" (107). Of course, the cause is erotic. One does not have to be a Freudian to recognize the role of the paper knife and the sensations she produces from it.

All becomes arousal as she feels her nerves strained tighter and tighter, her eyes opening wider, her fingers and toes twitching, and everything becoming more vivid. A key passage now occurs:

> Moments of doubt were continually coming upon her, when she was uncertain whether the train was going forward or backward or standing still altogether; whether it was Annushka at her side or a stranger. "What's that on the side of the chair, a fur cloak or some beast? And what am I myself? Myself or some other woman?" She was afraid of giving in to this delirium. But something drew her toward it, and she could yield to it or resist it at will. (107)

Anna is uncertain of the train's direction or speed, a sensation all of us who have ridden a train going through a tunnel with uniform walls know. Einstein later explained this sensation in terms of the relativity of motion. Within a uniformly moving frame of reference one cannot tell whether one is going forty miles an hour forward and the train next to one going the same speed backward, or one is going eighty miles an hour forward with the other train stopped, or any other combination adding up to an eighty miles an hour difference. Tolstoy uses this familiar experience of motional relativity to signal the moral relativity Anna begins to embrace. It is as if "some other woman" were committing her acts. Relativism acts like fatalism to take one beyond good and evil.

Although Anna yields to this delirium, she fears it, and understands that she is *not* fated to yield.[15] Despite what she will later tell herself and others, she knows she *can* resist: "she could yield to it or resist it at will" (107). The embrace of fatalism is a choice. (See Jackson and Browning).

Ears

When Anna arrives in Petersburg and sees her husband, one of the book's most famous passages occurs.

> At Petersburg, as soon as the train stopped and she got out, the first person who attracted her attention was her husband. "Oh, my God! Why do his ears stick out like that?" she thought, looking at his frigid and distinguished figure, and especially the ears that struck her at the moment as propping up the brim of his round hat. (110)

Of course, Karenin's ears could not be that bad or she would have noticed them before. The rest of what she sees in that passage—his frigid figure, a habitual sarcastic smile, his big, tired eyes—also reflect what she is now perceiving, not what is really there.

Critics usually interpret the "ears" passage as a sign of Anna's changed feeling about her husband after she begins to fall in love with Vronsky. They are correct to do so. But something else is also happening, although it becomes clear only in retrospect. As the novel proceeds, Tolstoy makes it evident that Anna, from this point on, *teaches* herself to see Karenin as repulsive and unfeeling. So this first reference to "ears" is not merely the *sign* of a changed feeling but also, as we learn later, the first in a long series of self-willed *causes* of changed feeling. The more she directs her attention to what she does not like, and the more she ascribes lack of feeling to Karenin, the more she comes to see him that way automatically.[16]

Looking, listening, and paying attention are actions, and perception is not simple taking in of what is there. We can look charitably or uncharitably. We can pay attention only to what is worst in a person; everyone possesses characteristics that can be seen as irritating or repulsive. Tolstoy wants to teach us that what we do at every moment of our waking lives—how we look and direct our attention—has supreme moral value precisely because it is so ordinary, precisely because it forms habits.

In one respect Anna does not resemble her brother. Stiva is incapable of guilt, remorse, and shame, but Anna is quite subject to these emotions. We have already seen her shame on the train ride home. When she arrives in Petersburg, she must insist to herself that she has nothing to confess. She will have guilty dreams of being caressed by both men. That old dream of the peasant she has had before now attracts to it all the stray images of the station at which she first met Vronsky and of the train ride home. Fueled by guilt, it recurs to her with increasing horror. There is no doubt that she feels she is behaving immorally and suffers as a result.

She therefore does what Stiva would never do: she teaches herself to misperceive. If she could learn to see her husband as incapable of feeling, then she would not feel guilty for hurting him. If he she could perceive him as a monster of cruelty—the sadist he is in the Garbo film—then her anger at him would be justified. And if she could teach herself to react to him with such repulsion that it is simply impossible for her to live with him, then abandoning him would no longer be a matter of choice. She would not be to blame. (See Gustafson, 118–32).

What Anna does is not uncommon, even if she eventually does it more thoroughly than most people. We create for ourselves the world in which what we want to do is justified, and we try not to see contrary evidence. We usually do not at any single moment make an explicit decision to misperceive, because if we did, the misperception would feel like a lie and would not work. Like salesmen with shoddy goods, we must first sell ourselves; we must actually believe our own lies. Therefore, if the misperception is large and important enough, and if it contradicts a great deal of our experience, it must be learned gradually, so that no single moment strikes us by its palpable falsity. By tiny, tiny alterations, repeated countless times, we must instruct ourselves, without seeming to do so, to make each perception imperceptibly different from the last.

Even though we never make a single decision to lie, this process is deliberate in the sense that each uncharitable act of looking is a choice. Occasionally, as Anna does, we may find ourselves seeing in the old way, and then, as we make a determined effort to adjust, we become too aware of the effort to see something as we wish. If this effort at adjustment happens too often, the awareness of it will prevent our belief in the misperception and the whole project will fail. To make the falsehood believable, we must consciously do what we are not consciously aware of doing, and so each act of perception must only minutely alter its predecessors. Choosing so that one will not remember having chosen, willfully creating a sense of fate, ignoring part of what one has previously seen and changing the rest: all these actions constitute what might be called *the paradox of self-deceit.*

Narrating from Within

Tolstoy indicates explicitly that Anna deceives herself in this way. He tells us that "she schooled herself to despise and reproach him" (337), calls the way she listens to and looks at Karenin "lying" and "falsehood," and provides contrasting evidence to her perceptions.[17] Tolstoy wants us to measure what she sees against what she could see and used to see. If readers recognize the gradual process by which Anna "schools herself," they may learn to avoid similar self-deceit.

In spite of Tolstoy's efforts, readers and critics have usually taken Anna's trained misperceptions of Karenin for fact. Given the explicitness of Tolstoy's statements to the contrary, it is worth asking why.

One reason is the way Tolstoy uses what I like to call "the *Emma* technique," because Jane Austen perfected it and made it especially visible in that novel. This technique became the heritage of realist novels generally, and it figures prominently in *Anna Karenina*. Tolstoy narrates a passage in the third person, but the thoughts and words belong primarily to a character. We have already seen him do so during Anna's train ride home and in the "ears" passage. It is as if the camera recorded events not from above, but through the character's eyes to trace what she sees. This technique runs risks, because readers may mistake a character's perspective for the author's.

With the risks comes the compensating advantage of allowing readers to follow a character's thoughts and feelings from within. Paraphrase of inner speech easily shades into direct quotation and sometimes develops into brief or extended stream of consciousness. When we encounter such direct quotations, we may usually conclude that what immediately precedes them is indirect quotation, a paraphrase of the character's thoughts rather than an enunciation of the author's.

As Mikhail Bakhtin pointed out, such passages also may permit more than one voice to sound. In addition to the character's internal voice, we may also hear the overtones of authorial irony. Where there is text, there may be commentary. (See DI.) We have witnessed such "double-voicing" when Stiva calls himself a "truthful" man and wonders why Dolly has not "taken an indulgent view" of his infidelities out of simple fairness. As we have seen, we may extend Bakhtin's idea: we may also get two perspectives if the author should tacitly invite us to consider how a second character would respond to the first character's thoughts, as he invites us to imagine how Dolly would react if she could overhear Stiva's meditations. In these ways, apparently simple third-person narration may become a revealing potential dialogue. To miss these possibilities is to overlook the distinctive quality of novelistic prose.

Jane Austen developed this technique from more rudimentary forms in order to dramatize the way in which, out of pride and prejudice, people misperceive. In *Emma,* she uses it at great length without a break, so that readers mistake the heroine's perceptions for author-testified fact. As Emma, who believes in her own shrewdness, guesses wrong, so do we. Only in retrospect do we see that our error has derived from not understanding that we were looking through the character's eyes. In all her novels, Austen teaches us about misperception by having us misperceive.

Like Jane Austen, Tolstoy instructs about our tendencies to misperceive, but unlike the author of *Emma,* he wants us to detect misperceptions as, or shortly after, they occur. In the plausibility of Anna's distortions we may recognize our own tendency to distort in similar ways. If this lesson is to be effective, we must see and correct her misperceptions often enough that checking for perceptual errors becomes a habit. Tolstoy therefore employs a variety of means to insure that we do not, or do not long, mistake Anna's inner speech for his testimony.

In particular, Tolstoy makes it amply clear that many third-person passages about Karenin are narrated from Anna's point of view. At times, he interrupts her inner speech to comment on it and mark the difference from honest looking. Or he indicates that the characterizations of Karenin are Anna's by allowing the passage to shade into direct quotation from her inner voice. Or he uses phrases and perceptions that we know are characteristic of Anna. The passage may mention "ears" or the way in which Karenin cracks his knuckles, a habit that Anna teaches herself to find repulsive. Tolstoy also directly calls what she says to herself lying.

After Anna's new image of her husband has set, she takes pleasure in the very act of lying. At first, falsehood was necessary to forestall guilt and shame, but now lying "had become not merely simple and natural in society but a positive source of satisfaction" (313). We see another stage in Anna's moral degeneration.

Until the childbirth scene in Part Four, most characterizations of Karenin come from Anna's perspective. Why have critics so often taken these as factual statements? Why have they, along with Anna, turned a person with flaws, limitations, virtues, and feelings into a moral monster incapable of feeling? Critics seem to have shared Anna's perspective and romantic views so thoroughly that they cannot imagine the author would differ. No matter what Tolstoy explicitly says, and no matter how much counterevidence he provides, they have preferred to see Anna as she sees herself. A tragic tale of a vital woman who defies traditional morality to pursue true love but comes to grief because of the cruelty of her unfeeling husband and the hypocrisy of conventional society: this story is too familiar, and too dear, to suspect.

In *Emma,* readers come to realize the deficiencies of the heroine's ways of perception. In Tolstoy's novel, too many do not. It is as if the character has successfully usurped the story from the author. The myth proves stronger than the novel set against it.[18]

Mimicry

Even in a novel this long, and even with frequent paraphrases of Anna's inner speech, Tolstoy cannot show every instance of false looking. He therefore includes actions that could only be the product of countless moments of hostile observation. We may thereby infer more instances than he shows directly.

Twice Anna expertly mimics Karenin. As "a wicked light gleamed in her eyes that had been so soft a minute before," she acts out a Karenin speech to Vronsky:

> "Eh, you love another man, and have entered into a criminal liaison with him?" (Mimicking her husband she threw an emphasis on the word "criminal." . . .) "I warned you of the consequences from the religious, the civil and domestic points of view. . . ." (200–201)

A hundred and eighty pages later, she has gotten even better. When Anna hears that Vronsky, coming to see her at her house, has met Karenin, she performs what her husband must have done:

> "And he bowed to you like this?"
> She drew a long face, folded her hands, and Vronsky suddenly saw in her beautiful face the very expression with which Aleksey Aleksandrovich had bowed to him. (380)

Now she can imitate, and to perfection, his body language as well as his tone of voice and choice of words. How much effort must she have taken, and how much hostile attention must she have paid, for her to mimic her husband so well? Mimicry presumes a multiplicity of improving approximations.[19]

Some Strategic Absences

Anna's mocking mimicry is a caricature of Karenin even though it represents his mannerisms well. Any good caricature, after all, resembles the original in some respects, and its very exaggerations may expose to ridicule qualities that really are absurd. Karenin does use bureaucratic classifications in situations where they are comically inappropriate. What makes caricatures unfair is not so much their exaggerations, which are easily detected, but their omissions, which may easily go unrecalled. The strategic absences matter because they mislead others or, in Anna's case, herself.[20]

Anna's portrait of her husband overlooks Karenin's capacity to feel, his love and devotion to her, his integrity, and other qualities we have seen or will discover in him. If we compare Anna's mocking imitation of her husband with her view of him at the novel's beginning, we see significant differences. Anna knows, and later says, that even though Karenin has trouble expressing feelings, he really does feel deeply. When he meets Anna on her return from Moscow, he greets her as if he were ironic: "'Yes, as you see, your tender spouse, as devoted as the first year after marriage, burned with impatience to see you,' he said in his deliberate, high pitched voice, and in that tone . . . of jeering at anyone who should say in earnest what he said" (110–11). As Bakhtin correctly reads this passage, Karenin has truly missed Anna, but the language of love is alien to him. (See DI, 328n26.) He can use it only "in quotation marks," as someone else's language that he is merely citing. He thereby imparts an ironic tone to what he really means. Two pages later, Karenin, tongue-tied and "no longer in a sarcastic tone," tells his wife: "You wouldn't believe how I've missed . . ." (114). Unable to finish his sentence, he gives her hand a long pressure while smiling meaningfully.

When Anna returns from her mission to repair her brother's marriage, Karenin tells her that even though Stiva is her brother, one cannot avoid considering him in the wrong. Anna admires this integrity and respects her husband's unwillingness to let family considerations interfere with his judgment: "She knew that characteristic in her husband and liked it" (118). When she sees Aleksey Aleksandrovich reading a work of French literature, she reflects that, for all his effort to keep up with the world of culture, he cannot really understand it. At this reflection, "Anna smiled as people smile at the weaknesses of those they love, and putting her hand under his, she escorted him to the door of the study" (118). These passages tell us that, at this point, she knows that her husband really loves her and that she loves him. In spite of his weaknesses and limitations, their marriage has been, if deficient, not the living hell she later calls it. Despite later assertions to the contrary, she understands that, for all Karenin's difficulty with the language of emotions, he is far from an "official machine" without feelings.

Aleksey Aleksandrovich Plans a Conversation

At the beginning of Part Two, Anna stops socializing with the circle she used to prefer in order to join the set of Princess Betsy Tverskaya, Vronsky's cynical cousin. At first, Anna "sincerely believed she was displeased" with Vronsky for pursuing her, but when he fails to show up at Betsy's once, her rush of disappointment indicates to her that this pursuit has become "her whole interest in life" (136). No longer self-deceived, but torn, she continually goes to Betsy's to order Vronsky to keep away from her, a contradiction he correctly understands as an avowal of interest. She soulfully laments that he has no heart, and he understands she means the opposite. She warns him that she has "forbidden" him to speak of love, but "at once she felt that by that very word 'forbidden' she had shown that she acknowledged certain rights over him, and by that very fact was encouraging him to speak of love" (148). If you love me, do not love me: that is the logic of such forbidding. Anna informs Vronsky that she has come purposely to tell him she does not want to see him any more, another version of the same self-canceling command.

By the time Karenin arrives to take his wife home, Anna and Vronsky, sitting apart from the rest of the company, are engaged in an intense exchange the tenor of which is unmistakable to everyone present, except Karenin himself. "This is getting positively indecent," one lady expresses what everyone senses. Karenin notices this reaction. Anna refuses to go home with him and stays for supper.

The next three chapters—Part Two, chapters 8, 9, and 10—constitute one of the book's key sequences. In chapter 8, Karenin considers what he has seen and tries to understand how he should speak of it with Anna. His reaction to Anna's "positively indecent" behavior is so frequently misunderstood from Anna's later perspective that it is worth considering.

Chapter 8 begins with Karenin at home, waiting for his wife and lost in thought:

> Aleksey Aleksandrovich had seen nothing striking or improper in the fact that his wife was sitting with Vronsky at a separate table in eager conversation with him about something. But he noticed that to the rest of the party this appeared to be something striking and improper, and for that reason it seemed to him to be improper. He made up his mind that he must speak of it to his wife. (151)

This passage does *not* say: Karenin understands the impropriety of Anna's behavior but does not mind it except insofar as others may have noticed it. Anna will later insist that Karenin feels neither jealousy nor pain but cares only about society's attitude. He cannot be hurt because he cannot feel at all. This self-serving judgment is almost unbelievable for any human being. It takes away Karenin's humanity and reduces him to something virtually inanimate. And it is palpably untrue, for Karenin, she knows, loves her, clearly shows jealousy, and suffers a great deal.

Karenin cares about what others say because that is the only way he can determine what is taking place. As some people are color blind, Karenin is blind to social relations. As he, Anna, and everyone else know, he lacks the ability to read social cues, especially those pertaining to deeper emotions. Unable to judge whether something improper is going on, he does what a color blind person would do to ascertain the hue of a new shirt: he relies on those who can see what he cannot. The judgment of others counts not because their assessment is all that matters, but because he cannot rely on his own. He really cares whether

Anna is involved with Vronsky, but knows that he is entirely at sea in making such judgments.

We now trace his inner thoughts interrupted by authorial commentary:

> Aleksey Aleksandrovich was not jealous. Jealousy, according to his notions, was an insult to one's wife, and one ought to have confidence in one's wife. Why one ought to have confidence — that is to say, complete conviction that his young wife would always love him — he did not ask himself. But he had no experience of lack of confidence, because he had confidence in her, and told himself he ought to have it. Now, though his conviction that jealousy was a shameful feeling and that one ought to feel confidence had not broken down, he felt that he was standing face to face with something illogical and irrational, and did not know what was to be done. Aleksey Aleksandrovich was standing face to face with life, with the possibility of his wife's loving someone other than himself, and this seemed to him very irrational and incomprehensible because it was life itself. (151–52)

The first two sentences belong to Karenin's inner speech: he tells himself that he is not jealous and brings to mind his conviction that jealousy is an insult to one's wife. The very fact that he denies jealousy shows that he experiences it. The author then comments ironically on Karenin's naive conviction that a young wife will always remain faithful to an older husband. Karenin is utterly illogical in concluding that because he has always had confidence he should now have confidence. Here, and throughout the chapter, Tolstoy shows us the jealousy Karenin feels while stressing the comedy of his naïve attempts to understand it. Tolstoy switches from internal perspective to external judgment without compromising either.

Karenin's problem is not a lack of feeling, but a lack of understanding. He fails to comprehend love relations, and he deals comfortably only with "the reflection of life" in official memoranda. He now has no choice but to experience the pain and make the decisions that real life entails. Feeling utterly inadequate to the situation, Karenin turns to still more bureaucratese, which, though providing temporary comfort, soon leaves him feeling less adequate than ever. The more he thinks, the worse he feels, and the more he tries not to think, the more jealousy haunts him.

The longer Karenin waits for Anna to return, the more her delay strikes him as significant. He paces back and forth, his legs enacting the vicious circle of his thoughts, as he tells himself he must say something. But what? Reflecting that jealousy is an insult to one's wife, he decides to say nothing. But this dictum about jealousy no longer carries any weight and so he realizes he must say something after all. To confront her, however, would be to accuse her and might constitute an unprovoked insult, and so on. Karenin is trying to be honorable by not accusing his wife of what may not be true. Yet he recognizes that silence is no longer an option. Many people more socially adept than Karenin have found themselves in this dilemma.

Karenin resolves the problem by returning to what he knows best and formulating a bureaucratic speech not so much from conviction as from the lack of any alternative. He really wants to speak of his feelings and her actions, but that is a language he cannot master, and so he prepares a translation. Besides, if he speaks simply of violations of rules, he can avoid the insulting (if false) accusation that she is really involved with Vronsky. He hopes that she will address the more serious issue without his having to express demeaning suspicions.

Most of us have experienced what Tolstoy often describes: the difference between the conversation we plan and what really happens. No matter how much we anticipate, the two never match. Our intentions may be derailed by purely contingent events, like a phone ringing or an urgent problem arising unexpectedly. In *War and Peace,* Pierre's interview with Davout is interrupted by an adjutant entering the room just as Davout is about to pardon Pierre. Davout's thoughts shift, and so, when he is reminded of Pierre, he hastily pronounces the death sentence he was on the verge of setting aside. Even without interruptions, conversations do not take place as planned, because the other person rarely reacts as we supposed. How could we predict reactions that partly depend on innumerable contingencies, internal and external, that affect the other person's mood and thoughts at a given moment? Why, one might just as well plan the course of a battle or construct a predictive social science.

Lying without Speaking

In chapter 9, Anna at last returns home. She arrives "playing with the tassels of her hood" and with her face "brilliant and glowing" as if from "a conflagration in the midst of a dark night" (154). Still under the spell of her intensely charged meeting with Vronsky, the last thing she wants to do is talk with her husband about it. But he has been waiting up to do so. If we reflect on Anna's conversational genius and Karenin's social idiocy, we will guess that Karenin will not get the serious conversation he desires, now or thereafter. She can easily parry all attempts to talk.

To avoid speaking, Anna engages in *false listening*. No matter what he says, she will either not hear it or misconstrue it. When she sees him, she obviously knows why he has stayed up, but she says, as if nothing has happened, "You're not in bed? What a surprise!" and, "without stopping, she went on into the dressing room." "It's late," she says, as if it were impossible to talk or there were nothing in particular to talk about. He stops her, says it is necessary for him to speak with her, but she answers, with surprise, "With me? . . . Why, what is it? What about? . . . Well, let's talk if it's so necessary but it would be better to get to sleep" (154).

With me? What about? she asks, as if there were someone else present and as if she did not know what there is to discuss. Lest there be any doubt that she is feigning, Tolstoy comments:

> Anna said what came to her lips, and marveled, hearing herself, at her own capacity for lying. How simple and natural were her words, and how likely that she was simply sleepy! She felt herself clad in an impenetrable armor of lying. (154)

What exactly is the lie? The word "lie" appears twice, but if one looks at the actual words Anna has used, there is no literal lie—just expressions of surprise. So what does the author mean by calling what she does lying and making clear that she herself knows that she is lying? Where is the falsehood, if not in her speech?

The answer is that *one can lie in how one listens as well as in how one speaks.* This Tolstoyan truth lies at the center of *Anna Karenina* and, if one does not grasp it, one misses both a key theme and an important engine of plot. It informs the book's treatment of honesty. Listening has moral value and can be done in good or bad faith. It is Anna's bad faith here, not anything she says, that makes her listening a lie.

What is true of listening pertains to looking. Both are ways of paying attention, and we are always choosing how to direct our attention. We decide how to look or listen, and what thoughts to entertain or pass over, at every moment of our waking lives. These small acts ultimately determine a life and constitute our most frequent and most important expressions of good or bad faith.

Exercising her Oblonsky skill, Anna responds to her husband with listening lies that are apparently "simple" and "natural." But the simplicity and naturalness are themselves knowingly contrived. Anna is a splendid actress and so Tolstoy explicitly warns us not to be taken in by her performance.

Their Past Marriage

Tolstoy then gives us one of the book's key passages, which I extract from a long paragraph:

> She looked at him so simply, so brightly, that anyone who did not know her as her husband knew her could not have noticed anything unnatural, either in the sound or the sense of her words. But to him, knowing her,

knowing that whenever he went to bed five minutes later than usual she noticed it and asked him the reason; to him, knowing that every joy, every pleasure and pain that she felt she communicated to him at once; to him, now to see that she did not care to notice his state of mind, that she did not care to say a word about herself, meant a great deal. (155)

Whenever he went to bed five minutes late she asked why, and whenever she felt joy or pain she communicated it to him: this does not sound like a relationship without love or a marriage from hell. It is a relationship so close that Anna notices the slightest break in routine. It must require a lot of "schooling" in misperception and selective memory to remember their eight years of marriage as completely unhappy.[21]

This characterization of their marriage probably belongs to the author because it is he, not Karenin, who characterizes the Oblonskys as given to fake simplicity and false naturalness, mentioned in the first sentence. The comment that no outsider could have detected the falsity also seems to come from the author's perspective, since Karenin reflects on the difference between past and present and not on the difference between what he and an outsider could see. Tolstoy sets up the description of the marriage so that we do not doubt it.

The fact that Anna herself recognizes her falsity in not speaking also suggests that even if we do take the sentence about their past marriage as a paraphrase of Karenin's thought, it is still largely true. Her refusal to talk contrasts with her past behavior and she knows it. If the sentence is Karenin's, he is at worst exaggerating. Anna at least asked him frequently, if not always, about why he was going to bed late, and she communicated many, if not all, of her feelings to him. We have in this passage evidence that the way Anna will later describe their marriage so as to justify her affair is false, as false as the way she listens here. Critics do not cite this passage.

One can easily fail to appreciate this passage because it is *openly camouflaged.* The crucial information appears in subordinate clauses of a long sentence in a long paragraph. But that is how this novel works: to teach us that we tend to overlook the most important information because it is less noticeable, the author frequently places that information where, though explicit, it is inconspicuous.

In a similar passage, we learn that a deeply injured Karenin, to protect himself, "locked and sealed up that secret place where his feelings toward his family—that is, his wife and son—lay hidden. He who had been such a concerned father had from the end of that winter become peculiarly cold to his son, and adopted toward him just the same bantering tone he used with his wife" (213). *He who had been such a concerned father:* clearly the author is speaking here, and he tells us that Karenin has been anything but uncaring about Seryo-zha. This information, too, is placed in a subordinate clause.

The Pallisers at Breakfast

Karenin tries to break through Anna's non-listening responses, but she easily escapes.[22] He tries to avoid accusing her: "'Your too animated conversation with Count Vronsky' (he enunciated the name firmly and with deliberate emphasis) 'attracted attention'" (155). Karenin makes sure to enunciate Vronsky's name because anyone who was jealous would find the name too painful to pronounce and so would use a pronoun or other substitute. By pronouncing Vronsky's name with deliberate emphasis, he means to preclude any accusation of infidelity. Anna deliberately misses the main point of this statement. Looking at Karenin "with laughing eyes" and an "impenetrable look," she replies:

> "You're always like that," she answered, as though completely misunderstanding him, and of all he had said only taking in the last phrase "One time you don't like my being bored, and another time you don't like my being lively. I wasn't bored. Does that offend you?" (155)

As though completely misunderstanding him: she understands him quite well, but there is no utterance that cannot be misunderstood. Anna answers as if his point pertained not to her behavior with Vronsky but to excessive animation in company.

Out of sheer frustration, Karenin shivers and cracks his knuckles. (See Gustafson, 121–22.) Anna now loathes this gesture and, to misdirect the topic of conversation, objects to it. "'Well, I'm listening to what's to come,' she said, calmly and ironically, 'and indeed I listen with interest, for I should like to understand what's the matter.' She spoke, and marveled at the confident, calm, and natural tone in which she was speaking, and the choice of words that she used" (156). Again we have direct authorial statement that she herself marvels at her own ability to prevaricate so naturally. Anna knows perfectly well "what's the matter" and she is fully conscious of what she is doing, enough so to appreciate her own performance.

At last, Karenin gives up all indirection, all bureaucratese, even all accusation, and speaks directly from the heart: "'Anna, for God's sake don't speak like that,' he said gently. 'Perhaps I am mistaken, but believe me what I say, I say as much for myself as for you. I am your husband, and I love you'" (156). Anna has not been counting on this tone, and she faces a choice: to continue with the falsehood or to consider his feelings and the fact that he loves her.

As it happens, this scene directly parallels one in the English novel Anna is reading on the train back to Moscow. We are told that this novel deals with fox hunts and speeches in Parliament. Anyone who knows the English novel will immediately recognize these incidents as the signature of Anthony Trollope. If one wanted to parody Trollope, one would be sure to include such events. Anna is most likely reading *Can You Forgive Her?*, the first of Trollope's six Palliser novels, the series in which most speeches in Parliament occur. The Palliser novels describe the marriage of a spirited woman, Lady Glencora, and an older man, Plantagenet Palliser, who is a prominent state official. Stiffly honorable, Palliser expresses feelings with difficulty. The parallel with Anna and Karenin is obvious.

Trollope's novel narrates three stories, in each of which a lively woman must choose between a "worthy man" and a "wild man." Lady Glencora, though married to Palliser, still loves Burgo Fitzgerald, whom she knew before her marriage. She has openly flirted with him and is considering running away with him. As in *Anna Karenina,* Palliser decides to do something quite difficult for him and speak with her about the matter. Like Anna, Glencora keeps mishearing him and changing the topic, until at last, he appeals, with real feeling, to her sense of the truth.

Like Anna, Glencora is struck by this speech from the heart. In response, Glencora does consider what he is saying. She realizes that she is at fault: she has listened to words of love from a former lover and so has been "false to her husband." "Her own spirit rebelled against the deceit which she herself was practicing" (Trollope, vol. 2, 188). Recognizing that, for all his stiffness and difficulty in love talk, he really does love her, she resolves to make the marriage work.

In the parallel situation, Anna makes the opposite choice. Karenin's heartfelt appeal and declaration of love directly parallel Palliser's, and Anna, like Glencora, is moved. But Anna decides not to respond in kind and to continue with her falsity. To do so, she must deny that he loves her, that he is even capable of love:

> For an instant her face fell, and the sardonic gleam in her eyes died away; but the word "love" threw her into revolt again. She thought: "Love? Can he love? If he hadn't heard there was such a thing as love, he would never have used the word. He doesn't even know what love is." (156)

She struggles to regard him as unfeeling in the face of what she, like Glencora, knows to be true. That is why Anna's face falls, the sardonic gleam in her eyes momentarily disappears, and she resorts to the sort of cliché—if he had not heard the word love, etc.—she must have heard repeated countless times in salons. From this point on, there is nothing Karenin could do to persuade her to speak and listen honestly.

The Shortest Chapter

The next chapter is the book's shortest because it reports non-actions. Its opening is quintessential Tolstoy: "From that time on, a new life began for Aleksey Aleksandrovich and his wife. Nothing special happened" (157). Although nothing special happens, many important things do not happen: Karenin repeatedly tries to speak with Anna and she always confronts his attempts "with a barrier that he could not penetrate, made up of a sort of amused perplexity" (157). He keeps hoping that "by kindness, tenderness, and persuasion" he might reach her, but, after endless failures, he at last begins to speak in that jeering tone he uses when uncomfortable and frustrated. She will not hear him and will not consider his feelings, which makes it easier for her to tell herself repeatedly that he cannot feel at all.

Vronsky

What matters most in understanding Vronsky is what did not happen to him.

> Vronsky had never had a real family life. His mother had been in her youth a brilliant society woman, who had during her married life, and especially afterward, many love affairs notorious in all society. His father he scarcely remembered, and he had been educated in the Corps of Pages. (62)

We see here how evil spreads. Vronsky's moral obtuseness derives not from a trauma but from an absence. He missed the family life where moral habits are formed, and there is no making up for that. His mother's affairs have shaped him, not because of what she has done, but because of what she in consequence has failed to do.

When Vronsky flirts with Kitty, even hinting at something more serious, he fails in all innocence to understand that such an amusement might cause Kitty serious injury or distress. He inflicts this pain with no intention to hurt, because he has never acquired the sensibility of a family. Vronsky is not even aware that he lacks something, a lack in itself.

In place of family sensibility, Vronsky has absorbed the ethos of military bachelors, which seems as natural to him as family considerations do to Kitty and Dolly. He divides people into two utterly opposed sorts:

> One, the inferior sort, vulgar, stupid, and above all ridiculous people, who believe that one husband ought to live with the one wife to whom he is lawfully married; that a girl should be innocent, a woman modest, and a man manly, self-controlled, and strong; that one ought to bring up one's

children, earn one's bread, and pay one's debts, and other similar absurdities. (121)

The other sort, the "real people," are elegant and plucky, abandon themselves to all passions, and "laugh at everything else" (121). Given his upbringing, Vronsky unsurprisingly laughs at bringing up one's children.

In Vronsky's contempt for paying one's debts, no less than in his contempt for earning one's bread, we see his disrespect for work. Most debts represent the work of others, and these are the ones Vronsky is least likely to pay. When we see Vronsky dividing up his debts and deciding which to ignore, the claims of people who have actually worked for him come last. Even though Vronsky would never steal, it never occurs to him that to refuse to pay tradesmen is to steal their labor.

Vronsky adheres punctiliously to his "code of principles." We hear this code paraphrased in Vronsky's language with Tolstoy's ironic countervoice equally audible:

> These principles laid down as invariable rules: that one must pay a card shark, but need not pay a tailor; that one must never tell a lie to a man, but one may to a woman; that one must never cheat anyone, but one may cheat a husband; that one must never pardon an insult, but one may give one, and so on. (323)

Vronsky would acknowledge each of these rules, but would never juxtapose them as the author does, because the juxtaposition suggests hypocrisy, which Vronsky, as a man of honor by his own lights, would abjure. What is interesting about this passage is that Vronsky really does have a sense of honor, and when he later tells Anna he never lies, by that time he means to anyone, women as well as men. He is quite sincere about that. He begins by adhering to his ridiculous code, but his moral sense gradually matures. Vronsky always tries to adhere to whatever principles he professes.

The absurdity of Vronsky's morality lies in the principles to which he is loyal, not in his loyalty. The harm he causes results not from malice but from an absence. He really does not know any better. Unlike Stiva, he has not trained himself to forget things he does not wish to remember. He does not need to, because he does not notice such things in the first place.

Vronsky's Attempted Suicide

Vronsky grows. When he breaks Frou-Frou's back, he realizes that he has committed "a fearful, unpardonable mistake" (211) and "for the first time in his life, he knew the bitterest sort of misfortune, misfortune beyond remedy, misfortune his own fault" (212). Vronsky does not refuse responsibility and the experience of deep regret changes him for the better. Difficulties in his evolving relationship with Anna are of course the main catalyst of his growth.

Throughout the novel, his sense of honor remains. But his understanding of what honor entails evolves.

After describing Vronsky's "code of principles," Tolstoy remarks that their chief advantage in Vronsky's eyes has always been their "unfailing certainty." Only now, with his love for Anna becoming much more than an affair, does he sense that his principles "did not fully cover all possible contingencies" (323). We hear in Tolstoy's irony the tacit suggestion that, apart from the silliness of the code, it is absurd to regard any set of principles as certain to cover all contingencies.

When Vronsky learns of Anna's pregnancy, he finds himself out of his depth. His mother, he knows, used to regard the liaison with Anna as proper polish for a society man, but now disparages Vronsky's deeper feeling as some "Werther-like desperate passion" (185). In defying her and his brother, Vronsky tries to make use of his earlier principles, but gradually alters them.

Vronsky eventually has to choose between his career, which he values, and Anna. As he wavers, he examines himself and his values. By the time he entertains the foreign prince who looks like a cucumber, Vronsky finds the guest's shallow love of amusement disturbing precisely because "he could not help seeing himself in him" (374). "Brainless beef, can I be like that?" Vronsky asks himself (375). The answer is that he was indeed just like that, but no longer is precisely because he can ask this question. Vronsky no longer lacks awareness that he lacks something.

When Anna seems to be dying from fever, she praises Karenin's goodness. Vronsky experiences profound shame and hides his face in his hands. Anna makes Karenin remove Vronsky's hands so he can see her husband, whom she calls a saint. When Vronsky recognizes that "the husband" who can forgive his enemies is morally superior to himself, his humiliation deepens. Vronsky "did not understand Aleksey Aleksandrovich but he felt it was something beyond him, even unattainable for him with his outlook on life" (436).

His outlook on life (*mirovozrenie*): humiliation calls Vronsky's whole world into question. He leaves feeling "disgraced, humiliated, guilty" and with no way to erase the shame. The shame runs so deep because it impugns both his dignity and his beliefs. "All the habits and rules of his life that had seemed so firm had turned out suddenly false and inapplicable" (436). He believes he has lost Anna because he has been "base and petty in his deceit" while Karenin was "magnanimous even in his sorrow" (437).

When Vronsky arrives home, he tries to sleep, but repeatedly envisions Karenin removing his hands. Vronsky recalls the foolish look on his face at that moment. Of course, he could not have seen this picture: he "remembers" the scene as he imagines it must have looked to someone else looking on—some representative of the world seeing his shame. Still worse, the one who really did witness this scene, and who certainly noticed what his face must have looked like, is Anna. Vronsky hears a voice telling him he did not appreciate and make enough of his time with her, and so regret is added to shame. Vronsky asks himself whether these are the feelings that provoke people to shoot themselves. Tolstoy then gives us an apparently unimportant detail:

> opening his eyes, he [Vronsky] saw with wonder an embroidered cushion beside him done by Varya, his brother's wife. He touched the tassel of the cushion, and tried to think of when he had seen her last. But to think of anything extraneous was an agonizing effort. (438)

Why, at such a moment, does Tolstoy include such a passage? We have already seen Tolstoy's appreciation of embroidery as a symbol of domestic values. Tolstoy also commented that embroidery gave him an idea for a whole chapter, which concerns Varya.

Varya plays a small but important role in *Anna Karenina*. She is another Dolly. As Dolly is Anna's brother's wife, Varya is Vronsky's brother's wife. Each sister-in-law is married to a perpetually unfaithful husband and each is generous, kind, prosaically wise, and dedicated above all to her children. If what is most important is least noticeable, and if undramatic Dolly appears less important than she really is, then Varya out-Dollys Dolly. She embodies the same values but plays a still smaller role in the novel's economy. In devoting a sentence and a half to Varya and her embroidery just before Vronsky shoots himself, Tolstoy hints at the values Vronsky's world view has omitted. Vronsky is amazed, but we should not be.

"Of course," Vronsky says to himself, "as though a logical, continuous, and clear chain of reasoning had brought him to an indubitable conclusion" (439). In this novel, nothing can ever be indubitable and the sense that an idea seems beyond doubt indicates mistaken thinking. Vronsky has gone from principles of unfailing certainty to a conclusion that seems unavoidable, but for Tolstoy people always live in a world of uncertainty. Tolstoy comments that what gave the thought of suicide the feeling of inevitability was not logical entailment but repetition of the same memories in the same order. On the whole and for the most part, certainty is a psychological state mistaken for a fact about the world.

A confusion of repetition with logical necessity, Vronsky's error derives from another Tolstoyan fallacy of perception. We usually find conclusions certain because we overlook contrary evidence and mistake an example for a proof. The embroidered cushion suggests what Vronsky's indubitable conclusion leaves out, everything that does not fit the story of romance, shame, and loss. As if to emphasize his theme of perception, Tolstoy immediately describes how, after Vronsky has shot himself and fallen, "he did not recognize his room as he looked up from the floor at the curved legs of the table, at the waste-paper basket, and the tigerskin rug" (439).

The servant who finds Vronsky is so panic-stricken that he leaves him bleeding to death while running for help. The person who comes to help, sends for three doctors, and stays to nurse Vronsky is: his brother's wife, Varya.

Vronsky's Loathing

Experiencing regret and shame, and spurred by his sense of honor and dignity, Vronsky continually grows wiser. By the time Dolly visits Vronsky and Anna, he really wants the family life he has never had and does not quite understand in practice. Vronsky is still shallow, of course, because he started out so shallow, and even though he has come far, he can never achieve what a good childhood would have made second nature. His mother's neglect of him has harmed Kitty, Karenin, Seryozha, and eventually Anna: and this destructive chain illustrates yet again how evil derives from an absence.

Shortly before the races, Vronsky visits Anna. He experiences, as he has often of late, a "strange feeling of inexplicable loathing" (197). Turning to a romantic script to explain this feeling, Vronsky attributes it to the necessity of "lying, deceiving, feigning, and continually thinking of others, when the passion that united them was so intense that they were oblivious of everything else but their love" (195). Other people "'haven't an idea what happiness is; they don't know that without our love, for us there is neither happiness nor unhappiness—no life at all,' he thought" (195). In this book, Tolstoy often shows characters thinking or speaking the most tired clichés without a blush because the clichés seem like simple facts to them. The straightforward phrasing of such hackneyed thoughts reflects the power of a myth allowing for no alternative way of looking at things. When readers take these passages as untinged by irony, the same myth governs them.

Vronsky and Anna are repeatedly false in saying that what bothers them is the necessity of being false, just as Stiva is false when he tells himself something similar at the novel's opening. They lie about not wanting to lie. Anna and Vronsky are engaged in adultery and, still worse, they fail to consider the effect of their actions on Karenin and Seryozha. Anna positively enjoys the game of deceit. Nevertheless, they assure themselves and each other that their discomfort comes from the necessity of deception.

Tolstoy explicitly specifies the real cause of Vronsky's inexplicable loathing. It is Seryozha, who looks at them with questioning eyes because he does not understand whether he is supposed to love Vronsky, whom his mother regards as her greatest friend, or look on him with aversion, as his father, his governess, and nurse do. Seryozha blames himself for not knowing. His shyness and uncertainty, precisely because they cannot be written off as the hostility of the world, force Anna and Vronsky to suspend their neglect of the nonromantic consequences of their actions. "This child, with his innocent outlook upon life, was the compass that showed them the point to which they had departed from what they knew but did not want to know" (197).

Vronsky Tries to Talk

When Vronsky arrives before going to the races, Anna, fearing he won't take the fact seriously enough, tells him that she is pregnant. Vronsky immediately experiences "with tenfold intensity that strange feeling of loathing of someone" (199). His own child-to-be compels Vronsky all the more strongly to know what he does not want to know, to pay attention to the real effects of his situation on others. He replies by telling Anna that "our fate is sealed" and that they must put an end "to the deception in which we are living" (199), a statement that, for all its clichéd phrasing, insists on an action: "leave your husband and make our lives one" (199).

But Anna does not want to take any action. She is afraid to lose her social position and her son, and would rather postpone the necessity of an action as long as possible. "She who had so feared he would take her condition too lightly was now vexed with him for deducing from it the necessity of taking some step" (200). She dreams a double dream, the inner one about the terrible peasant and the outer one about how she is told that the inner dream means she will die in childbirth. We know from her reaction to the trainman's death that she believes in fate and omens. Now the self-interpreting dream, with its precognition of inevitable death, serves to make any decision unnecessary. She meets all Vronsky's attempts to discuss what action they will take much as she has met Karenin's attempts to talk: by misunderstanding, by deflecting the issue, and with amused perplexity. He cannot break through.

Make our life one? "It is one as it is" (199). You must change a situation in which you torture yourself over everything—"the world, your son and your husband" (200). "Oh, not my husband. . . . I don't know him, I don't think of him. He doesn't exist" (200). Vronsky finds it incredible that she would not even think of her husband and says so, but he cannot get her to return to his main point, the necessity of making a decision.

Vronsky had several times already, though not so resolutely as now, tried to get her to consider their situation, and every time he had been confronted by the same superficiality and triviality with which she met his appeal now. It was as though . . . she, the real Anna, retreated somehow into herself, and another, strange, and unaccountable woman came out, whom he did not love, and whom he feared, and who was in opposition to him. But today he was resolved to have it out. (200)

He can resolve to have things out as much as Karenin does, but he will have no better success. He confronts a master of deflection, and, like Karenin, he experiences this false listening as if it were the product of a second Anna. With frivolous irony, she now does her first imitation of her husband and turns the conversation to Karenin's inability to feel:

> "He's not a man but a machine, and a spiteful machine when he's angry," she added, recalling Aleksey Aleksandrovich with all the peculiarities of his figure and manner of speaking and setting against him every defect she could find in him, softening nothing for the great wrong she was doing him. (201)

Tolstoy is explicit: she seeks out his peculiarities—ears, knuckles, anything about his figure and manner of speaking—and deliberately sees them in the worst light, finds every possible defect and sets it against him, and softens nothing because of the great wrong that she is doing to him. The author makes a point of differing from her and, just when she says Karenin is unfeeling, Tolstoy points out how unfeeling she is in not considering what he suffers because of her great wrong. If there is a great wrong, as the author attests, then it is untrue that Karenin does not suffer. This passage goes uncited by those who read the novel from Anna's point of view.

Anna uses the false listening she has practiced with Karenin to deal with Vronsky. As the novel progresses, she does so more and more, and Vronsky is less and less able to do anything about it. When they live together, Anna's false-hood accelerates. That is why, as Dolly notes, she has developed the gesture of dropping her eyes, as if not to see things; why she takes opium; and why Vronsky has to ask Dolly to implore Anna to obtain the divorce she refused when Karenin promised it long ago. Evidently, Anna has parried every one of Vronsky's attempts to discuss the matter seriously. We learn as well that she is concealing matters of the greatest importance to him. Worrying that his future children will be Karenin's, and imploring Dolly to make his worry clear to Anna, he evidently does not know what Anna tells Dolly in response: that there will be no more children because she is using birth control. By concealing crucial information from him, Anna is being false with another kind of silence.

When Anna later telegraphs Vronsky to come home quickly because their daughter is seriously ill, we recognize that she is capable not only of self-deception and false listening, but also of overt falsehood. When Vronsky hurriedly returns—one cannot ignore such a summons even if one is pretty sure it is not true—Anna cannot even remember what supposedly ailed the little girl. Anna and Vronsky grow more and more distant, and she, noticing the distance, blames him for not loving her enough, for condescending silence, and for wanting to abandon her for another woman. When he notices the "other Anna" and tries to break through to her real self, she accuses him of cruelty and domination, but when he takes her deceptions as simple truths she imagines either that he is being deliberately cold or that he no longer cares to know what is true. Vronsky does not know what to do, and no heartfelt appeal works, any more than Karenin's did.

Responsibility at a Remove

Here is one way to tell Anna's story: She teaches herself to misperceive so as to avoid guilt. Practicing false listening and false looking, she gradually allows these habits to develop a dynamic of their own, like her growing addiction to opium. At first she knowingly marvels at and enjoys her expert practice of falsehood, but at last she grows almost unable to tell when she is lying. For stretches of time, Anna either loses the ability to distinguish reality at all or can see it only intermittently.

Anna's story dramatizes the novel's theme of honesty. Honesty is difficult; dishonesty can be complex. A lie does not necessarily come into being at the moment when the falsehood becomes visible. At that moment, the liar may be genuinely sincere because he or she has long since acquired a habit of misperception. That habit has resulted from countless small choices to see in a distorted way or to omit seeing what one does not want to see.

Falsehood may take place at a temporal remove. We make a psychological, as well as moral, mistake when we equate intention or responsibility with a choice that immediately precedes the action. We may be responsible without such an immediately prior choice. By teaching ourselves not to see, we become responsible for what we miss, even if we do not appreciate exactly what is missed.

In his crime reporting, and in articles published while *Anna Karenina* was being serialized, Dostoevsky argued much the same point. He applied it to habits of thinking that can lead, at a remove, to violent crime. That idea shaped the plot of *Crime and Punishment*, published a little more than a decade before *Anna Karenina*. Tolstoy, if we are to judge by an essay he wrote much later, understood Dostoevsky's point. This essay is the one that describes life as a series of tiny, tiny alterations.

As Tolstoy (I believe correctly) paraphrases Dostoevsky's thought, Raskolnikov did not decide to murder the old woman just before doing so. He lived his true life at a distance, and he made that decision at a distance. When murdering the old woman, Raskolnikov discharged "the cartridge with which he had long been loaded" (R&E, 81). His decision was made and he lived his true life not when he held the axe in hand, or made the loop in his overcoat by which the axe could secretly hang, or argued for the morality of certain kinds of murder. He made it when he was just lying on his sofa and thinking about things not at all related to the old woman: "when he was doing nothing and . . . only his consciousness was active: and in that consciousness tiny, tiny alterations were taking place" (R&E, 82).

Anna's practiced misperceptions, originally designed to assuage guilt over her affair, cause harm not only to Karenin and Seryozha, and later to Vronsky and her daughter Annie, but also to herself. It is not the infidelity itself that destroys her, and the novel, strangely enough, never seems to condemn her for infidelity per se. It is rather her various kinds of falsehood, from sheer neglect of others' feelings to various forms of self-deception and false listening, that the author faults the most.

Races and Circuses

Tolstoy narrates the long sequence devoted to the horse races in an odd way. Instead of recounting the events in chronological order, he first gives us the story as Vronsky experiences it and then goes all the way back to tell us the story from the perspective of Anna and Karenin. First we see the race itself, then the spectators watching the race. Tolstoy's choice to set aside chronology even creates some awkwardness.[23] Since Anna appears in both stories, her conversations before leaving home, first with Vronsky and then with Karenin, are separated, although they must have occurred one after the other. We get her reaction to Vronsky's accident long after the accident itself. Why does Tolstoy narrate in this way?

The answer, I think, is that Tolstoy wants to dramatize his core theme that *looking is an action*. With the race already described, the second story can focus on looking. It dwells on the voyeuristic interest of the audience at the injury and death of horses and riders. "It's too exciting," declares Betsy with interest, and another lady answers: "It's exciting, but one can't tear oneself away. . . . If I'd been a Roman woman, I would never have missed a single circus" (221). One could hardly pick a better-known example of immoral watching than the Roman circus. To include a discussion of it among characters who wish they could have been a Roman audience is to offer almost too obvious a statement that looking is an action with moral value.

Karenin himself states the point explicitly: "there are two aspects . . . those who take part and those who look on; and love for such spectacles is an unmistakable proof of a low degree of development in the spectator" (221). *Those who take part and those who look on:* Tolstoy narrates each "aspect" separately to single out the moral implications of the latter.

What Anna Sees and What Tolstoy Says

Each narrative begins just before the races. Part Two, chapter 27 initiates the second narrative, pertaining to Anna, Karenin, and the audience. It begins, as other sequences do, with Anna upstairs "standing in front of the mirror" and dressing. Karenin arrives, and she "went down to meet him with a bright and radiant face; and conscious of the presence of that spirit of falsehood and deceit in herself which she had come to know of late, she abandoned herself to that spirit and began talking, hardly knowing what she was saying" (217). She speaks "very simply and naturally" with him. He does not detect the falsehood and gives her words "only the direct significance they bore" (217). For this very reason, "Anna could never recall this brief scene without an agonizing pang of shame" (217).

This reference to her shame, like several others, indicates that her self-deception is not complete. In this case, the statements she makes under the influence of that "spirit of falsehood and deception" shame her precisely because they are totally unnecessary. Karenin is not playing the game, so there is no pressure that might justify the falsehood. Asking her husband for money, Anna crimsons to the roots of her hair, and when he kisses her hand good-bye, "she was aware of the spot on her hand that his lips had touched, and she shuddered with repulsion" (219). Here repulsion is shame transferred to another.

Shame and repulsion in turn propel the spirit of self-deception that cause them. Anna's spirit of falsehood grows, all the more so because she is agitated both by the races and, especially, by the danger to Vronsky. Chapter 28 opens with passages that narrate from within what she sees and tells herself. They dramatize her active false looking.

When Karenin arrives, Anna is already sitting with Betsy, herself an incarnation of falsehood. Anna

> caught sight of her husband in the distance. . . . She was aware of her husband approaching a long way off. . . . She watched his progress toward the pavilion, saw him now responding condescendingly to an ingratiating bow, now exchanging friendly, nonchalant greetings with his equals, now assiduously trying to catch the eye of some great one of this world, and tipping his big round hat that squeezed the tips of his ears. All these ways of his she knew, and all were hateful to her. "Nothing but ambition, nothing but the desire to get ahead, that's all there is in his soul," she thought; "as for

those lofty ideals, love of culture, religion, they are only so many tools for advancing." (219)

It should be obvious that the point of view here is Anna's, not the author's, as the reference to ears indicates. So does the way the sequence of perceptions shades into direct quotation from her inner speech. She, not the author, sees his bow as ingratiating, she sees him trying to catch the eye of some great one of this world, and she denies that he is interested in anything but his career.

Karenin is no toady, as this description of him assumes. Although Tolstoy mocks Karenin's belief in the value of his official work, he credits him with sincerity. Like Trollope's Palliser, Karenin may be absurd in confusing official accounts with reality, but he honestly devotes himself to the public welfare as he sees it.

In the interval between the races and during the races themselves, "Anna heard his high measured tones, not losing one word, and every word struck her as false, and stabbed her with pain . . . she heard that loathsome, never-ceasing voice of her husband" (231). *"That"* (*etot*) loathsome voice: this observation clearly expresses Anna's perspective. A key passage follows. It begins with a direct quotation from Anna's inner speech and continues with the author's direct commentary on it:

> "I'm a wicked woman, a lost woman," she thought; "but I don't like lying, I can't endure falsehood, while as for *him* [her husband] it's the breath of his life—falsehood. He knows all about it, he sees it all; what does he care if he can talk so calmly? If he were to kill me, if he were to kill Vronsky, I might respect him. No, all he wants is falsehood and propriety," Anna said to herself, not considering exactly what she wanted of her husband, and how she would have liked to see him behave. She did not understand either that his peculiar loquacity that day, so exasperating to her, was merely the expression of his inward distress and uneasiness. As a child who has been hurt skips about, putting all his muscles into movement to drown the pain, in the same way Aleksey Aleksandrovich needed mental exercise to drown the thoughts of his wife which in her presence and in Vronsky's, and with the continual iteration of his name, would force themselves on his attention. (220)

How could Karenin not be disturbed by an event in which Vronsky's name is on everyone's lips? Karenin is not catching the eyes of some great one of this world, but distracting himself from an understandable pain; and far from not caring, he is in such distress that he must do whatever he can to ease it. He is in emotional pain the way a hurt child is in physical pain.

By this time, the reader has had enough evidence to recognize Anna's supposed hatred of falsehood as a Stiva-like self-justification. Only just before coming to the races, Anna, having consciously sensed "the presence of that spirit of falsehood and deceit in herself which she had come to know of late . . . abandoned herself to that spirit" (217). We have witnessed her marveling at her ability to be false, and even reveling in the very practice of it. We have also seen that one reason she does not leave Karenin is that she does not want to give up her social position. It is she, not he, who acts with an eye to reputation, and so her accusation reflects what she wants to deny about herself. The unfaithful wife who characterizes her husband as unfeeling while hurting him, who revels in falsehood while insisting on her hatred of falsehood, and who acts out of concern for social opinion while claiming it is her husband who cares only for propriety: all these instances of hypocrisy, I think, call into question critics' description of Anna as a rebel against falsehood.

By stressing Anna's "spirit of deceit and falsehood" and by correcting her perception of Karenin, Tolstoy makes his evaluation of her self-justifications clear. I would say "unmistakably clear" were it not that critics have so often made the mistake of missing Tolstoy's explicit comments. It is as if these comments did not exist at all. I am at a loss to understand how Boris Eichenbaum, one of the most famous literary scholars Russia ever produced, and the author of several volumes on Tolstoy, could have stated that in *Anna Karenina* "Tolstoy does not intrude his judgments and estimations. He watches life from on high" (N, 815). This view of the novel preceded Eichenbaum and continues to this day. Perhaps its very repetition has contributed to overlooking Tolstoy's frequent "intrusion" of judgments.

Watching Watching Watching

During the race, Anna keeps her binoculars focused on Vronsky, and does not even flinch when another rider is killed. Karenin watches how she is watching, and tries to tell himself that what she is doing is perfectly "natural," in spite of "what was so plainly written" on her face (222). She becomes aware of his eyes fixed on her, and turns to watch him watching her, and meets his eyes with a frown that seems to say, "Ah, I don't care" (222). He sees that look, which means that he watches how she watches how he watches her watching Vronsky. The entire scene becomes a drama in which looking is the only action.

A False Confession

When Anna sees Vronsky fall, she breaks into weeping, and Aleksey Aleksandrovich stands so as to screen her from other eyes. He leads her to the carriage while commenting on the "cruel spectacles," but she replies curtly and rudely. Offended, he tells her that her behavior has been unbecoming. "Perhaps I was mistaken. If so, I beg your pardon" (225), he says, still hoping that she will tell him his suspicions are utterly without merit, but she replies:

> "No, you were not mistaken," she said deliberately, looking desperately into his cold face. "You were not mistaken. I was, and I could not help being in despair. I hear you, but I am thinking of him. I love him, I am his mistress; I can't bear you; I'm afraid of you, and I hate you. . . . You can do what you like to me." (225)

It would be hard to imagine any way to make such a disclosure less considerate of his feelings: there is almost a sadistic magnification of his pain here.[24] And, amazingly enough, despite announcing her infidelity, she is still being false, characteristically, by what she leaves out. Anna will immediately write to Vronsky to tell him, in the cliché of such scenes, "I have told my husband everything!" but she has not. She has not told him she is pregnant, which is surely a significant omission of a fact that she has been considering, and has discussed with Vronsky, that very day.

For the First Time

Karenin sets just one requirement for Anna to continue living under his protection, receiving his financial support, and maintaining her social position as a married woman: she must not see Vronsky at their house. She nevertheless summons Vronsky when she thinks Karenin will be away, and the two men meet in the doorway. Karenin lifts his hat and leaves, while Vronsky thinks: "if he would fight, would stand up for his honor, I could act, could express my feelings; but this weakness or baseness. . . . He puts me in the position of a deceiver, which I never was and never meant to be" (376). Vronsky feels he is put in the position of a deceiver not because he is committing adultery but because Karenin will not challenge him, that is, will not allow himself to be maimed or killed by his wife's lover. Yet Vronsky is not being insincere. Just as he would have been genuinely surprised if told that he was misleading and hurting Kitty, so he cannot put himself in Karenin's position. He also cannot see that a duel, which would allow him to "express his feelings," could only make things worse for Karenin.

It is when Vronsky describes this encounter in the doorway that Anna mimics the way her husband bows. Vronsky expresses bewilderment that Karenin has not challenged him, since "he feels it, that's evident" (380). Karenin's pain is so evident that Vronsky, who is neither psychologically acute nor sympathetic to Karenin, can plainly see it, but Anna replies "sneeringly":

"He? . . . He's perfectly satisfied."
"Why are we all miserable, when everything might be so happy?"
"Not him. Don't I know him, the lie in which he's utterly steeped?
. . . Could any person, who feels anything, live as he is living with me? He understands nothing, and feels nothing. Could a man of any feeling live in the same house with his unfaithful wife? Could he talk to her? Speak to her familiarly [or: speak to her in the "thou"—in Russian, *ty*—form]? And again she could not help mimicking him: "'Anna, *ma chère;* Anna, dear!'" [*ty, Anna!*]
He's not a man, not a human being—he's a puppet! No one knows him; but I know him. Oh, if I'd been in his place, I'd long ago have killed, have torn to pieces a wife like me. I wouldn't have said, 'Anna, *ma chère'!* [*ty, ma chère*] He's not a man, he's an official machine. . . ."
"You're unfair, very unfair, dearest. . . . But never mind, don't let's talk of him." (380)

A puppet, an official machine, not a human being: Anna's dehumanization of Karenin could hardly go further, and even Vronsky calls the portrait unfair. In so doing, he proves more accurate than many critics and adapters for film or stage.[25]

Karenin is in fact not entirely inclined to call her my dear, or *ty,* but spends the night in a fury that she has disregarded his one request. He senses, beyond the pain caused by the affair, a severe insult to his dignity that could easily have been avoided. He confronts her angrily. Anna has just told Vronsky that she could understand if her husband expressed rage or tore her to pieces. According to her, such a reaction, unlike his calmness and his "*ty, ma chère,*" would show that Karenin is not an official machine but a human being with feelings. But now that he shows rage, she replies "with a rush of hatred" that it is unfair of him to take advantage of her, to strike one who is down [*bit' lezhachego*]. Karenin replies:

"Yes, you only care for yourself! But the sufferings of a man who was your husband have no interest for you. You don't care that his whole life is ruined, that he is thuf . . . thuff. . . ."
Aleksey Aleksandrovich was speaking so quickly that he stammered, and was utterly unable to articulate the word "suffering." In the end he pronounced it "thuffering" [*pelestradal*]. She wanted to laugh, and was immediately ashamed that anything could amuse her at such a moment. And

for the first time, for an instant, she felt for him, put herself in his place, and was sorry for him. (384)

For the first time (v pervyi raz) she felt for him, put herself in his place, and was sorry for him. Think how long it has taken for her to flirt with Vronsky, have an affair with him, and learn to mock and mimic her husband, and *not once* in all that time has she considered his feelings or put herself in his place. This is the sort of absence that speaks worlds. It shows Anna's deep narcissism and illustrates the kind of negligence that, for Tolstoy, causes the most evil. It is positively cruel.

The moral problem with the failure to place herself in Karenin's position has nothing to do with the affair itself. Anna could have had the affair and still have regretted hurting her husband, and she could have put herself in his place, at least once before. This omission convicts her far more severely than the affair itself.

Even now, she puts herself in his place only "for an instant." A moment later she tells herself: "No, can a man with those dull eyes, with that self-satisfied complacency, feel anything?" (384). As in the scene that parallels the discussion of the Pallisers, this reorientation from momentary sympathy to dehumanization is a *choice*.

I Tried to Hate

We have seen that when routines are broken, habitual patterns of thought may be reconsidered, and earlier ones may reassert themselves. So it is with Anna when, after giving birth, she suffers from an apparently fatal fever. She drops all efforts to misperceive her husband and recognizes that she has contrived her view of him as unfeeling. She does more than return to her more favorable opinion of Karenin as we saw it in Part One: she makes clear that she knows he is even better than that.

Anna sends a telegram to summon her husband, and when he arrives, does not initially notice his presence. She says of him: "I would forget, he would forgive . . . He's so good, he doesn't know himself how good he is" (433). At first she wants to give Annie to a nurse so as not to hurt Karenin with the sight of another man's child, but then she realizes that he is so good that such care is unnecessary. "You say he won't forgive me because you don't know him. I'm the only one, and it was hard even for me. . . . Has Seryozha had his dinner? I know everyone will forget. He would not forget" (433). Anna understands: it is hard to get to know Karenin, but if one does, one will find that he feels deeply even if he has trouble expressing his feelings. She has always known that. He is no official machine. The statement that "he would not forget" Seryozha rings especially powerfully in a novel that identifies evil with negligence.

When Anna at last sees her husband, she describes herself and her efforts at misperception exactly as the author has done. She tells him:

> But there is another woman in me, I'm afraid of her: she loved that man [Vronsky], and I tried to hate you, and could not forget about her that used to be. I'm not that woman. Now I'm my real self, all myself. I'm dying now, I know I shall die. . . . Only one thing I want: forgive me, forgive me completely, I'm terrible, but my nurse used to tell me; the holy martyr—what was her name? She was worse. (435)

I tried to hate you: Anna affirms that she deliberately misperceived her husband, that, as the author has earlier said, she "schooled herself to despise" him. *I . . . could not forget about her that used to be. I'm not that woman. Now I'm my real self, all myself:* Anna declares that she, the real Anna, always knew that Karenin is not the puppet her contrived substitute made him out to be. The simile of "two Annas," one of whom knows what is real and the other of whom indulges in self-deceiving falsehood, can be traced to the relativity passage in Part One, when Anna, in the train ride home, is drawn to a delightful delirium. She asks herself: "And what am I myself? Myself or some other woman?" Whenever Anna marvels at her capacity for falsehood, we sense a split in which the observing Anna knows that the speaking and listening Anna is lying.

It is almost as if Anna had overheard the author's explicit statements about her falsehood and is here endorsing them. Even when she recovers from her fever, wants to return to Vronsky, and again finds her husband repellent, she does not deny his goodness and his capacity to feel and love. It is therefore not credible to deny what she says in the childbirth scene because she is in a fever. If that were all, then, as she recovered her health and once again preferred Vronsky, she would again see her husband as a sadistic official machine. But she does not, because she cannot return to the falsehood that she herself has exposed, just as one cannot again believe in a mirage once one has detected what it really is. As we shall see, she now explains her hatred for her husband quite differently.

The Only Character Who Saves a Life

Anna's feverish praise of Karenin's goodness contributes to his transformation. Quite unexpectedly, to himself and to the readers but not to Anna, he experiences genuine feelings of Christian love and forgiveness for his enemies. In chapter four, I will discuss his reaction to her praise, his conversion, and the effects of his Christian forgiveness on others. Here it is sufficient to note that Tolstoy leaves no doubt that the conversion is sincere. "He did not think that the Christian law that he had been all his life trying to follow enjoined him to forgive and love his enemies; but a joyous feeling of love and forgiveness for his enemies filled his soul . . . he sobbed like a little child" (434). *He did not think:* Tolstoy means to exclude the interpretation that Karenin sanctimoniously decides to make an insincere Christian statement (I'm a Christian, I forgive you, so there!). No, the feeling of love and forgiveness just fills his soul. Anna predicts the conversion and recognizes it as genuine.

Karenin's feeling leads him not only to forgive Anna and Vronsky, but also to take a special interest in the newborn little girl. Tolstoy then gives us, buried in a long paragraph and placed in a sentence with several other subordinate clauses, another openly camouflaged fact:

> At first, from a feeling of compassion alone, he had been interested in the delicate little creature who was not his child, and who was cast to one side during her mother's illness, and would certainly have died if he had not troubled about her, and he did not himself observe how fond he became of her. (440)

Annie *would certainly have died if Karenin had not troubled about her:* this statement must come from the author, not Karenin, because the main point of the sentence is to tell us what Karenin did *not* notice. Karenin is the only character who saves a life in this novel, and yet this fact, which might mitigate hostile portraits of him, typically goes unmentioned.

Divorce and the Children

When Anna returns to health and "the softening effect of the near approach of death" (441) has passed, she again feels ill at ease with her husband. He continues to care for the baby she neglects. Betsy, whose very presence signals Anna's return to falsity, urges her to meet Vronsky again, and, looking ironically at Karenin, makes the same suggestion to him. When he is left alone with Anna, his use of the familiar "thou" form again irritates her, and she cannot conceal her discomfort with his very presence. She returns to her former course of behavior. But she can no longer justify it by calling him unfeeling.

Critics often overlook the remainder of Part Four, without which, I think, Anna's subsequent behavior cannot be understood. Omitting it decisively alters the novel's plot. One of the novel's most insightful pro-Anna critics does mention the concluding sentence of Part Four. That sentence reads:

A month later Aleksey Aleksandrovich was left alone with his son in his house at Petersburg, while Anna and Vronsky had gone abroad, not having obtained a divorce but having absolutely refused one. (457)

The critic observes:

Oblonsky persuades Karenin to a divorce; then Karenin, with Dolly's help, mounts many reasons against it, all of them wrong; but confused and sensitized to Christian forgiveness, Karenin agrees to grant a divorce all the same; Betsy Tverskaya then manages to catch Vronsky just before he leaves for Tashkent; a passionate reunion takes place between the two lovers Anna and Vronsky, both still convalescent. And then—in a stunning show of compression and authorial self-control, Tolstoy withholds all further information and ends Part Four with the astonishing comment that, a month later, *Anna s Vronskim uekhala za granitsu, ne polichiv razvoda i reshitel'no otkazavshis' ot nego* (Anna and Vronsky had gone abroad, not having obtained a divorce but having absolutely refused one). So a divorce was offered and refused. But how did it happen and into what time-and-space warp in the novel did this crucial event disappear? (Emerson, 170).

Tolstoy was indeed capable of the stunning authorial control this critic mentions. Nevertheless, in this case I see no time warp. Stiva asks for a divorce on Anna's behalf and Karenin agrees—and more. Under Russian law, adultery was the only pertinent grounds for divorce, and the adulterous party could not remarry. Karenin agrees not only to a divorce, but also to plead guilty to a fictitious charge of adultery so that Anna could remarry. That is, to help her, he will injure his dignity and commit perjury, which is not only illegal but also a sin against God. To contemporary readers, the idea of sin may seem quaint, but it is important to Karenin. Even nonreligious people usually understand why one would not want to perjure oneself. The perjury will also prevent him from ever marrying again. Karenin is willing to do all this, and he does not stop there.

Against his most cherished desires, he also agrees to grant Anna custody of Seryozha. "To consent to a divorce, to give her her freedom, meant in his thoughts to take from himself the last tie that bound him to life—the children whom he loved" (453). In that plural, children, the author reminds us of Karenin's love for Annie, whom Anna herself will neglect. Annie is legally his daughter, so his consent is needed for Anna to keep her. In Karenin's decision to grant her a divorce with both children, he gives up "the last tie that bound him to life." Anyone who regards Karenin as single-mindedly devoted to his career might pause over this paraphrase of Karenin's inner speech.

Karenin writes Anna a note, which he shows to Stiva, in which he offers her anything she wants: "tell me yourself what will give you true happiness and peace of mind. I put myself entirely in your hands and trust to your feeling of justice" (451).

In making this offer, he overrides his concern that granting Anna custody of Seryozha might not be good for Seryozha. His first thought in response to Stiva's request is to think not of himself but of his son.

> What would become of his son in case of a divorce? To leave him with his mother was out of the question. The divorced mother would have her own illegitimate family, in which his position as a stepson and his education would not be good. Keep him with him? He knew that would be an act of vengeance on his part, and that he did not want. (453)

Stiva does not give a thought to Seryozha's welfare, but Karenin rightly does. Of course Seryozha's position as Vronsky's dependent would not be good. In seeing arguments on both sides of the question, Karenin shows real sensitivity to its moral dimensions and the effect of his decision on others. I am perplexed at how one can say, categorically, that all these reasons are simply "wrong." The question is complex and the answer not obvious. Indeed, one might almost say that when Karenin overrides his worries about his son's future, Christian love is leading him morally astray.

The author does not regard all reasons against granting a divorce and custody of Seryozha as wrong. He indicates the opposite. When Stiva goes to speak with Karenin, the author remarks that Stiva becomes "suddenly aware of a sense of embarrassment unusual in him" (450). Stiva cannot identify the reason for his embarrassment, but the author explains it as the effect of conscience. It is because acts of conscience are so rare in Stiva that he cannot recognize one. "This feeling was so unexpected and so strange that he did not believe it was the voice of conscience telling him that what he was about to do was wrong" (450).

Why Anna Refuses a Divorce

Why then does Anna absolutely (or resolutely) refuse the divorce and custody of her son? Far from leaving the refusal unexplained, Tolstoy makes the reason clear. In a Dostoevskian way, Anna resents Karenin for his very goodness. For Anna, the offer of a divorce with custody of Seryozha, precisely because it was made out of genuine forgiveness and love, necessarily establishes Karenin's moral superiority over her. Still more troubling to her, it renders her indebted to his goodness. She cannot tolerate that. She tells Stiva:

> "I have heard it said that women love men for their vices," Anna began suddenly, "but I hate him for his virtues. I can't live with him, do you understand? The sight of him has a physical effect on me; it enrages me, I can't, I

can't live with him. . . . Would you believe it, that knowing he's a good man, a splendid man, that I'm not worth his little finger, still I hate him. I hate him for his generosity." (448)

Her witty inversion of the maxim that women sometimes love men for their vices has evidently been prepared, and she has dwelled on the thought until it has taken perfect form. Before the birth of her daughter, Anna hated her husband for being unfeeling and spiteful, now it is for being loving and generous. In either case, the sight of him causes repulsion, and so, she concludes, she simply *cannot* live with him.

But then why not accept the divorce and her son? She makes the reason explicit a few sentences before the end of Part Four. She tells Vronsky: "Stiva says that *he* has agreed to everything, but I can't accept *his* generosity" (456–57; italics in original). To accept his generosity would mean to owe him something.[26] She states that she hates him precisely for his goodness and generosity. She refuses his offer of a divorce, and the offer of whatever she might want, out of pride.

For the sake of that pride, for the sake of not being indebted to "*his* generosity," she is willing to leave her son behind. One has to ask how much she cares for her son's welfare if such a consideration could lead her to abandon him.[27] It is not as if she leaves Seryozha behind because she decides he would be better off with his father. If she thinks he would be better off with her, then surely she should take him, even if doing so leaves her indebted to Karenin's generosity. We see her narcissistic cruelty in the very fact that her reason for not taking Seryozha has nothing to do with what is best for him.

When Dolly visits Anna and Vronsky in the country, Anna tells her: "it is only these two beings [Vronsky and Seryozha] that I love and one excludes the other. I can't have them together, and that's the only thing I want. And since I can't have that, I don't care about the rest. I don't care about anything, anything" (669).

Critics often take Anna at her word and assume she could not have had both lover and son. (For exceptions see Browning, 330–31, Murav, 80, and Wasiolek, 145.) But this statement is false. In fact, when she tells Dolly that her two loves exclude each other, Anna has still not asked Karenin for the divorce he offered, as we know, because in this very scene Dolly is trying, at Vronsky's behest, to persuade her to do so. The same reason that she refused Karenin's offer before still motivates her: asking for a divorce with or without Seryozha "means that I, hating him, but still recognizing that I have wronged him — and consider him magnanimous — that I humiliate myself to write to him" (669). Now this refusal tacitly to acknowledge Karenin's magnanimity affects not only Seryozha and herself but also Vronsky, who wants to marry her, and Annie, who remains legally Karenin's child.

Tolstoy could hardly have placed her refusal of a divorce more prominently than in the last line of Part Four. Her motive, not to be indebted to Karenin's generosity, appears just before that concluding line and again in this exchange with Dolly. But the story she tells, though contradicted by the text, has proven so compelling that critic after critic has accepted it. The tragic choice between lover and child: apparently, the appeal of a plot too mythic for doubt even to be entertained, not only overrides contrary evidence but makes it invisible.

In criticizing the romantic myth, Tolstoy was not taking on a straw man. On the contrary, from his day to ours, it has proven powerful enough to triumph over his explicit critique. For the sake of that myth, Anna teaches herself to misperceive reality. Under its sway, many readers do the same with Tolstoy's novel. All the more reason, then, for us to reexamine the myth and reveal it as the ideology it is. Only then can we do what the novel teaches and see more wisely.

Anna's Suicide and the Totalism of Meaning

Nothing But Love

The novelist and critic Dmitri Merezhkovsky regarded Anna as the incarnation of pure passionate love. Anna was not really alive until she met Vronsky:

> From the first appearance of Vronsky, almost from the first silent glance at him, and to her last breath, Anna loves and only loves. We scarcely know what she felt and thought, how she lived—it seems that she did not exist before love; one cannot imagine an Anna who does not love. She is entirely love, as if her whole being, body and soul, were fashioned out of love, like the body of Salamander out of fire or Ondine out of water. (N, 804–5)

Salamander and Ondine (or Undine) are mythological creatures discussed by Paracelsus. The first is an elemental being inhabiting fire and the second a water nymph who becomes human only when in love. Undine is condemned to death if her lover betrays her. She inspired several romances in the nineteenth and twentieth centuries (EoL, 986, 1148).

For Merezhkovsky, Anna differs from other Tolstoy characters because she "has no words of her own." Although we remember her feelings, we can recall "not one personal, peculiar word, exclusively her own, not even about love" (N, 806). She is not at all stupid, but "her complete absorption in passion is such that she shields us precisely from intelligence, consciousness, higher selflessness, and the unsensual aspect of the soul. Who or what is she beyond love?" (N, 806).

For Merezhkovsky, as for many later critics, Anna uncannily resembles Vronsky's horse Frou-Frou, who manifests an elemental surplus of energy and demonstrates love for her master even unto death. Through the death of mare and woman, "the inescapable crime of love, the eternal tragedy, the childish play of the death-bearing Eros will be fulfilled" (N, 809). Fate sends Vronsky a warning when he breaks Frou-Frou's back. It claims the life of Anna, as it has taken Frou-Frou's, because she is "full of the innocent surplus of life (is not her whole guilt in that she is too beautiful 'And glows and loves because / Not to love is impossible')" (N, 810; Merezhkovsky is citing Pushkin).

I have paraphrased Merezhkovsky's thesis for two reasons. The less important one is that it is an unusually pure example of a romantic reading. Merezhkovsky accepts the myth of romantic love even though, or rather precisely because, he knows it is a myth, as his references to Salamander, Ondine, and Eros suggest. The more romantic clichés he can find, the happier he is. Wittingly or not, most romantic readings of the novel have echoed Merezhkovsky.

Merezhkovsky's idea that Fate killed Anna could not be more hackneyed. One can almost overhear Anna agreeing that she could not but have acted as she did because she is all love and for her not to love is impossible. As much as Anna could wish, this reading absolves her from all responsibility. It does so by negating that she has any will at all. For whatever she may be at fault, she is not to blame.

Dehumanizing Anna

> A person never coincides with himself. . . . the genuine life of the personality takes place at the point of non-coincidence between a person and himself.
> — MIKHAIL BAKHTIN (PDP, 59)

The more important reason I have cited the passage from Merezhkovsky is that it foregrounds another of Tolstoy's themes. Like Anna, Merezhkovsky thinks in terms of extremes—indeed, of totalities. Anna is *all* love, lives *only* when loving, is unthinkable except when loving. For Tolstoy, such extremism seriously errs, and the belief that a person can be only one thing fundamentally distorts the nature of human existence.

As Tolstoy tells the story, totalism and the belief that a person can be one thing cause Anna great harm. Her troubles with Vronsky worsen primarily because she imagines that love must consume the whole of a person, with no thoughts or interests left over. If Vronsky shows interest in anything else, then he does not love her, is staying with her out of duty, and is looking for an excuse to leave her.

As her suicide approaches, Anna develops a model of interpretive totalism: nothing is chance, the world is fundamentally simple, and everything says the same terrible thing. The truth explaining everything finds expression in Vronsky's friend Yashvin's philosophy of gambling: he wants to strip me of my shirt, and I of his. With these words, Anna believes that she has found a sort of negative enlightenment allowing her to see through all concealments to the naked, horrible truth—a metaphor Tolstoy uses literally when Anna mentally undresses a woman she sees and shudders at her imagined ugliness. In this dark light, there is nothing but the struggle for existence, and as Anna looks from her carriage at every stray passerby or object, she finds in each confirmation of her terrifying insight.

The totalism of meaning repeats. For Anna. each person is completely isolated, the world is all hatred, and all supposedly higher things, like religion or culture, exist only in order to conceal the awful truth. At the races, Anna has said to herself that all Karenin's interests, in religion or anything else, are fake, and now she extends this misreading to everyone and everything.

For Tolstoy, a story that is too neat, explains too much, and makes the world all of a piece must be false.

If Anna were nothing but love, she would not be human at all, which is presumably why Merezhkovsky compares her to mythic figures. We would sense her as a pure symbol or allegory. In that case, we could not identify with her suffering, as most readers do. In a romance, a person may be all one thing, but not in a realist novel, and least of all in Tolstoy, because no human being is simple and entirely consistent. If Merezhkovsky were right, Anna would have no individual psychology, and she plainly does. She is palpably herself, not a mere incarnation of some single emotion. Merezhkovsky loves Anna, but in a way that dehumanizes her even more than she dehumanizes Karenin.

Impurity and Inconsistency

> Nothing is harder for me than to believe in men's consistency, nothing easier than to believe in their inconsistency. He who would judge them in detail and distinctly, bit by bit, would more often hit upon the truth.
> —MONTAIGNE (239–40)

"But pure and perfect sorrow is as impossible as pure and perfect joy": in Tolstoy nothing is pure, and no one is just one thing. Events often happen just "for some reason." Each of us has qualities that do not fit with other qualities. The effect of contingent incidents, some characteristics of each person might just as well not be there.

Contingency and impurity define Tolstoy's vision. Merezhkovsky's dehumanization of Anna removes the Tolstoy from Tolstoy.[28]

We recall: in *War and Peace*, Pierre's dying father looks at him "with a gaze the intent and significance of which no man could have fathomed. Either it meant absolutely nothing more than that having eyes one must look somewhere, or it was charged with meaning" (W&P, 118). In Tolstoy, we can presume neither meaning nor meaninglessness, because both are always possible.

After Pierre's father dies, and Prince Vasily connives for the inheritance, something unexpected happens. Vasily's main interest in life lies in manipulating others, almost for the sheer sport of it. He seems to care about nothing else.

We are therefore surprised when Vasily emerges from the room where Pierre's father has died, staggers to the sofa where Pierre is sitting,

> sank down on it, and covered his eyes with his hand. Pierre noticed that he was pale and that his jaw twitched and quivered as if he were in a hectic fever.
>
> "Ah, my friend," he murmured, taking Pierre by the elbow, and there was a weakness and sincerity in his voice that Pierre had never heard before. "How greatly we sin, how we deceive—and all for what? I am nearly sixty, my friend—I, too—. It all ends in death, all. Death is a terrible thing . . ." And he wept. (W&P, 122)

Pierre has never seen Vasily sincere before, and we will never see him sincere again, but here he is momentarily but believably sincere. A reader who guessed that Tolstoy, like so many other writers, would use this moment to initiate a process of beneficial change in Vasily would sentimentalize Tolstoy. This instant of sincerity has no consequence. Like so many incidents in Tolstoy, it goes nowhere, and the novel is all the more realistic for that.

We differ from ourselves.

Tolstoy is especially bold in this scene. The preceding chapters have focused on the comic struggle over the old man's will, and all of a sudden we get a moment of real pathos. Few writers would risk such an abrupt switch in tone and fewer still could prevent a slight shadow of comedy from falling on Vasily's unexpected sincerity. Tolstoy's surprising shift follows his character's. The moment does not appear false because an appreciation of impurity and uncertainty characterize the author's vision. Tolstoy is consistent in showing inconsistency.

The Temptation to Allegory

War and Peace and *Anna Karenina* avoid excessive consistency. Where even the best novelists would reach for an allegory, symbol, or pathetic fallacy (nature mirroring a character's emotions), Tolstoy does not, because he regards such "artistry" as fake.

It is not that these two novels never use symbols or allegory. It is rather that they avoid patterns that palpably derive from the author or reflect an overarching design imposing itself on a particular situation. We do not see foreshadowing, which is a form of backward causation testifying to the design of the work as a whole.[29] But we do see characters repeating themselves insofar as they are more or less consistent. Symbols must show no more than a character himself could see, the way Levin, observing the gradually changing shapes in clouds, can think that, in the same way, his views of life have changed.

Significance lies within the created world and so never seems like artistry, which comes from without. Tolstoy foregoes patterning absent from life. Both novels avoid tying up all loose ends as the work draws to a close. We cannot count up all the unmarried males and females and predict weddings. Tolstoy explained: "I cannot and do not know how to confine the characters I have created within given limits—a marriage or a death after which interest in the narration would cease. I couldn't help thinking that the death of one character only aroused interest in other characters, and a marriage seemed more like a source of complication than diminution of the reader's interest" (D, 1365). Neat endings—like neat anythings—lie.

The world is not wholly random, and so Tolstoy does give us partial symbols, imperfect allegories, and a vague sense of patterning—but never more than that. Levin knows perfectly well that nature is not telling him something with those clouds. He realizes that any shape he finds there will only barely resemble something in life and will not stay. It cannot be counted on. Readers of these novels should count on nothing more either.

Why should everything say the same thing? Is it not possible, for instance, that a character who is deeply sad could enjoy fine weather? As the critic Barbara Hardy points out, that is exactly what happens when Levin and Stiva go hunting. With Kitty's humiliating refusal on his mind, Levin cannot at first bring himself to ask Stiva about her. When he does, he learns that she has been ill. Levin is shocked, but at that moment a bird appears, and he becomes absorbed in the shooting and in his dog, who brings the warm bird in his mouth. Hardy observes:

> This is almost the opposite of James's presentation of phenomena in terms of obsession. The scene is free because Tolstoy is saying that men's griefs are complex, are not always wholly absorbing, that work or play can be exhilarating even at such a time. Because the phenomena are so vividly present— the creak of growing grass, the exhilaration of the hunt—the scene is free from symbol. The sharing of the bird [by Stiva and Levin] might, in a novel by Stevenson or James, be made indicative of the common family interest, but even this rejected interpretation sounds ludicrous here. (N, 894)

Hardy is correct. She is also on the mark when discussing Levin's irritation over Ryabinin's dishonest purchase of Dolly's forest. Whereas another writer would make one of Levin's two emotions, humiliation over Kitty and his feeling of respect for the land, a shield for the other, Tolstoy allows them both to be equally sincere. One cannot say which one is primary, as one could in most novels.

Hardy does not discuss Tolstoy's philosophical concerns, but her account of his character descriptions accords with his belief in contingency and his sense of open time. Readers' feeling that Tolstoy writes as if nature herself held the pen derives in part from his refusal of "artistic" solutions and his use of patterns that are only partial.

Let me go one step further: Tolstoy sets up potential allegories so that, after we begin to trace them, he can disappoint us. His characters and readers may expect something allegorical, overly symbolic, dramatic, or critical, but Tolstoyan reality disappoints them.[30] Nikolai Levin answers the priest who pronounces him dead. We prove mistaken whenever we expect something too neat, too appropriately dramatic, or too literary.

Frou-Frou's Suicide?

For the same reason, the horse race scene does not constitute an allegory of Anna's story, and the death of Frou-Frou does not foreshadow hers. Merezhkovsky speaks for most critics when he finds allegory and a "warning" to Vronsky here, but if this scene worked that way, Tolstoy would be a much lesser writer. We would sense him as artificial, not as supremely realistic.

Of course there are similarities between Anna and the mare. After all, Vronsky has chosen them both. These similarities may illustrate Vronsky's psychology, but they do not make the scene an allegory. Tolstoy tempts us to allegory so that we can mark where it fails.

Perhaps critics have detected the similarities between Anna and Frou-Frou but ignored the differences because they expect allegory much as they expect romantic love. As Anna sees the trainman's death as an omen, critics see that scene as foreshadowing and the races as both foreshadowing and allegory. Tolstoy wants to teach us to resist such interpretations of life and of his novel.[31]

Tolstoy offers just enough resemblance between Anna and Frou-Frou to tempt us to allegory, but if we yield we will miss his point. To begin with, Tolstoy provides interesting reasons, pertaining to the dynamics of attention, for Vronsky's "unpardonable mistake." These reasons have nothing to do with the causes of Anna's death. Just before the races, Anna has told Vronsky she is pregnant, and Vronsky has been seriously affected. When he leaves, his distraction leads to a mistake that almost makes him late to the race:

> When Vronsky looked at his watch on the Karenins' balcony, he was so greatly agitated and lost in his thoughts that he saw the figures on the watch's face but could not realize what time it was. He came out onto the highroad and walked, picking his way carefully through the mud, to his carriage. He was so completely absorbed in his feeling for Anna that he did not even think what time it was, and whether he had time to go to Bryansky's. He had left him, as often happens, only the external faculty of memory which points out each step one has to take, one after the other. (203)

In this state, Vronsky wakes his coachman. Vronsky observes a lengthening shadow but does not recognize it as a sign of advancing time. He admires a cloud of midges, tells the coachman to drive to Bryansky's, and only after five miles does he realize that he is late.

Most of what we do, we do by habit, and when the mind is distracted, habit takes over. We do not then perform our actions unconsciously—habit requires a minimum of attention and Vronsky takes each step without mistake—but we use all the rest of our attention to focus on what distracts us. That is why Vronsky can see the figures of his watch and not realize what time it is or ask if he is late. If, when we are in such a distracted state, great attention were suddenly wanted, we well might have an accident. Doing everything by habit and "the external faculty of memory," we would lack the presence of mind to respond where habit is insufficient and a sense of the overall situation is needed. In a horse race, or anything else requiring great physical and mental presence, the smallest lack of concentration at a single moment can make all the difference. Without thinking, Vronsky shifts his weight wrong and breaks the horse's back. Nothing similar happens with Anna.[32]

With Frou-Frou, Vronsky is totally in control. But anyone who remembers how Anna deflects Vronsky's attempts to talk will realize that she controls their relationship. She has been attracted, indeed, by his puppy-dog attitude of submission. Vronsky has to get Dolly to persuade Anna to ask for a divorce: he not only cannot get his way but he cannot even talk to her seriously about the subject. Anna's death is an act of will, even of revenge, but Frou-Frou does not commit suicide. Frou-Frou really is helpless, but to see Anna's relationship with Vronsky that way is, I think, to be reading some other book.

The Dynamics of Quarrels

The sequence leading to Anna's suicide contains nine chapters and extends for some thirty pages. It dramatizes extremism. Anna's thoughts are governed by an extreme view of love, by the desire to take dramatic action, and, above all, by a belief that there is a key, which she possesses, to understanding everything that ever happens. Nothing is contingent and nothing can evade her interpretive scheme: the psychology of interpretive totalism governs Anna's thoughts and leads to her death.

From Tolstoy's perspective, Anna makes a version of the same mistake as those who believe they have a key to history. She resembles Pierre in *War and Peace* when he adopts Masonic numerology. Like Anna, Pierre believes that he grasps the deepest significance of events and that he has been chosen for a special fate. As a result, he is almost executed. The wages of totalism is death.

Anna and Vronsky find themselves engaged in a set of quarrels that seems unstoppable. He grows more and more irritated by her accusations, but is entirely unequal to the situation. The central problem derives from her idea of love:

> In her eyes, the whole of him, with all his habits, ideas, desires, with all his spiritual and physical temperament, was one thing—love for women, and that love, she felt ought to be entirely concentrated on her alone. Yet that love was diminishing; consequently, as she reasoned, he must have transferred part of his love to other women or to another woman—and she was jealous. . . . Not having an object for her jealousy, she was on the lookout for it. (769)

Love, to be real, must be total and allow for no other interests. If Vronsky has other interests, then his love must be diminishing and diminished love (as she also reasons) cannot be love at all. Since he can only be "one thing—love for women," then he must love someone else. Thus, she is always accusing him of interest in another woman and, despite her recognition of his honesty and devotion, usually believes what she imputes.

This totalism sets the drama that follows. Anna interprets everything Vronsky does as a sign he does not love her, but that interpretation is so horrible that she cannot face it. She keenly feels it would mean her death. So she must make it up with him and admit, without believing it, that she has been wrong in their quarrels. Such an admission can only be humiliating and fuel a desire to prove that he is wrong. She alternates between the horror of death and the horror of humiliation.

If Vronsky gives in to her, Anna sees his surrender as condescending. This fresh humiliation begets another quarrel. He cannot understand what to do, since neither giving in nor justifying himself does any good, and he grows more and more irritated. He decides at last simply to be silent while going about the business needed for them to return to the country, as she has wished. She sees this silence as a sign of indifference and therefore as proof that he loves someone else. That deduction again provokes the dialectic between horror and humiliation. Tolstoy is at the height of his powers as he describes her state of mind. As the sequence progresses, the author enters more and more frequently into her consciousness and describes the world as she sees it.[33]

Because she thinks she has the key to understanding everything that happens, Anna imagines what Vronsky must really mean whenever he says something. She then treats that interpretation as if he had actually expressed it. When Vronsky says that he does not believe in the full sincerity of her unnatural interest in Hannah, the English girl Anna has taken under her protection, Anna thinks: "I know what he meant: he meant—unnatural, not loving my own daughter, to love another person's child. What does he know of love for children, of my love for Seryozha, whom I've sacrificed for him? But that wish to hurt me! No, he loves another woman, it must be so" (771). He has said nothing about her not loving her daughter, but she herself knows that she does not, and so she takes the just accusation as if it were said. So in their next quarrel she directly accuses Vronsky of having said she does not love their daughter, and he, expressing bewilderment, can only repeat what he did say. Of course, she has not sacrificed Seryozha for him but refused her son so as not to be indebted to Karenin. But she has repeated this version to herself so often, and it fits her romantic self-justification so well, that she has come to believe it.[34]

The more he expresses frustration at her accusations, the more she concludes that he no longer loves her. "He hates me, that's clear. . . . He loves another woman, that's even clearer. . . . I want love, and there is none. So all is over . . . and it must be ended" (776). When a telegram comes from Stiva, Vronsky at first tries to read it in private because he suspects that Karenin may have refused a divorce, but when Anna insists on seeing it, he shows it to her. "So he may hide and does hide his correspondence with women from me," she thinks. Everything means the same thing.

When he tells her he cares about having a definite answer from Karenin, she tells him that "definiteness is not in the form but in the love" (777). Utterly at a loss at this new way of accusing him of not loving her, Vronsky thinks: "My God! Love again" (777). She asks him why he wants the divorce and misconstrues his answer:

> "Oh, you know what for; for you and for the children to come."
> "There will be no children."
> "That's a great pity," he said.
> "You want it for the children, but you don't think of me?" she said, quite forgetting or not having heard, that he had said, *"For you and for the children."*
> The question of the possibility of having children had long been a subject of dispute and irritation to her. His desire to have children she interpreted as a proof he did not prize her beauty.
> "Oh, I said, for you. Above all, for you." . . .
> "Yes, now he has laid aside all pretense, and all his cold hatred for me is apparent," she thought, not hearing his words, but watching with terror the cold, cruel judge who looked mockingly at her out of his eyes. (777; italics in original)

He is not mocking her but pained—at the quarrel, at the impossibility of saying something she will hear, at her cruel declaration they will not have children, and, above all, at the suffering she is undergoing and he is powerless to ease. She has told Dolly that childbirth will mar her beauty. Now she attributes that thought to him, and so his desire for children with her becomes—amazingly enough—proof that he does *not* love her. That conclusion follows inexorably from her notion of love and from the totalism of her interpretations.

When she is alone, she spends the whole day—except for two hours at the dressmaker's—vacillating between hope of reconciliation and fear of humiliation. Again she concludes that "clearly" he loves another woman.

> And remembering all the cruel words he had said, Anna supplied as well the words that he had unmistakably wished to say and could have said to her, and she grew more and more exasperated.
>
> "I'm not holding you," he might have said. "You can go where you like. You were unwilling to be divorced from your former husband, no doubt so that you might go back to him. Go back to him. If you want money, I'll give it to you. How many rubles do you want?"
>
> All the cruelest words that a brutal man could say, he said to her in her imagination, and she could not forgive him for them, as though he had actually said them. (780)

Her habits of false listening, of misremembering, and of believing her own inventions, which she developed with Karenin, have now gone to an extreme with Vronsky. The words he had "unmistakably" wished to say: the word "unmistakably" clearly belongs to Anna, not the author. The reference to her refusal of a divorce indicates that, despite what she said to Dolly, she remembers that it was she who decided against the divorce and custody of Seryozha.

Since she knows without fail the meaning of everything Vronsky says, there is no reason for her not to take as said things that must have been meant.

Why the Epigraph is Troubling

For obvious reasons, most critics try to explain the novel's biblical epigraph, "Vengeance is mine, I will repay."[35] It has proven a "puzzle" (as is often said) to some critics who accept the romantic reading. For it seems to condemn Anna. If one breaks the law of God or commits acts that go against the nature of things, then, by an inner logic, one will meet destruction. Nothing suggests that this destruction is tragically glorious.

To make matters worse, Tolstoy himself endorsed this reading that condemns Anna. One Russian critic, Vikenty Veresaev, recounts how he discussed *Anna Karenina* with Tolstoy's son-in-law, Mikhail Sukhotin, appropriately enough, on a train. Veresaev, who had recently come up with his own interpretation of the epigraph, asked Sukhotin to get Tolstoy's reaction. In Veresaev's view, Anna's suicide results from her not behaving romantically *enough*. Having given herself over to the force of passionate love, she does not embrace it consistently. "If she had given herself purely and honorably to that force, a new life of integrity would have opened before her. But Anna became afraid of human condemnation, of losing her social position" (N, 817).

Veresaev out-Annas Anna. For him, Anna's fate demonstrates that life will destroy anyone who does not surrender to love without reserve. The epigraph enunciates this romantic moral.

After presenting this interpretation to Tolstoy, Sukhotin wrote to Veresaev that "unfortunately, from his answer it seems that I was right and not you" (N, 818). Tolstoy responded: "Yes, that is clever, very clever, but I must repeat that I chose that epigraph simply, as I already stated, in order to explain the idea that the bad things man does have as their consequence all the bitter things that come not from people, but from God, and that is what Anna Karenina experienced" (N, 818).

A few years after the novel was completed, Tolstoy endorsed an article by M. S. Gromeka that offered an interpretation unfavorable to Anna's passion. For Gromeka, the novel illustrates that one can neither violate the laws of human nature with impunity nor reconstruct those laws on the basis of abstract philosophical preferences. In Gromeka's opinion, quasi-liberal views of "freedom" in love receive a death blow in this novel. Married love remains the only viable kind and it alone is good for children, according to Gromeka. (See Gromeka.)

One can almost see the intellectuals of Tolstoy's day and ours wince. Could Tolstoy reject romantic love and endorse so conservative a set of beliefs? Unfortunately, he did. Tolstoy said of Gromeka's thesis: "He explained what I unconsciously put into the work. It is a most beautiful article. I am delighted by it. Finally *Anna Karenina* has been explained" (N, 801n1). Romantic readings need to discount this statement.

Of course, Tolstoy was likely exaggerating his approval of Gromeka's article. After all, Tolstoy did not believe a single interpretation could explain this or any other significant work. Perhaps he loved teasing prevailing liberal opinion. But an exaggeration is still largely an endorsement, all the more so because Tolstoy claims Gromeka caught even his unconscious intention.[36]

How, then, can one maintain an opposite view? Surely Tolstoy must be rescued from his assertion of what Eichenbaum and so many others call "bourgeois" morality. (In such formulations, the word "bourgeois" cannot be taken literally: it is not opposed, for instance, to aristocratic morality, which is actually discussed in *Anna Karenina,* as the word is little more than a grunt signifying disapproval.)

To save Tolstoy from himself, critics commonly plead that he began with the intention of writing a novel condemning Anna but then (as is said) he "fell in love with her" and wrote a different book. But in that case, why did he retain the epigraph condemning her? And why did he endorse the anti-Anna interpretation after completing the novel? The usual answer is that Tolstoy's novel belies his own intention. He meant to say one thing, but actually said another. Tolstoy not only changed his intention in the course of writing but did so without being aware of it.

Let me say that I do not regard the idea that an author could change his mind in the course of writing as implausible. Nor do I think it absurd that a work can say what the author wished to deny. Works do evolve in the course of writing. Tolstoy himself once deemed a Chekhov story excellent even though what Chekhov meant to say would have made the story a weak one. Because Chekhov is a true artist, Tolstoy explained, he wrote a story whose complexity mercifully exceeds and contradicts his intentions.

I also agree that an author's own pronouncements on his work, though not to be set aside lightly, cannot be decisive if the text contradicts them. That is why I have relied on the text itself, not the author's comments or earlier note-book versions, in elucidating it. What is most important is not what the author says about the work but what he does in it.

The problem for the opponents of "bourgeois morality" is that the epigraph is part of the work. That is why Eichenbaum chooses to call it vestigial, a hold-over from an earlier stage of creation that *should have been* eliminated. It is a literary analogue to the human body's appendix, a novelistic House of Lords that somehow survived by sheer inertia. This interpretive strategy is unsatisfying because it must reject a part of the work that could not have slipped by a forget-ful author. If the epigraph must be rejected as incompatible with the work, why not other passages? How many incompatibilities can a reading eliminate? Shall we reject as vestigial all the places where the author states that Anna is lying? At what point does pruning of undesirable passages constitute rewriting the book to suit one's a priori interpretation?

These questions demonstrate why "vestigiality" has lost the struggle for in-terpretive survival and why critics have found it helpful to reinterpret, rather than overlook, the epigraph.

Two Interpretations of the Epigraph, and an Unexpected Third One

"Vengeance is mine, I will repay." These words, a translation into English of the Slavonic words Tolstoy cites, appear in both the Old and New Testaments. In Paul's epistle to the Romans (12:19) they allude to Deuteronomy (32:35). The double source lends itself to two interpretations.

Only one obviously condemns Anna. In Deuteronomy, God threatens the enemies of his people with vengeance, and so the line seems to threaten Anna with punishment for breaking God's law or worshiping a false god. But Paul chooses to stress that people should forgive their enemies because vengeance belongs to God. Taken this way, the epigraph seems to fault not Anna but the society that condemns her. The second interpretation more easily fits with a romantic reading.

I believe that the second interpretation is viable, but that it does not cancel the first. I see no contradiction between the beliefs that bad actions lead naturally to harmful consequences and that those consequences should be left to God. Paul clearly cites Deuteronomy as consistent with this view.

Both interpretations apply, but during the sequence leading to Anna's suicide, a third one unexpectedly presents itself.

Anna several times revels in the thought that if she commits suicide, she can punish Vronsky for his cruelty: "the one thing that mattered was punishing him. . . . she began musing with enjoyment on how he would suffer, and repent and love her memory when it would be too late. . . . she vividly pictured to herself how he would feel when she would be no more" (781). It is as if *she* were saying the words of the epigraph: Vengeance is mine, I will repay. If so, Anna is assuming the role of God.[37]

The desire for vengeance stays with her when she goes to Dolly in despair and finds to her consternation that Kitty is present. Anna immediately reflects that Vronsky was in love with Kitty, and so Kitty is a rival. Anna knows that Kitty dislikes her, and both recall that only recently Anna has flirted with Levin. In a Dostoevskian way, Anna resents Kitty precisely because she has wronged Kitty with two men. Anna resents Kitty all the more because Kitty sees her in a wretched condition. She indulges towards Kitty the spiteful feelings already directed at Vronsky.

Kitty notices Anna's hostile look but, attributing it to the changed position of someone who had once patronized her, feels sorry for Anna. With her keen eye now set toward any possible insult, Anna detects this compassion, which could only feel condescending and redouble her spite. Anna turns to Kitty: "'Yes, I am glad to have seen you,' she said with a smile. 'I have heard so much of you from everyone, even from your husband. He came to see me, and I liked him very much,' she said, unmistakably with malicious intent" (791). When Anna leaves, Kitty tells Dolly how sorry she is for Anna. Anna is mortified.

Totalism and Isolation

Part Seven's last three chapters trace Anna's thoughts. As she meditates, Anna arrives at her new interpretive key to all human life. Tolstoy has described Yashvin as a person not just without principles but with positively immoral principles, and Anna applies Yashvin's philosophy of gambling to everything:

"'He wants to strip me of my shirt, and I him of his.' Yes, that's the truth!" (791).

Anna's new idea is that life is Darwinian in the pejorative sense that it is a struggle for survival. (Darwinism is invoked a few times in the book.) Everyone uses everyone else and all desires except the satisfaction of appetites are fake. No one really cares about anything but self and no one can even know anyone else. We are all self-contained monads, locked in a prison house of ego. Empathy is impossible, and we would not use it if we could, because we are not just indifferent to each other but actually hate each other. Anna has gone from the narcissistic heaven of romance to a narcissistic hell of isolation.

Anna believes that her interpretive scheme, "the piercing light which revealed to her now the meaning of life and all human relations," strips away all pretense and reveals what is really there.[38] Her extremism now becomes a sort of interpretive totalism. In Anna's view, her ability to see into people has become an infallible method for seeing through them. Most of these chapters are narrated in an almost stream-of-consciousness fashion, and so we eavesdrop on how in her thoughts she applies this new vision to every stray object she comes across. Nothing is contingent, nothing escapes the vision, everything says the same thing.

On the carriage ride home, she sees two men talking with warmth and asks herself: "can one ever tell another what one is feeling?" (790).[39] A man who mistakes her for an acquaintance lifts his hat: "He thought he knew me. Well, he knows me as well as anyone in the world knows me. I don't [even] know myself" (790).

Children are buying ice cream, and Anna thinks that they want "that filthy ice cream" the way we all want sweets. "And Kitty's the same—if not Vronsky, then Levin. And she envies me, and hates me. And we all hate each other. I Kitty, Kitty me. That's the truth. 'Tyutkin *coiffeur. Je me fais coiffer par* Tyutkin . . .'" [Tyutkin, hairdresser, I have my hair done by Tyutkin: the name alone is in Russian]. The French pretensions of the Russian hairdresser—is she passing his shop?—seem to symbolize all pretensions. Behind everything is lie or hate. Anna reflects that Dolly, out of sheer envy, probably takes a secret delight in Anna's misery, and that Kitty doubtless considers her an immoral woman. "How I can see through her! She knows that I was more than usually nice to her husband. . . . If I were an immoral woman I could have made her husband fall in love with me . . . if I'd care to. And, indeed, I did care to" (790). No less than everyone else, Anna is filled with deceit and hate: the difference is that she knows it and pretends nothing else. Earlier in the book we saw her lying about not lying, and now she concludes that there is nothing but lying.

She has seen Karenin's ideals as simply so many tools for advancing, and now she pronounces everything higher to be sham. Religion is a fake. "They're ringing the bell for vespers, and how carefully that merchant crosses himself! As if he were afraid of dropping something. Why these churches and this ringing and this humbug? Simply to conceal that we all hate each other" (791).

When Anna arrives home, she asks if Vronsky has answered her note and her telegram. He has answered the latter and said he cannot be home before ten, and she does not consider that his telegram was an answer to hers but that he never got her imploring note. She resolves to "tell him all" and then go away. "Never have I hated anyone as I hate that man!" (791). His hat makes her shudder with aversion, as do the servants, the walls, the food laid out for her, and everything else in the house. Everything connected with Vronsky is now "ears." Packing a few things, she decides to take a train to see him for the last time and then leave. She returns to the carriage, and again we trace her thoughts about everything the carriage passes, and again everything means the same thing.

Contrary Evidence?

Anna tries to catch the thread of her earlier thoughts: "Tyutkin, *coiffeur?*— no, not that. Yes, of what Yashvin says, the struggle for existence and hatred— that's the one thing tying people together" (362). Mentally addressing a party going to the country, she tells them it's a useless journey, because there is never any escape, everywhere everything is the same, and one cannot get away from oneself. (See Weir.) Seeing a drunk, she imagines inebriation to be just another futile attempt to escape the hell of self.

Now she turns "that glaring light in which she was seeing everything" (792) on Vronsky's initial pursuit of her and understands his motives in the same cynical way. She cannot deny that he loved her, but she imagines that from the start he was motivated mainly by vanity, the sense of triumph, and the pride of conquest. Of course, that is more or less true of Vronsky at the beginning of their relationship, but not later. Now, having misrepresented him as wholly romantic from the start, she sees him as vain all along. As she becomes aware of each falsity, whether in herself or in Vronsky, she takes it as evidence that everything is false. Her lies exact their punishment all the more strongly because she has denied them for so long, because she takes every insight to the extreme, and because her interpretive totalism allows in principle for one and only one meaning.

Anna thinks: "He loves me, but how? *The zest is gone* [English in the original]" (793). The fact that she acknowledges his love at all indicates that her interpretive totalism is not yet complete. It is still a project, and she must work on it or other meanings will seep through. This incompleteness turns out to be of immense importance, because it keeps alive the possibility that Anna could check her mad mental ride to destruction. As in the train ride in Part One, she can yield to or resist the delirium.

Vronsky may still love her, but Anna knows for a certainty that he would be glad if she went away. "This was not mere supposition, she saw it distinctly in the piercing light which revealed to her now the meaning of life and all human relations" (793). She correctly recognizes that what she wants from Vronsky is total, "passionate," and "selfish," the love of a mistress who does not care to be a wife. That is, presumably, yet another reason she delayed so long in seeking a divorce. The sort of love she values fits no better with marriage than with child-birth. "If I could only be anything but a mistress, passionately caring for noth-ing but his caresses; but I can't and I don't care to be anything else. And that desire arouses aversion in him" (793) because he wants a marriage and children, she reasons. The aversion she detects arouses Anna's fury.

Anna is partly aware that her interpretation of Vronsky is forced, and she has not yet forgotten all contrary evidence. Even if she were to live, that process might never be complete, just as she never absolutely banished all appreciation of Karenin. As evidence contrary to her totally bleak portrait of Vronsky occurs to her, she must therefore reason it away. Of course he is not in love with Kitty or the Princess Sorokina or anyone else, and of course he will not leave me, she admits, but that is not because his love is total. His devotion simply reflects his sense of honor and duty, which is insulting. Except for romantic love, no other motive—honor, family love, or anything else—can matter, and romantic love, if it was ever there at all, is now gone.

As she tries to overcome contrary evidence, Anna takes a further interpretive step: "And where love ends, hate begins" (793). This is the extremist view taken to the extreme. If the slightest deviation from one extreme appears, then we are at the other.

Anna the Philosopher

Although Anna resembles a paranoid in finding the same hostile meaning in everything, she is not paranoid because she does not imagine a conspiracy of evil directed at her alone. On the contrary, she globalizes. There is nothing but isola-tion and hatred for everyone, and Anna regards herself as unique only in seeing through deception more clearly than others. Anna becomes a philosopher as Tolstoy illustrates where interpretive totalism of any conceivable kind may lead. Any belief that one has the key to everything, that there are no exceptions, that contingency does not exist, that the world is simple enough to be described in terms of a few laws, that under the complexity of things a single truth abides: all these extreme and totalistic presumptions spell disaster. *Levin comes to learn the complexity of things, and Anna the simplicity.* In the parallel plots, Tolstoy gives us two distinct ways of understanding the world. As in his portrait of Pierre's mad systematizing, he means Anna's final philosophy to stand for all attempts to see the human or social world in a single light. Utopianism is nothing but inverted cynicism. The portrait of Anna is now directed not only at romance but also at the predominant trends of Western thought since the seventeenth century.

Anna sees hatred not as a fact of her own experience but as universal: "I don't know these streets at all. Hills it seems, and still houses, and houses. . . . And in the houses always people and people. . . . How many of them, no end, and all hating each other" (793). She now asks whether any escape from this universal law is possible. Suppose, for instance, that Aleksey Aleksandrovich should give me a divorce and Seryozha, she imagines. At the mere thought of Karenin, she pictures "with extraordinary vividness" the image of him that evokes repulsion — "his mild, lifeless dull eyes . . . his intonation, and the cracking of his knuckles" (794). Divorced, she could marry Vronsky, but that would if anything make him love her even less. And Seryozha would not stop asking about her two husbands.

She concludes that there can be no exception to universal hate. "Aren't we all flung into the world only to hate each other, to torture ourselves and each other?" (794). The falsity of her assertions about Seryozha — that she had no choice but to abandon him — now seems to prove to her that she does not love her son any more than Vronsky loved her or than anyone ever loves anyone else. Again her lies exact their retribution and again her extremism makes her judgment unqualified.

The Madness of Reason and the Choice of Fatalism

Having arrived at the station, Anna enters the waiting room and again she is torn between hope for a reconciliation and a sense of the humiliation that would entail. When she is in the train, her bag bouncing on the springy seat, she notices through the window a "deformed peasant covered with dirt . . . stooping down to the carriage wheels," and she remembers her terrifying dream. A couple enters the carriage, and Anna, surveying them, thinks she sees their whole hideous history. As the train begins to roll, the man crosses himself and Anna, again denying that any belief in something beyond self could be sincere, thinks angrily: "It would be interesting to ask him what meaning he attaches to that" (796).

As the train rolls, she returns to her awful thoughts and takes yet another step:

> "Where did I leave off? On the thought that I couldn't conceive a position in which life would not be misery, that we are all created to be miser-

able, and that we all know it, and all invent means of deceiving each other. And when one sees the truth, what is one to do?"

"That's what reason is given man for, to escape from what worries him," said the lady in French, lisping affectedly, and obviously pleased with her phrase.

The words seemed an answer to Anna's thoughts. (796)

It is Anna who perceives affected lisping and this perception accords with the cynical interpretation she gives to the words. The lady presumably thinks of reasoning one's way out of a dilemma, but Anna thinks of reasoning oneself to suicide.[40] In her very descent into madness, Anna becomes another of the "rational suicides" of Russian literature, all of whom are only pseudorational because too great a faith in reason is itself a form of madness.

Anna still plans to see Vronsky one more time, and she still has hopes, but the thought of death grows ever stronger. The more extreme her diagnosis of the human condition, the fewer alternatives remain. Her extremism and her belief that she has the interpretive key lead inexorably to suicide—unless she can start thinking differently.

The suspense of this scene derives from the fact that the possibility of other insights is not yet foreclosed.[41] Romance and Anna presume fatalism, but Tolstoy's novel does not. Belief in fatalism is a choice. The reader, too, can yield to it or resist it at will.

Foreshadowing

When Anna gets off the train, she is given Vronsky's answer to her note. He expresses regret that he did not receive her note earlier and again promises to be back by ten. But what she sees, or thinks she sees, is that the note is written in a careless hand, which is insulting and proof he does not love her. It would not matter what he wrote. If one decides to read with hostility, all messages are hostile, as all is yellow to the bilious eye.

The platform begins to sway as another train comes in, and the purely physical sensation of swaying makes Anna imagine that she is in the train again. Her thoughts follow the lead of her body.

And all at once she thought of the man crushed by the train the day she had first met Vronsky, and she knew what she had to do. With a rapid, light step she went down the steps that led from the water tank to the rails and stopped close to the approaching train. (798)

She knew what she had to do (chto ei nado delat'): she fulfills the "evil omen" she pronounced at the train station where she first met Vronsky. It is crucial to note here that it is she, not the author, who fulfills the omen. This is not a novel with foreshadowing, but one in which the character believes in the real-life counterpart to foreshadowing, omens. Like the heroine of a tragic romance, Anna lives as if she were in a world governed by fate and foreshadowing, and so she thinks she knows how the story must end and "what she had to do."

To read the trainman's death as foreshadowing is to mistake the work's point. For the author, the world of romance is false. We are deluded if we believe that somehow our story is already written, in the way a novelistic character's story may be planned in advance. Life is not a book, and this book is designed to show the mistake of thinking it is. Anna is not the heroine of a romantic novel with omens and foreshadowing; she only thinks she is. She is, in fact, a genre expatriate from romance placed in a work and in a world antithetical to the entire romantic vision.[42]

Annie

Anna now stares at the wheels to time her jump. She considers: "There, in the very middle, and I shall punish him and escape from everyone and myself" (798). Anna has thought constantly of Vronsky, and occasionally of Seryozha and how she abandoned him. But she has not once, in this entire sequence, thought of her daughter. She does not so much as ask herself what will happen to Annie without her. But the danger is obvious: in addition to losing her mother, Annie may well be returned to her legal father Karenin, who is now no longer gentle and forgiving but half-crazed.

Even more than what Anna does think about, such as her desire to harm Vronsky with her suicide, it is what she does not think about that matters here. She was able to conduct her affair with Vronsky without once putting herself in Karenin's position until the moment when he stammers about "thuffering." The worst evil of her suicidal thoughts is what they omit, her daughter.

In Part Eight, after Anna's death, we meet Vronsky, accompanied part of the way by his mother, heading off to the Eastern War in order to commit suicide. He repeats several times that death is his goal, and he refuses a letter of introduction offered by Sergey Ivanovich because, as he explains, "to meet death, one needs no letter of introduction" (812). In going to the war, and still more, in choosing to die, Vronsky, too, abandons Annie. We learn that Vronsky has in fact given his daughter to Karenin, and now, though he has second thoughts, reasons that "he can't take back his word" (811). His misery, his regret, his sense of honor: anything is more important than his daughter. We sympathize with his grief, as we sympathize with Anna's terrible suffering, but who sympathizes with Annie's prospects in the care of Karenin and the Countess Lydia Ivanovna?

She is not an orphan by chance, but by the choice of both of her parents. Vronsky does not appreciate his own cruelty. Evil manifests itself as an absence.

The Red Bag

Anna's leap to death is perhaps the most psychologically acute suicide in world literature. She wants to jump in front of the car approaching her, "but the red bag which she began to take from her arm delayed her, and she was too late; the car had passed. She had to wait for the next" (798). She is about to kill herself, so why does she care about the bag? Tolstoy's realism is at its height here.[43]

Most of what we do we do by habit. Anna is used to putting her bag down carefully before doing anything that might damage it, and so, without thinking, she does so here. Her body takes the action for her. I know of no other author who would imagine this detail, and there is no other who understands so well the way our body "thinks" and shapes our actions and thoughts.

It does so in an even more remarkable way in the next sentences:

A feeling such as she had known when about to take the first plunge in bathing came upon her, and she crossed herself. That familiar gesture brought back into her soul a whole series of memories of her childhood and girlhood, and suddenly the darkness that had covered everything for her was torn apart, and life rose up before her for an instant with all its bright past joys. (798)

Because she assumes the position of jumping, her "body memory" makes her cross herself. Without willing it, but because of the "mind of her body," she performs the very action she has just been mocking. This purely physical action in turn recalls memories of childhood. These memories pertain to life before Vronsky, and even before Karenin. They thereby recall what the life story she tells herself has left out—life "with its bright past joys"—and so implicitly contradict her belief that there can be nothing but misery.

If Anna would only attend to these memories, she would not kill herself. But again the body rules. Just as she has taken care of her handbag without having mentally decided to do so, now she does what we typically do when a thought occurs to us just before we have finished a difficult task. She holds the thought until the task is completed. She does not take her eyes from the wheels of the second car.

And exactly at the moment when the midpoint between the wheels drew level with her, she threw away the red bag, and drawing her head back into her shoulders, fell on her hands under the car, and, with a light movement, as though she would rise immediately, dropped on her knees. And at that very moment she was terrified at what she was doing. "Where am I? What am I doing? What for?" (798)

Only Tolstoy would think of having her jump with a light movement, as if she would rise immediately. She throws away her bag as if it matters, as if she would not get it wet in the water, and then she jumps as if diving, and her body acts as if she would immediately rise to the surface.

Only now can she turn her attention to the implications of her childhood memories and regret that she has jumped. Anna's suicide is all the more horrible because her last moment is one of colossal regret at what she has done. Perhaps there is more misery in this moment than in the rest of her life combined. How many suicides experience such a horrible last instant, invisible to all others and known here only by grace of an omniscient author? No matter how much we may disapprove of Anna's behavior, and no matter how much we have sympathized with her before, it is impossible not to sympathize even more deeply with her last instants.

The Epigraph's Fourth Meaning

"She tried to get up . . . but something huge and merciless struck her on the head and dragged her down on her back"(798–99). *Something* struck her: that is how *she* would sense things, so the line is from her perspective. She tries to take back her action but she cannot. Now she is the one who prays: "'Lord forgive me everything!' she said, feeling it impossible to struggle" (799). She has renounced prayer and mocked it, but, like Levin in the childbirth scene, prays anyway. Her denials of meaning, like Levin's denial of God, clearly do not reflect what she really believes. Like her childhood memories, the prayer testifies to what her story has omitted, and again magnifies the horror of her last moment.

That horror itself recalls the terrible peasant working the iron. We have been told that the most frightening aspect of this dream is how the peasant ignores her, and now the engine of death does the same.[44]

Part Seven concludes:

And the candle by whose light she had been reading the book filled with troubles, deceptions, grief, and evil lighted up for her all that had previously been in darkness, flickered, began to grow dim, and was put out forever. (799)

The light is that glaring light that falsely seemed to illuminate the meaning of everything. The metaphor of reading a book, which might easily seem hackneyed, here reminds us of Anna's way of living as if she were a novelistic heroine. Tolstoy makes the simplest of images eerily appropriate.

Anna dies not because she is somehow punished by society, God, or the author for infidelity. The main cause is her own way of thinking: her belief in romance, her extremism, and above all, her cultivated habits of contrived misperception. She does not arrest her falsehoods when she can, and so her death is a sort of delayed consequence to the process that began with "ears." She has chosen to seek vengeance on Vronsky, omitted considering her daughter, indulged her spite towards Kitty, failed to consider seriously contrary evidence, and decided to follow the "omen." Each act or non-act contributes to her jumping.

Now the epigraph acquires a fourth meaning: it is as if Anna were pronouncing retribution upon herself.

CHAPTER FOUR

Levin

Why Reforms Succeed or Fail

Political economy told him [Levin] that the laws by which the wealth of Europe had been developed, and was developing, were universal and unvarying. (362)

The Significance of Russian History

Perhaps the most important worldwide story of the past few hundred years concerns the response of non-Western societies to Western power. To maintain independence, to compete economically, to rescue their people from poverty, and to play a role commensurate with their numbers and cultural achievements, many societies have had to face the same problems: Is it possible to adopt Western technological and scientific achievements while still maintaining other aspects of traditional culture? Or does that technology so depend on the political institutions, cultural values, social practices, and habits of thought that gave rise to it that it cannot be successfully borrowed alone? Does modernization of an economy require the Westernization of everything else? How Western must a society become to compete with the West?

These questions have confronted countries as different as Japan, Turkey, Botswana, India, and China.[1] Western military and economic power has exerted such pressure that virtually every non-Western culture has had to respond. Depending on how it is understood, the process of change embraced or resisted has been called either "Westernization" or "modernization."

The term Westernization suggests breaking with traditional life to imitate the cultures of the West. Modernization, with its temporal rather than geographical implications, describes stages of transformation that are universal even if the West took the first steps. If terms are used this way, then the principles of modernization are no more Western than the laws of physics. A modernizing country does not copy, but catches up, and since all are running on the same track, it may surpass those with a head start. Still more encouraging, native traditions may prove at least as compatible with economic transformation as

143

Western ones. Why copy European culture if "Asian values" offer even better conditions for technological progress?

Considered from a global perspective, Russian history may be especially significant because Russia was the first country to face these questions squarely. It set the pattern of debates and defined the alternative answers. Everywhere there have been analogues to "Slavophiles" and "Westernizers."

Peter the Great chose an extreme solution, to Westernize (not just modernize) Russia as rapidly and as thoroughly as possible. He forced his country to change radically almost overnight. To do so, Peter compelled the aristocracy to adopt Western mores wholesale. Within a century, the aristocracy's first language was French. Readers of *War and Peace,* the opening chapters of which are set in 1805, will remember that the upper classes used Russian primarily to talk with peasants. Even in *Anna Karenina,* set some sixty years later, Kitty's brother-in-law Lvov passes instinctively from Russian to French, which is easier for him. He can count on everyone in his social class understanding him.

Under Peter, social life changed suddenly and dramatically. Schools were established, and the Academy of Sciences was founded before there were Russians literate enough, let alone scientifically accomplished enough, to understand what such an academy was. It had to be staffed with foreigners. Government, the church, the military, and daily social activities underwent rapid and radical transformation. The new Julian calendar dated events as Europeans did, rather than from the creation of the world. The *Book of Deportment* explained European manners to noblemen who now had to practice Western manners from the use of cutlery to the conduct of conversations in salons. The famous pictures of Peter shaving the beards of noblemen suggest not only untraditional grooming but also an affront to the religious idea that man was made in the image of God. To make such alterations, Peter imposed his will by sheer force.

Perhaps most significant of all, women emerged from seclusion and became partners in social and intellectual life. As a result, Western readers of *Anna Karenina* do not feel they encounter a world radically different from the one described by George Eliot or Balzac, and today American readers are no more distant from Anna's Russia than from Trollope's England. By contrast, the makers of the modern Arabic and Turkish novel, a form borrowed from the West, had to deal with the radically different status of women in their countries. Almost everywhere, Westernization has proven especially unsettling insofar as it changed the rights and roles of women. In Iran and elsewhere, horror at such changes has fueled attempts to reverse Westernizing reforms. As Atatürk and the Shah of Iran may be seen as latter-day Peters, Khomeini fits the pattern of an extreme "anti-Westernizer."

Toryism and Whiggism

Modernization does not necessarily require uprooting an old culture and replacing it with a new one. The Russian Slavophiles, who have too often been confused with later extreme nationalist groups, questioned not modernization, but the choice to sacrifice the rest of Russian culture to import technology. In their view, Peter had no need to force a radical break with the past by imposing a "revolution from above." Instead of rejecting Russianness, why not adapt the new practices to existing culture? Is it really necessary to wear Western clothing in order to use a modern plow or rifle?

According to the Slavophiles, Peter brought Russia into the modern world in the wrong way because he was in a hurry. The Slavophiles deplored rapid change. In their view, a culture develops gradually, over centuries, custom by custom and practice by practice. It cannot be imposed all at once. Abstract rights and plans dictated from above simply do not take, and impatient rulers usually institute a "dictatorship of virtue" enforced by a reign of terror: liberty, equality, fraternity, or death. No matter how many rights are nominally guaranteed, a new tyrant is bound to arise.

The Slavophiles preferred the English model. In Britain, rights evolved over time and change took place step by step. If English law was less consistently "rational" than French revolutionary principles, it was more solidly grounded because it reflected the mores of the people. Of course, not all Englishmen were gradualists. The Slavophiles theorized that British history has been an ongoing struggle between "Toryism" and "Whiggism," which they understood as universal ideas in conflict everywhere. Everywhere people face a choice between gradual and rapid change, between custom and abstract principles, and between transformation by force and by the test of experience. For the Slavophiles, Peter was the ultimate "Whig."

St. Petersburg

In Russian thought, St. Petersburg, the new capital Peter built on conquered swampland, came to symbolize sudden change and Western rationalism imposed from above. Utopian architects had long dreamed of a perfectly planned city whose geometric symmetry would represent the triumph of reason over custom, mind over nature, and design over contingency. Petersburg was the first such city built in the modern world. Its clear lines contrasted with haphazard Moscow, which represented gradualism, custom, and embeddedness within the historical process.

The hero of Dostoevsky's *Notes from Underground* will not leave the capital even though he knows it is bad for his health precisely because he devotes his life to a struggle with abstract rationalism. He famously declares that "there are intentional and unintentional cities" and Petersburg is "the most abstract and intentional city in the world" (NFU, 6). It is inhabited by "retort-men." In *Crime and Punishment*, Dostoevsky plays with the idea that Raskolnikov's rationalist theories justifying murder derive from the spirit of the city in which he lives. It is almost as if Petersburg were committing the murders through him. On his way to the crime, Raskolnikov even dreams of city planning.

In a complex way, *Anna Karenina* develops the "anti-Whiggish" position. Tolstoy foresaw what we have witnessed, the failure of so many plans to modernize. His position was a conservative one, long rejected as perverse. But at the beginning of the twenty-first century, his insights seem increasingly pertinent. Levin's evolving ideas serve as a vehicle for Tolstoy's.

Aristocracy

Levin's upbringing has shaped his views about social change, his sense of time and tradition, the value he places on work, and his belief in aristocracy properly understood.

At the beginning of the novel, the author explains that "the families of the Levins and the Shcherbatskys were old noble Moscow families, and had always been on intimate and friendly terms" (25). Levin, an orphan who prepared for the university with Kitty's older brother, found in the Shcherbatsky household "that inner life of an old, noble, cultivated, and honorable family of which he had been deprived by the death of his father and mother" (25). He falls in love with the whole Shcherbatsky family before deciding he loves Kitty in particular. The Shcherbatsky sense of tradition and domestic life, their values developed over generations, and the breeding that is second nature to them all mark the family as Moscow people: one could not introduce them as "an old Petersburg family." By the time Tolstoy wrote this novel, the symbolism of the two cities had grown so familiar that he would have sensed no need to explain it. We recognize without being told that Karenin's bureaucratic utopianism—his belief that all problems can be solved by adjusting institutions—represents a comic form of Petersburgism.

Stiva's values also derive from a degraded Petersburg sensibility, and his disagreements with Levin reflect the larger debate symbolized by the cities. Levin objects strenuously to Stiva's sale of his (or rather Dolly's) forest to Ryabinin because it contradicts Levin's fundamental values. For Levin, the aristocracy's inherited ownership of estates entails a duty across generations. One is not so much an owner as a caretaker of the land and one has a responsibility not to see it degraded.

But Stiva lives entirely in the present and acknowledges no obligation over generations. If he did not live so much in the present, he would not be selling the forest in the first place. For one thing, he would not be spending his money on actresses, and for another, he would be fulfilling his obligation to his family, which includes passing on to them what he has received from the previous generation. Levin is continually irked by Stiva's neglect of Dolly and the children in part because family, like land, represents duties extending beyond one's own lifetime. Levin reminds Stiva that the Oblonsky children will have nothing with which to make their way in the world.

The way in which Stiva sells the forest tells the same story. For ready money, he sells it for much less than it is worth. Ryabinin plans to buy it, cut down the trees, sell them for much more than the purchase price, and leave the land degraded. Stiva abets this degradation of the land by taking so much less than the value of the trees on it. Levin asks Stiva why he has not counted the trees, but Stiva replies that such work is beneath him as an aristocrat. This reply irritates Levin still more, not only because he works the land himself, but because he understands aristocracy in the opposite way, as an obligation to know the land, value it, and preserve it.

Duty and Culture

Stiva regards Levin's idea of aristocracy as "reactionary" (183), an attempt to preserve an outmoded class structure. Levin makes clear that his attachment to the aristocracy extends only so far as its members fulfill their duties and live proper lives. Otherwise, they have no right to the land and to their social status. When Levin asks about Kitty, and Stiva explains that Vronsky was attractive to her because he is "a perfect aristocrat," Levin's pride and principles suffer injury together. Levin explodes: "You consider Vronsky an aristocrat, but I don't. A man whose father crawled up from nothing at all by intrigue, and whose mother—God knows whom she was mixed up with" (183). For Levin, Vronsky is no aristocrat because of his family's morals and Stiva (implicitly) is no aristocrat because "you think it despicable of me to count the trees in my forest, while . . . I prize what's come to me from my ancestors or been won by hard work" (183). Far from taking offense, Stiva enjoys the sheer performance value of Levin's outburst. "Levin's excitement gave him genuine pleasure" (183). This pleasure, too, is of the moment.

Later in the novel, Tolstoy plays Stiva's degraded Petersburgism for still more humor. In Part Seven, Stiva journeys to the capital to secure a job with a higher salary and to arrange his sister's divorce. He combines the two purposes by asking Karenin not just for the divorce but, while he is at it, for his influence in obtaining the new position.[2] Stiva also goes to Petersburg because Moscow is a "stagnant swamp," and in the capital people have the right attitude toward life (757). We hear Stiva's thoughts paraphrased ironically (double-voiced) by the author:

> After living for some time in Moscow, especially in close relations with his family, he was [always] conscious of a depression of spirits. . . . he reached a point when he positively began to be worrying himself over his wife's ill humor and reproaches, over his children's health and education. . . . even the fact of being in debt worried him. But he had only to go and stay a little while in Petersburg . . . where people lived — really lived — instead of vegetating as in Moscow, and all such ideas vanished and melted away at once. (757–58)

Why, that very morning Stiva has met a prince who openly maintains two families. This prince deliberately introduced his eldest son to the second family so as to "broaden his ideas" (758). In Petersburg, no one imagines that people should make major sacrifices for their children. "Here people understood that a man is duty bound to live for himself, as every man of culture should live" (758). In this paraphrase of Petersburg discourse, one hears the author's countervoice in the reference to self-indulgence as a duty and hedonism as respect for culture. Petersburgers, Stiva reflects, know that a job is not about actually working, but about making connections that result in income without work. Meeting his relative Prince Piotr Oblonsky, Stiva hears with pleasure Piotr's contrast between really living by pursuing pretty women and thinking, in the old Russian way, of one's eternal salvation. All the Oblonskys, it appears, are amoral creatures of the moment.

A Strange Sort of Duty

When Levin attends the local elections that so interest Vronsky and Oblonsky, he finds himself talking with the "reactionary landowner" he met at Svyazhsky's. The two "reactionaries" discover they are both thinking about the same problem. Why do they spend so much effort working the land when they could make more money either in government service or by treating the land as a source of cash in the present? Why not follow modern commercial advice: cut down the lime trees, sell them, and let out the land to peasants in plots? Today's form of this advice would be to demolish an old neighborhood in order to build condominiums. Both Levin and the landowner recognize the advice as economically sound, but neither can bring himself to follow it. Why?

Levin gropes toward an explanation: "It's a sort of duty one feels to the land"

(685). Stiva would regard the concept of duty to an inanimate object as nonsense. Levin means an obligation extending over time, but Stiva would find that concept even more absurd. The other landowner offers an analogy. Imagine that you are planning a garden where a centuries-old tree stands in the way. Do you cut it down? The answer depends on one's sense of time and one's confidence in the value of plans. Suppose one cuts down the tree to make way for progress and then discovers that the up-to-date plan, though it made the land attractive at first, later makes it ugly. The new garden may come to resemble those initially spiffy inns that, as Levin notices, soon look even worse than the dirtiest old inns because they are pretentious as well as shabby. One cannot then go back and restore the tree, just as one cannot, after knocking down old buildings, change one's mind and build new old buildings. If one respects the past and anticipates the limitations of even the most enticing plans, one will find a way to improve the land without cutting down the old tree. Instead of regarding it as an obstacle, one should treat it as a given and devise an arrangement in which the tree occupies a prominent place. Such a garden may not be geometrically neat or fit abstract rules, but it is rooted in something more than present taste and can be altered if necessary.

The same values apply to all social change. Levin discovers that an approach respecting one's duty to the land also leads to better economic results in the not very long run. He arrives at this conclusion by reflecting on his own experience, by studying the failure of other approaches, and by the thinking he does to write his book. That book turns out to be of immense importance in understanding the novel's themes and their relevance today.

Levin's Book

> In addition to farming . . . Levin had begun writing a book about agriculture, the plan of which turned on taking into account the character of the laborer on the land as one of the unalterable data of the question . . . (161)

Pause for a moment on the strangeness of Tolstoy's decision to devote so much of his novel to ideas about agriculture. Russian novels stand out as peculiar enough for including long speeches on God, death, immortality, determinism, fatalism, moral relativism, political nihilism, and many other topics that the Russians called "accursed questions." Stendhal famously remarked that topics like these no more belong in a novel than a pistol shot belongs in a concert. They disrupt, but cannot be ignored. Even today, when we have grown to appreciate the aesthetics of Russian philosophical novels, their tendency to leap from action to treatise and from complex motivation to psychological essay strikes most Western readers as an oddity.

Accursed questions may be tolerable, but agriculture? What possible reason could there be to include digressions on a topic so obviously unpoetic or unnovelistic, even by the prevailing standards of the Russian novel? The agricultural passages left Tolstoy open to parody, especially by the radicals.[3] Tolstoy did not hesitate to offend prevailing opinion, but why pick a topic so apparently marginal to do so?

The answer is that Tolstoy uses Levin's evolving ideas about agricultural reform as exemplary in two ways. First, they show the process of honestly thinking through a difficult question with no pat answers. We shall discuss that process in part two of this chapter. The present part focuses on the applicability of Levin's ideas not only to agricultural improvement but also, and much more broadly, to all modernization and reform.

Since World War II, some countries, like South Korea, Taiwan, and Singapore have successfully pulled themselves out of poverty, whereas others, like Tanzania, Ethiopia, Burma, and North Korea have not. Why? Attempts to help undeveloped countries, whether by individual countries, the United Nations, or the World Bank, have often left them worse off than before.[4] The reasons that efforts at modernization succeed or fail figure among the most pressing questions today.

Levin's theories (or antitheories) pertain not only to modernization but also to social reform generally. Why do most reforms, however well intentioned, leave conditions no better, and sometimes even worse, than before? As attempts to modernize an economy often hold it back, plans to reduce unemployment, poverty, and crime often increase them. Some social diseases are partly iatrogenic, caused by the very attempt to cure them. It would be altogether too convenient to ascribe most of these failures to acts of sabotage by evil men. Something deeper and more complex is involved.

As we shall see, Levin's ideas also illuminate several related problems: how to make oneself a better person, what Christian love entails, the difference between real and fake art, and the way to think authentically. Most of this novel's questions, and many of the ways in which the book speaks to our lives today, become clearer if we understand the implications of Levin's book.

What Is Agriculture?

I call the book that Levin is writing *What Is Agriculture?* because, like Tolstoy's later tract *What Is Art?*, it is not just another study but "a criticism of all the old books" (170) on its topic. In his daydreams, Levin at first hopes that his treatise will be able to "effect not merely a revolution in political economy, but to annihilate that science entirely" (363), much as *What Is Art?* aims at utterly destroying all existing aesthetics.

In *Anna Karenina,* Tolstoy treats such grandiose hopes with gentle but unmistakable irony. Only when he abandons his utopianism can Levin really think through his ideas. After all, his book above all concerns the folly of all utopian plans and general laws. One needs not a revolution but attention to detail, and one needs to respect local conditions while giving up the hope for a single answer that applies everywhere. Successful change is not sudden and universal but slow and piecemeal.

After Kitty rejects Levin, he takes refuge in his book. Because it is a replacement for the family happiness he craves, it tends to dreamy extremes. Levin fantasizes:

> The whole system of culture, the chief element of the conditions of the people, must be completely transformed. Instead of poverty, general prosperity and content; instead of hostility, harmony and unity of interests. In short, a bloodless revolution, but a revolution of the greatest magnitude in the little corner of our district, then the province, then the whole world. (364)

And all these changes, he imagines, will be accomplished by "me, Kostya Levin, who . . . was refused by the Shcherbatsky girl. . . . I feel sure Franklin felt just as worthless" (364). When Levin marries, and no longer needs the book to assuage his loneliness, utopian dreams cease to obscure its essentially anti-utopian thesis.

The Root Cause

Russia always seems to be trying to modernize and catch up with the West at breakneck speed. That ambition marked the time of *Anna Karenina* as well as the eighteenth century and the Soviet period. It is with us today. Is it possible that Russia never seems to catch up precisely because it insists on doing so overnight? Perhaps Russians have tried to change in the wrong way?

Like so many landowners in Russian literature and society, Levin tries to introduce new and better methods resembling those used so successfully in Western Europe, but these efforts almost always come to nothing. He wonders why beneficial changes are so hard to realize, and his quest for a solution becomes a significant part of his story.

When Levin first returns to his estate after Kitty's rejection, "the bailiff came in and said that everything, thank God, was doing well; but informed him that the buckwheat in the new drying kiln had been a little scorched" (100). The language here is the bailiff's, and Levin understands that "a little scorched" means totally ruined. Because Levin himself has designed and built this kiln, the news particularly annoys him. He knows that if the buckwheat was scorched, "it was simply because precautions had not been taken, for which he had hundreds of times given orders" (100). Clearly, the problem is not technological: no machine will work if not operated properly. But why is it that the peasants routinely misuse this and all other machines that Levin has introduced?

Levin learns that for some reason his plan for sowing clover early cannot be put into practice. His new English seed oats suffer from a touch of mildew, because, for some reason, his specific orders have not been carried out. Later, his new hay-pitching machine breaks. Levin the reformer and modernizer encounters a series of disappointments.

If Levin resembled so many intellectuals in his time and ours, he might seek "the root cause" (as we would call it today) of all these failures. Much as the generals and historians satirized in *War and Peace* mistakenly seek the cause of historical events in a single decision, and much as revolutionaries often reduce the complexities of social ills to a single conspiracy or institution, so intellectuals often view complexity as a delusion to be explained away by a few simple underlying laws. It is just this habit of thought that feeds utopianism, because if the diversity of evil and misery had a single cause, then one could eliminate it by changing only one thing. What could be easier? Abolish private property, alter the way children are educated, pass laws to regulate morals according to a given code, and evil will disappear or, at least, radically diminish. Behold, I make all things new. But Levin learns that there is no single cause for what has gone wrong.

Looking back on the twentieth century, we may wonder whether the root cause of the worst human misery is the belief that there is a root cause of human misery.

In fact, many things happen contingently, just "for some reason."

Friction

When Levin attends the elections, he tries to handle some business for his sister, but discovers that somehow it cannot be done. In Dostoevsky, the reason would be "administrative ecstasy," the sheer delight bureaucrats take in making petitioners cringe, plead, or wait. But nothing of the sort happens here, and the problem is not one of intent at all. No one has any interest in thwarting Levin, so he cannot understand what goes wrong.

When conspiracy theorists find they cannot accomplish something as easily as expected, they typically ask *cui bono?* (who benefits?) to discover the obstacle. Some person or group must have caused the failure. Defeat means sabotage. This way of thinking presumes that behind every action there must be an intent, whether conscious or unconscious. Such a view rules out the possibility that mere contingency or friction accounts for the difficulty.

The military theorist Carl von Clausewitz deemed *friction,* in this special metaphorical sense, an essential concept in understanding armies. Without using this word, Tolstoy regarded the same phenomenon as pertaining not just to war but to everything social. "If one has never personally experienced war," Clausewitz explains,

> one cannot understand in what difficulties constantly mentioned really consist. . . . Everything looks simple; the knowledge required does not look remarkable, the strategic options are so obvious that by comparison the simplest problem of higher mathematics has an impressive scientific dignity. Once war has actually been seen the difficulties become clear; but it is extremely difficult to describe the unseen, all-pervading element that brings about this change of perspective. Everything in war is very simple, but the simplest thing is difficult. The difficulties accumulate and end by producing a kind of friction that is inconceivable unless one has experienced war. (Clausewitz, 119)

The unseen, all-pervading element: For Tolstoy, similar difficulties arise when dealing with bureaucracy, introducing changes in agriculture, and implementing reforms. A Tolstoyan perspective is easily imagined today. Social problems look so simple: people in underdeveloped countries are poor, so give their governments foreign aid; workers are unemployed, so hire them to perform needed government services; schools do not educate, so raise teachers' salaries; the state regulatory commission keeps energy prices too high, so partially privatize the system: answers seem so obvious, but in practice reforms rarely have the intended effect. They produce unintended consequences, which themselves have consequences; and, as Isaiah Berlin liked to point out, no one can foresee the consequences of consequences of consequences. Experience may teach one to expect certain kinds of difficulties, but some can never be anticipated. There is always friction: "Countless minor incidents—the kind you can never really foresee—combine to lower the general level of performance, so that one always falls far short of the intended goal" (Clausewitz, 119).

No one is deliberately impeding Levin's efforts for his sister. By the same token, no one is trying to thwart his agricultural reforms. Sabotage is out of the question. "All this happened not because anyone felt ill will toward Levin or his farm; on the contrary, he knew that they [the peasants] liked him [and] thought him a simple gentleman (their highest praise)" (340).

Friction defeats the reforms. But where does this friction come from and how might one best deal with it?

The Elemental Force

The bailiff and peasants recognize in advance when a plan is bound to fail, and at last Levin, instead of growing angry, pays attention to what they say:

> The bailiff listened attentively, and obviously made an effort to approve of his employer's projects. But still he had that look Levin knew so well that always irritated him, a look of hopelessness and despondency. That look said: "That's all very well, but as God wills." Nothing mortified Levin so much as that tone. But it was common to all the bailiffs he had ever had. They had all taken up that attitude toward his plans, and so now he was not angered by it but mortified, and felt all the more roused to struggle against this, as it seemed, elemental force continually ranged against him, for which he could find no other expression than "as God wills." (165)

The elemental force: this concept is central to both Tolstoy's great novels. Tolstoy uses a few similar terms for it. In *War and Peace,* he refers to an elemental force shaping individual lives (W&P, 648) and to "the elemental life of the swarm" constituting the cumulative effect of countless people's small actions governed by no overarching law. In *Anna Karenina,* he calls the elemental force a "brutal force" when its outcome is cruel. The rough equivalent of friction for Clause-witz, the elemental force applies more widely.

Clausewitz's explanation stops at friction, but Tolstoy takes the elemental force as a starting point for understanding why some plans are more likely to fail than others.

In order to grasp the course of events more easily, we tend to reduce the countless infinitesimal forces making up the elemental force to a single cause. After all, it is impossible to enumerate innumerable actions, and so historians and social scientists naturally look for some super-cause that sums up all those small actions. They may presume laws or postulate narrative neatness. Tolstoy relentlessly exposed the logical fallacies in both forms of simplification, which, at some point, either assume what is to be proven or proceed as if it were already proven.

Historians, social theorists, and biographers favor generalizations or sym-metries permitting a clear analysis or simple story. They find what they seek. Their success demonstrates not that complexity has been adequately explained but that when a discipline demands a certain sort of explanation it is bound to be "discovered." In disciplines pretending to be social sciences, it is repeatedly discovered that things are not as complex as they appear.

Even the phrase "elemental force" may mislead if we think of it as a single thing rather than as the cumulative effect of many irreducibly different things.

Why the Elemental Force Cannot Be Resisted

The Emperor Caligula is supposed to have wished that Rome had a single head so he could cut it off with a single blow. Utopians believe that evil has a single cause. This sort of thinking feeds revolutionism, terrorism, and dictatorship, as it did in Russia; for who would not break a few eggs to make such an omelet? Improvement, even perfection, looks so easy. But it isn't. Evil, like Rome, has millions of heads. Its name is legion.

Social good also has millions of heads. Neither social evil nor social good results from some particular choice, rule, or law. Over time, practices arise for local and contingent reasons and then solidify into habits, which in turn govern most actions. Habits are layered one upon another as different circumstances arise. Some persist even when useless or counterproductive. Every society has "vestigial organs" that bear witness to its history. Dictated by no plan, habits and practices in their totality adhere to no law and form no symmetrical structure. In their messy accumulation, they shape what happens, for good or ill.

Anything with a history has had to contend with countless events that have happened just "for some reason." It has had to develop an unsystematic repertoire of responses. Every culture possesses such a repertoire, which represents the habits of millions of people responding to innumerable situations. Taken together, the culture's habits and practice form a *field of possible action,* a sort of gestalt, that exerts pressure on every one who acts. In any such field, some actions are more likely than others. The field of possible actions may change, but it does so slowly, one set of habits or practices at a time. It cannot change all at once, because there is no single thing to change. No one has planned it, so no one can easily alter it.

In *War and Peace,* the wise General Kutuzov understands the elemental force and the limitations it places on his power. Commanding an army bears no resemblance to playing a war game in which one devises a strategy and executes it by moving pieces across a map. Kutuzov manages armies not by planning but by gently guiding where the elemental force already tends. He works within the small array of possible outcomes that the elemental force allows. The novel's other wise general, Bagration, does not even guide, but simply pretends to be giving orders while doing his real job: inspiring men so that, with high morale, they may perform better in unpredictable situations.

To attempt more would be folly. No one can resist the elemental force for long because it is everywhere and always, a swarm of pressures acting without guidance. Because the elemental force consists of a hundred million diverse causes, there is no defense to prepare against it. The sum total of habits is invincible, not because someone powerful is resisting, but because no one is resisting. To fight it is to take up arms against the sea.

Why Minds Wander

Reforms that require violating the elemental force fail: this is a Tolstoyan maxim. If we examine what happens when Levin tries to introduce new machines, we can observe the process of failure more closely. A key factor is the impossibility of paying perfect attention.

Attention is a severely restricted resource. We cannot pay close attention to many things at once. Moreover, attention wanders no matter how much we may try to keep it focused. These two limitations require us to leave most actions to habit, either because we are mainly concerned with some other action, or because when something distracts us, habit takes over. It is therefore of crucial importance what habits govern our behavior when we are not closely focused on what we are doing.

The impossibility of keeping one's attention focused is part of a more general human characteristic: scanning. We cannot keep our hands and feet perfectly steady because they have an inbuilt tremor. If they did not, photographers would not need tripods. Eyes constantly scan. Minds constantly monitor thoughts and perceptions. Bodies switch position. The reason for these involuntary movements is the same reason there are no animals with wheels. The world is radically uncertain, and dangers can come from anywhere, so if our minds and bodies did not scan, we would die. Imagine a dreamy gazelle or, today, a truck driver without peripheral vision. Tolstoy is quite aware of these dynamics of mind and body even if he would not give an evolutionary explanation for them.

We perform many actions involuntarily not because an unconscious intention guides us, as a classical psychoanalyst might suppose, but because actions may be governed by no intention at all. Sometimes our minds wander and our hands twitch not because we unconsciously wish them not to hold steady, but because it is impossible for them *not* to wander or twitch for very long without enormous effort. To suppose that our minds would stay focused unless we used psychic energy to make them wander is like supposing that an object in motion requires force to stay in motion. The inertia of our minds and bodies, what happens without effort or intention, leads us not to focus but to scan, and so to leave tasks to habit.

A set of questions distinguishing two world views presents itself. Is the fundamental state of the social world regular or messy, predictable or unpredictable? Which requires explanation and which takes work, orderliness or disorderliness? If we ceased to apply effort, would the books on library shelves soon become more or less arranged? Do potholes fix themselves? One may regard Tolstoy's novels as an extended polemic against the assumption, borrowed from the aspiration to a construct a Newtonian social science, that order may be presumed, and that contingency is an illusion. Tolstoy's psychology, not just his philosophy, derives from his belief in contingency and uncertainty.

Learning to Mow

When minds wander, habit takes over. When Vronsky goes to Bryansky's, he sees the hands on his watch but does not realize he is late, because he is operating by habit. His mind is elsewhere, on his meeting with Anna, and so, although he reads the time, he does not pay the extra attention needed to deduce its significance. Having already decided to go to Bryansky's, he lets habit direct his subsequent actions until his mind wanders to what he is doing, and he at last realizes that he is late.

We must be able to do some things by habit or we could not do several at once. Lyndon Johnson is supposed to have quipped that Gerald Ford was so dumb he could not walk and chew gum at the same time, but most of us can listen to the radio, sip a drink, and chat, all while driving a car, which is itself a single verb applied to many interrelated actions. We can perform all these actions simultaneously because most are done by habit and therefore require a minimum of attention. They can be done almost automatically.

When we first learned to drive, that was all we could do because driving was not yet a habit and required all our attention. People do not think about how they walk, but each of us had to learn how to perform this now automatic action by a painful process of trial, error, and practice. We all walk differently, and people drive or use tools with a range of precision depending on how they have learned the skill in the first place. In most circumstances, we are satisfied with what will suffice even if it is less than ideal. Repetition, including all the less than perfect motions we have used to get the job done, creates the habits that constitute our style of driving, walking, eating, or countless other common behaviors.

Tolstoy describes this painful acquisition of a skill when Levin learns to mow. First Levin must concentrate his whole mind, and still can hardly wield the scythe. At last he reaches a point of blissful self-forgetfulness, where trusting the body's own memories works better than paying close attention to every movement. But that is not the final step of learning. The old peasant, who really mows well, does not have to blank his mind for his body to perform correctly. He can adjust the body's motions as contingent circumstances and uneven terrain present themselves, as no one in a state of forgetfulness could do. He is fully present. The old peasant can notice a mushroom, pick it up, and put it away for his wife, all without breaking stride.

Because attention is so limited a resource, it takes all our effort to break an old habit, and one cannot break more than one at a time. Attention allows only a small range of freedom. We again see why childhood, when most habits are acquired, is so important.

We command our minds and bodies the way Kutuzov commands the army.

Reform by Template

When Levin wants to introduce new machines and better methods of working, he runs against the habits of the peasantry. With the best will in the world, nobody can work for long hours without his attention wandering frequently. If one introduces a machine that will work properly only if one constantly pays attention to it, but will break if one's mind wanders and old habits take over, then the machine will break.

A few years ago, cars of a certain brand started lurching forward dangerously. The manufacturer contended that the car would not lurch if the driver only paid constant attention, and isn't that what drivers should do anyway? Not at all, and to demand as much is to demand the impossible. The manufacturer might just as well have insisted that drivers float six inches above the seat.

Our minds wander even during the most intense and engaging activities, and when they do, we operate by habit. The elemental force of habit is decisive. The machines that Levin and other landowners introduce were tested on English farmers. The reason they break in Russia is not that Russians are incompetent or uneducated, as Svyazhsky supposes, but that Russian work habits differ from English ones. One cannot simply import machines with no regard to the people who are to use them. Levin's book insists that culture matters. The people who work are not just providers of so many units of interchangeable man-hours. He knows that this view contrasts with the "political economy" of his day, much as it contradicts prevailing economic theory in ours.

Before Levin learns that the laborer's culture matters, he deems it reasonable to insist that every peasant should continually "keep his wits about him, so as not to break the winnowing machines, the horse rakes, the threshing machines, that he should always attend to what he is doing" (340). Levin has to learn the impossibility of this demand, and Tolstoy wants us to apply this insight more generally. No plan for reform or modernization will succeed if it runs against the elemental force or ignores the interaction of habits and attention.

At first, Levin thinks modernization is possible by copying a foreign model or applying abstract principles. Like other modernizing Russian landowners, he encounters a silent antagonism without malice. When Levin at last grasps what is happening, he reflects that "when capital is applied in the European way the produce is small . . . this simply arises from the fact that the laborers want to work and work well only in their own peculiar way, and that this antagonism is not incidental but invariable, and has its roots in the national spirit" (362–63). Reform by template fails because it necessarily turns into

> a cruel and stubborn struggle between him and the laborer, in which there was on one side—his side—a continual intense effort to change everything to a pattern he considered better; on the other side, the natural order of things. And in this struggle he saw that with immense expenditure of force on his side, and with no effort or even intention on the other side, all that resulted was that the work did not go to the liking of either side, and that splendid tools, splendid cattle, and land were spoiled with no good to anyone. (339)

"With no effort or even intention": that is the sign of the elemental force at work.

How Reforms Can Take

But then how are reforms to be implemented? Levin is no fatalist, and he is not looking for an excuse to stay with the old ways. Quite the contrary, he wants to solve a puzzle that is much more than an intellectual exercise. It pertains to a defining aspect of his life, his work. He knows that it has implications for many other people. Having learned what impedes change, he now asks not what would be the best state of affairs, but how to foster improvements without running into the elemental force.

On his way to Svyazhsky's, Levin stays with a prosperous peasant family. These peasants began by renting three hundred acres, then bought them and rented three hundred more. They evidently run the farm quite productively. Levin is impressed that they have even introduced new tools and methods. Their potatoes have flowered before Levin's, and they use a modern plow. Levin is especially struck that after thinning out the rye they have used the thinned rye as fodder for the horses. Levin has himself tried to do this, "but always it had turned out to be impossible" (344), a phrase indicating there was no single discernible reason for the impossibility, just the sort of "for some reason" that shows the elemental force at work.

How does this family do what Levin and the other landowners cannot? Levin senses that the solution to his puzzle lies here, and he eventually finds it. No one at the farm has begun with a template for modernization. Rather, they have used traditional methods with as much diligence and intelligence as they could, taken advantage of opportunities as they presented themselves, and then, when they ran into problems, improvised from the immediate conditions. Changes have come by a patchwork series of local fixes. Sometimes these changes have involved new tools, but the tools were never chosen simply because they were better in some abstract sense. Rather, they happened to solve a problem that clearly needed solving when no other available solution seemed to work.

Changes have come from the bottom up. They have not been conceived theoretically and then imposed, but have been jury-rigged without an overall plan. Experience has been the guide. The idiosyncrasy of local circumstances, whether of the terrain, the condition of the family and the specific people doing the work, or the purely contingent opportunities provided by past practices and present surroundings, has played a major role. Each change has in turn altered prevailing conditions and so provided opportunities for more changes. Arising in this haphazard way, the opportunities that present themselves follow no prescribed order. Sometimes old technology works better than new, and sometimes a solution that would have worked elsewhere will not work here.

When Asymmetry Works

> Glory be to God for dappled things . . .
> And all trades, their gear and tackle and trim.
> —HOPKINS ("Pied Beauty," 240–41)

Reform requires knowing existing conditions intimately. It demands attentive "presentness" to changing circumstances. Success depends on *phronesis,* practical reasoning, and *metis,* cleverness and resourcefulness, but not *episteme,* abstract theoretical reasoning. Practical wisdom is case-based, and its results are haphazard and messy. It resembles the British constitution, not the French Rights of Man, and looks like Moscow, not Petersburg. All its ways are crooked. It demands intelligence that does not aim at total solutions, never undertakes change just to change, and refuses to favor one solution over another because it looks neater. Its solutions do not please geometrically.

As neat plots signify falsity, symmetry portends failure.

The aesthetic of abstract theory favors purity. The beauty of practice is pied.

Small local changes work better than overarching ones in part because one can reject or modify them with little effort or expense. One can also try out different solutions in various places to see which one will work better. Besides, since conditions vary even over small distances, the best general solution may still work less well than a series of local ones, each adapted to its milieu. Perhaps most important of all, asymmetry and variety provide a large number of possibilities for future change. Because the future is uncertain, and one never knows what needs will prove most pressing, it pays to preserve flexibility.

The less certain the situation, the greater the value of flexibility and variety.

As chance favors the prepared mind, opportunity favors the heterogeneous situation. Incentive is only one reason that centrally planned economies have proved so inefficient. Perhaps even more important, central plans do not have the flexibility or rapidity of response to take advantage of local opportunities or avoid sudden obstacles. For that, one needs decision-makers on the spot. Each decision-maker can adapt to local, quickly changing circumstances without petitioning Moscow for a change in the Plan.

If the world were predictable and uniform, antelopes would have wheels and communism would work.

One of Jane Jacobs's central insights about city planning is that too much planning in the usual sense increases, rather then reduces poverty, and ruins rather than improves cities. Instead of imposing a unified vision, one does better by preserving a mix of old and new buildings, appreciating the value of different neighborhoods, avoiding codes that limit a given activity to one place, and valuing local initiative. These recommendations, when first made, ran counter to the received wisdom of a discipline whose roots are utopian and whose triumphs included St. Petersburg. Utopians favor symmetry and uniformity, but a historical process produces a patchwork of asymmetric and heterogeneous parts that offend utopians' aesthetic sense. Jacobs's classic book, *The Death and Life of Great American Cities,* self-consciously presents itself as a modern application of anti-utopian thinking. Levin would have heartily approved of it.

Discounting History

I cannot summarize the ideas of all the significant thinkers who, knowing Tolstoy or not, have arrived at Tolstoyan insights about modernization. So I will focus briefly on two. James C. Scott's *Seeing Like a State: How Certain Schemes to Improve the Human Conditions Have Failed,* published in the Yale University Press Agrarian Studies Series, mentions or quotes *War and Peace* three times, each pertaining to the impossibility of scientific social planning.

Scott begins by considering the "huge development fiascos" in Eastern Europe and some Third World countries.

> But "fiasco" is too lighthearted a word for the disasters I have in mind. The Great Leap Forward in China, collectivization in Russia, and compulsory villagization in Tanzania, Mozambique, and Ethiopia are among the great human tragedies of the twentieth century. . . . At a less dramatic but far more common level, the history of Third World development is littered with the debris of huge agricultural schemes and new cities (think of Brasilia or Chandigarh) that have failed their residents. . . . I aim in what follows,

to provide a convincing account of the logic behind the failures of some of the great utopian social engineering schemes of the twentieth century. (Scott, 3–4)

What Scott calls "high modernist" ideology, which promises mastery of nature and human nature, plays a key role in these failures. High modernists display unbridled confidence that they can redesign the social and economic order according to "scientific" principles. But their supposed science is not scientific at all, since it is unskeptical and unresponsive to failed experiments. Its criteria are not evidentiary but largely aesthetic: for high modernists, "an efficient, rationally organized city, village, or farm was a city that *looked* regimented and orderly in a geometrical sense" (Scott, 4).

High modernists typically favor central planning and huge, visible schemes, like giant dams, factories, farms, and grid cities. To implement their plans, they would give vast power to state officials and theorists who develop and apply the proper ideological principles. It is no wonder, then, that intellectuals and politicians have so often found high modernist thinking appealing. After all, the more theory is needed, the more valuable are theorists, and the more state power must be used to implement the theory, the more power politicians and bureaucrats can accumulate.

High modernists characteristically express contempt for anything that has merely been thrown up by history rather than arrived at by rational means. The historical process and the heritage of the past impede scientific solutions. Received ways of thinking, local knowledge, reliance on traditional practices, and a devotion to practical reasoning all preserve superstitions. The products of history are dappled things, but the rational future is crystalline, pure, geometrical, and easily legible.

There will be no more crooked streets or crooked people. Nothing will be merely ad hoc, no concession will ever be made to local preferences, and a universal, rational method will decide everything. History is bunk.

In placing the greatest weight on the future, high modernist plans typically discount the future's uncertainty. They presume that the laws of society have at last been discovered and that they reveal everything significant to be fundamentally simple, comprehensible, and predictable.

Anyone who knows Dostoevsky and Tolstoy will recognize that this ideology was already commonplace in nineteenth-century Russia and is explicitly criticized by these two novelists. I suspect Dostoevsky became a conservative in large part because radicals professed this pseudorationalist ideology.

In *Crime and Punishment,* rationalist ideology is discussed as "socialism" (though the capitalist Luzhin also professes a bastardized version of it). Razumikhin, whose names means "reasonable" as opposed to "rational," expresses the author's critique of it. Socialists all believe that

> a social system that has come out of some mathematical brain is going to organize all humanity and make it just and sinless in an instant quicker than any living process. That's why they instinctively dislike history, "nothing but ugliness and stupidity in it," and they explain it all as stupidity. That's why they so dislike the *living* process of life; they don't want a *living soul!* . . . the soul won't obey the rules of mechanics, the soul is an object of suspicion, the soul is retrograde! . . . [But] You can't skip over nature by logic. Logic presupposes three possibilities, but there are millions! (C&P, 298–99)

Untangling the Labyrinth of Possibilities

Scott's pantheon of high modernists includes Le Corbusier, Lenin, Trotsky, Saint-Simon, Walter Rathenau, Robert Moses, Julius Nyerere, and the Shah of Iran. Saint-Simon's ideas were widely known in nineteenth-century Russia. Lenin and Trotsky fit the model of a Russian *intelligent* (member of the radical intelligentsia) satirized by Dostoevsky in *The Possessed*. In general, Russian *intelligents,* with their hubristic belief in a science of history, in extreme measures, and in the rational transformation of human psychology and natural terrain, display the characteristics of Scott's high modernists.

For Scott, Le Corbusier exemplifies high modernist ideology. When Le Corbusier's plans for the total redesign of cities were rejected by one country, they could be immediately reworked for another, since local customs, traditions, climate, even topography, were deliberately not taken into account. Neither was the existing city as it had developed "irrationally" over time. On the contrary, history and tradition were the enemies. "Architecture," Le Corbusier insisted, "is the art above all others which achieves a state of platonic grandeur, mathematical order, speculation, the perception of harmony" (Scott, 106). In remaking cities, "we must refuse to afford even the slightest concession to what is: to the mess we are in now" (Scott, 106). Proper design must above all be *legible* in the sense that cities should feature right angles, constantly repeating patterns, the complete separation of functions, and numerous similar prescriptions that became standard for city planning. What counts most is the view from the air.

Le Corbusier expressed horror of open-endedness, unforeseen change, and unsymmetrical growths: "An infinity of combinations is possible when innumerable and diverse elements are brought together. But the human mind loses itself and becomes fatigued by such a labyrinth of possibilities. Control becomes impossible. . . . Reason . . . is an unbroken straight line" (Scott, 107).

Plans on this gigantic scale require absolute state power to implement. High modernists tend toward authoritarianism because they view the mess of give-and-take politics as irrational. "The despot is not a man. It is the *Plan,*" Le Corbusier wrote, "the correct, realistic exact plan. . . . This plan has been drawn up well away from the frenzy in the mayor's office or the town hall, from the cries of the electorate or the laments of society's victims" (Scott, 112).

The century-old tree that Levin and the other landowner would build around, high modernists would immediately cut down.

Destructive Conservatism

Scott's book deals primarily with plans to rationalize agriculture, and his arguments often sound as if they were drawn from *Anna Karenina.* Scott takes his examples of disasters from twentieth-century attempts to implement plans that treat the culture of the farmer, the heritage of local practices, and the particularities of the land as irrelevant. Speaking of the failure of one such plan, concocted by American experts working in a Chicago hotel room for the Soviets, Scott observes: "The farm, unlike the plan, was not a hypothesized, generic, abstract farm but an unpredictable, complex, and particular farm, with its own unique combination of soils, social structure, administrative culture, weather, political strictures, machinery, roads, and the work skills and habits of its employees" (Scott, 201). He could almost be citing Levin's book.

In Tanzania, the World Bank and socialist ideology combined to support Julius Nyerere's *ujamaa* villages campaign, which, beginning in 1973, forcibly resettled cultivators and nomads into centrally planned villages, laid out uniformly and symmetrically along main roads. Such planning made the population legible, that is, capable of being controlled and receiving public services, while supposedly permitting all the advantages of scientific agriculture. Here again we see a definition of science that is ahistorical and essentially aesthetic. All the local variations and accommodations that made the countryside illegible and messy when viewed from the capital and by outsiders appeared to be the result of mere "destructive conservatism" (as a World Bank report maintained) rather than the accumulated wisdom of practical experience. It never occurred to the scientific planners that what works in Kansas might not work in East Africa, that local habits might represent valuable knowledge about local conditions, that farmers were not suppliers of so many interchangeable units of labor, or that agricultural specialists, for all they had to offer, might also have something to learn from the locals.

Pulled away from the lands with which they were familiar, the cultivators were de-skilled and all their experience with specific terrain was lost. The peasants had possessed a flexible repertoire of strategies, to be deployed according to countless local variables, not the least of which was their own differing needs and habits. By contrast, the centralized plan was "a static, free-frame answer to a dynamic and variegated . . . environment" (Scott, 228). *Ujamaa* villages looked orderly on a map, but placing peasants far from fields made crop watching and pest control impossible, while concentrating population and livestock led to epidemics. Ecological disaster and agricultural failure were still worse in the more brutal Ethiopian villagization, which, under Mengistu, resettled over four million people a year. But there was one government success: as in Russia after collectivization, the rural population (or what was left of it) was a lot more controllable.

Disciplines

My second thinker who has arrived at Tolstoyan insights about modernization is the philosopher Stephen Toulmin. As it happens, Toulmin and I have often discussed *Anna Karenina,* his favorite novel. He has thought about Tolstoy's influence on other thinkers, notably Isaiah Berlin and Ludwig Wittgenstein.

Like Levin, Toulmin argues against the universalizing aspirations of social science, while pointing out how the logic of disciplines tends to exclude contrary evidence. "Too often. . . . any assumption that the standard methods of economic analysis are applicable similarly to all situations introduces distortions that we can escape only by 'de-universalizing' them, and limiting their application to well-recognized and carefully analyzed conditions" (RtR, 60).

Toulmin offers the example of Balinese agriculture, which was governed for eight hundred years by a system of water temples whose priests controlled irrigation schedules. In the late 1960s and early 1970s, the Indonesian government introduced new strains of a miracle rice. It instructed farmers to abandon traditional planting methods and the temple irrigation system went out of use. As in many of Scott's stories, crop yields initially soared, but in a few years insect pests and funguses multiplied. Foreign consultants found it hard to accept that abandoning traditional practices contributed to the disaster because to do so would mean admitting the efficacy of priests and prayers. Importing a foreign way of thinking, expert opinion classed the water temples as purely religious, whereas they had served a real agricultural function. However the Balinese may have explained the temples, traditional irrigation practices reflected centuries of trial-and-error experience. Toulmin observes: "Professionals who are committed to particular disciplines . . . too easily assume that economic and technical issues can be *abstracted* from the situation in which they are put to use, and so can be defined in purely disciplinary terms" (RtR, 65).

No more than Levin does Toulmin advise abandoning technological improvement. He means that to make those improvements successfully planners must take into account local conditions, experiential knowledge, and "the elemental force." The Bali modernization plan erred first by disregarding these factors and then by proceeding rapidly on a massive scale. The more one regards the future as uncertain and allows for unanticipated consequences, the more cautiously one acts. Assuming friction and unforeseeable obstacles, one starts on a small scale, looks for problems, and tries out corrections before slowly introducing reforms to a larger area. Instead of trusting the plan as one would rely on physical laws, one accumulates experience and adapts. Instead of rationalizing, one tinkers.

As the family of successful peasants in *Anna Karenina* introduces new methods, so eventually Bali arrived at a compromise including both the water temples and new varieties of rice. The way to improve local conditions is to make new methods available and then allow people to choose ones they recognize as both superior and conformable to existing practice. One respects local knowledge and the power of the elemental force.

War and Peace vs. *Anna Karenina*

Between *War and Peace* and *Anna Karenina* Tolstoy's approach to reform changed. Levin's approach to agriculture partly resembles but also significantly differs from Nikolai Rostov's:

> Nikolai was a plain farmer: he did not like innovations, especially those from England, which were then coming into vogue; he laughed at theoretical treatises on agriculture . . . he always kept before him the estate as a whole. . . The chief thing to his mind was not the nitrogen in the soil, the oxygen in the air, nor any special plow or manure, but the peasants who worked the land. (W&P, 1370)

At first Nikolai only pretends to manage, while in fact learning peasant habits, methods, practices, and opinions. He familiarizes himself with the peasants' forms of expression and the hidden meanings behind their words. Only then does he begin to manage in earnest. He appoints as bailiff the very person the peasants would have chosen. He works to keep families together, to reward work and punish laziness, and to make sure peasant crops succeed as well as his own. This method produces "the most brilliant results" (W&P, 1370).

All these practices resemble Levin's, except that Nikolai cares nothing for better technology. Nikolai succeeds because he respects the elemental force but he does not even try to modernize. By contrast, Levin learns that respecting local practices not only produces good results but also offers the best way to introduce superior methods.

Speed

Like modernization, other reforms can succeed if and only if they are carried out in the right way.

One may object that Levin's position insures that change happens slowly. People simply cannot wait for such a patient procedure to operate. Levin might reply that "fast" reforms are even slower because they usually do not work and are often counterproductive. Adjusting the flight plan and changing the speedometer do not shorten the journey.

In *The Gulag Archipelago,* Alexander Solzhenitsyn cites a revolutionary proclamation of 1862 that calls for terrorism because "we cannot afford delay—we need speedy, immediate action!" Solzhenitsyn replies:

> What a false path! They, the zealots, could not afford to wait, and so they sanctioned human sacrifice. . . . to bring universal happiness nearer! They could not afford to wait, and so we, their great-grandsons, are not at the same point as they were . . . but much further behind. (Solzhenitsyn, 91)

Levin's Idea, Its Corollaries and Analogues: Self-improvement, Christian Love, Counterfeit Art, and Authentic Thinking

Anna Karenina explores and extends the implication's of Levin's ideas. They link diverse passages of the book and, seriously considered, constitute Tolstoyan advice for living better lives.

After examining some obstacles to thinking more wisely, the present chapter considers (1) Kitty's attempt to become a better person and self-improvement generally, (2) Karenin's Christian love and why he cannot maintain it, (3) the distinction between fake and true art clarified in the Mikhailov scene, and (4) the difference between fake and true thinking, as described in Levin's intellectual encounters with Sergey Ivanovich, Stiva, and Svyazhsky.

Extending Levin's Idea

Levin's book on agriculture suggests a number of conclusions. Social reform must respect the elemental force and proceed from the bottom up. Theory must be regarded as a series of tentative generalizations from practice and must never dictate to practice. Experience on the ground with specific problems must guide experiments with new practices, which must in turn be modified in light of unforeseeable results. Expect to tinker. Over time, successful change will look not like a planned city but like a patchwork of jury-rigged solutions layered one on another. Because local culture matters, too much uniformity in one's prescriptions will prove a hindrance. One needs wisdom as well as science, and practical knowledge counts more than theory. Anything utopian will fail. Except on rare occasions, think like Aristotle and Montaigne, not like Plato and Leibniz. Unless there is strong evidence to the contrary, take the future as radically uncertain, to the point where one cannot even assign statistical probabilities. Maintain flexibility. Overspecialization works only in a world of certainty and only over the short run until the unexpected presents itself.

On the whole and for the most part, plans are slowed, diverted, frustrated, or reversed by friction. Nothing is pure, and everything is interrupted. Most resistance comes not from conspiracy but just "for some reason." It is unwise to presume that difficulties proceed from a contrary intention, whether of an opponent or of one's own unconscious. Of course, intentional opposition exists, but resistance arises without it, from friction, habit, and the elemental force.

Above all, changes that take and enable future changes must respect initial conditions. One cannot simply impose a theoretically derived template or a model copied from elsewhere.

Where questions of morality are involved, change by template is likely to prove not only unsuccessful but also hypocritical. It virtually guarantees insincerity, artifice, self-deception, or deception of others.

When originality is desired, templates create only its counterfeit. Instead of real thinking, they give us pseudothought, and instead of genuine art, mere novelty. Tolstoy possessed the keenest sense for the fake, in behavior, in art, and in thought. He wants to teach us to recognize it, to understand its appeal, and to reject it in spite of all its charms.

As the political advocacy or self-help sections of chain bookstores illustrate, it is all too easy to invent schemes for reform or self-improvement that flatter one into self-righteousness. The formula for successful writing in these genres satisfies the reader's desire to be morally superior by insinuating that in the very act of reading, he or she already is. All you need to do is more of what you are already doing. Just clear away the debris, and the straight path is obvious. Those with saleable formulae tell us how easily the right rules can teach spontaneity, model sincerity, and insure originality.

Rules can show students how to imitate good literature, but not how to be creative. They at best offer tools useful when one already is creative. Enough talent and practice can teach people to copy a school of thought, but not to think. Teaching people to master a theory with its accompanying vocabulary and rhetorical moves is the easiest thing of all, as so many graduate programs in the humanities demonstrate. But really to better oneself, to be creative, and to think through a problem with genuine concern for the truth: these complex actions are a lot harder—or so Tolstoy would have us believe.

Three Ways Not to Answer

Levin unwittingly applies his insights in the process of arriving at them. His core idea is that in order to reform one must begin with experience and follow it wherever it may lead, and he does so in correcting his own thoughts. His idiosyncratic ideas develop idiosyncratically. Levin really wants to discover the best solution to social problems, not to show how much he knows or how progressive he is. He discovers that in this respect he is almost unique.

When Levin presents his ideas to others, they sometimes classify them as belonging to one or another school instead of hearing what he is saying. Or they reply: "But Kaufmann, but Jones, but Dubois, but Micelli? You haven't read them: they've thrashed out that question thoroughly" (362). Tolstoy has here invented a German, an Englishman, a Frenchman, and an Italian, foreign authorities who can be named without specifying how their ideas apply. We might call this sort of answer the *argument by bibliography*, a fallacy that readers today may recognize.

Such replies insure against confronting any facts one has not already learned to explain away. Levin encounters another avoidance maneuver when, upon arriving in Moscow, he drops in on Sergey Ivanovich. Levin finds his half-brother with an irritable professor who has come all the way from Kharkov to debate a question "then in vogue: Is there a line to be drawn between psychological and physiological phenomena in man, and if so, where?" (27). That question, differently phrased, is still in vogue, and perhaps always will be, so long as materialism purports to account for conscious human life. Are our thoughts and actions totally reducible to physiological, neurological, or chemical phenomena? Or do we have a mind irreducible to the brain? Is there a realm of choice and meaning beyond the reach of causal explanation? Levin grasps both sides of this issue. As a student of natural science, he understands the reductionist paradigm. On the other hand, as a person increasingly troubled by questions of meaning, he intimates that this paradigm cannot address what really matters in life.

As Levin listens to the discussion, "he noticed that they connected these scientific questions with the spiritual, that at times they almost touched on the latter; but every time they came near what seemed to him the chief point, they promptly beat a hasty retreat, and plunged again into a sea of subtle distinctions, reservations, quotations, allusions and appeals to authorities, and it was with difficulty that he understood what they were talking about" (28). Such evasions are always with us. For academics, questions that really matter seem hopelessly naïve, and so academic discourse comes to resemble an intellectual game, like the chess problems that engage Sergey Ivanovich.

It pretends to thought when there is little thinking.

Sergey Ivanovich maintains the antimaterialist position, but he shows no appreciation that it matters beyond intellectual debate. The professor paraphrases the opposing side, maintained by "Wurst, and Knaust, and Pripasov," a triumvirate that has become a Russian byword. Arguments by authority typically display a similar structure. These Russians from the 1870s cite two Germans and a Russian, and today we Americans would perhaps cite two Frenchmen and an American.

Levin at last decides to force the important question they have been avoiding: "'According to that, if my senses are annihilated, if my body is dead, I can have no existence of any sort?' he queried" (28). The question is a faux pas:

The professor, in annoyance, looking as though the interruption had caused him great suffering, glanced at the strange inquirer, more like a bargeman than a philosopher, and turned his eyes upon Sergey Ivanovich, as though to ask: What's one to say to him? But Sergey Ivanovich, who had been talking with far less heat and one-sidedness than the professor, and who had sufficient breadth of mind to answer the professor, and at the same time to comprehend the simple and natural point of view from which the question was put, smiled and said:

"That question we have no right to answer as yet."

"We have not the requisite data," chimed in the professor, and he went back to his argument. (28–29)

In this scene, Levin experiences the condescension of those who have let disciplinary formulae replace real thought. The two intellectuals reply as we literature professors might answer a student who asked how Tolstoy's or Shakespeare's or George Eliot's ideas might speak to their worries about how to live. We smile and let them know, as kindly as we can, that such questions are childish. Thus, in addition to argument by bibliography, intellectuals use *the argument by disciplinary exclusion,* which classes unprofessional concerns as naïve. We demonstrate sophistication by what we do *not* ask.

The most common answer Levin receives whenever he presents his ideas or questions is a form of *argument by association,* a kind of name-calling. Dear Kostya, those are the objections a conservative would raise, and you don't want to be mistaken for one of them, do you? This kind of answer irritates Levin, as it plainly irritated Tolstoy, because it excludes contrary evidence on principle. No matter how logically deficient one's position might be and no matter how clearly experience seems to falsify it, one does not have to consider these shortcomings because the mere mention of them betrays reactionary sympathies. "'You're a reactionary, I see," says Stiva to refute Levin, who replies: "Really, I have never considered what I am. I am Konstantin Levin, and nothing else" (181).

Anna teaches herself to exclude contrary evidence in order to assuage her guilt and allow herself to do what she wants. The intellectuals in the novel use analogous means to avoid questions they do not want to answer or objections they do not want to entertain. These parallel forms of cultivated non-seeing constitute an important link between the novel's two major stories.

Kitty and Self-improvement

As Kitty learns about love from her mistake with Vronsky, she learns about self-improvement from her experience with Madame Stahl. Though she does not know it, her lesson resembles Levin's idea about social reform and extends it in interesting ways.

After the ball, Kitty falls ill. Her illness is plainly moral. It expresses shame that she has shown her love to a man who carelessly dismissed it. She regrets that she refused the man she should have accepted, and she feels guilty for having hurt him. Anna, whom she has trusted, has played her false. Reflecting on her own behavior, Kitty has come to see the ritual of flirting and courtship as a shameless display of goods for sale. Aware that she herself has used her prettiness to entice, she becomes repulsed by the very thought of Stiva. She no longer understands the proper role of sexuality in a good life and, out of her own shame and confusion, insults Dolly for returning to her husband.

Kitty craves something to live for other than the pursuit of a husband. At the spa, she imagines that she has found it in philanthropy. Tolstoy, like Dostoevsky, Dickens, and other novelists, understands how self-deception may accompany a sincere desire to help others. But Kitty is still too young to suspect her own motives. She also has not learned that one cannot become a better person by copying a model or imitating someone else.

Improvement by copying: Kitty's efforts repeat the mistake that Levin has identified. As the landowners are trying to Westernize Russia, she is trying to "philanthropize" herself. Both select a model that appears good and, without taking into account existing conditions, decide to impose it by assiduous imitation.

One cannot become better by template, and one cannot simply graft another personality or another set of social institutions onto one's own. Whatever is, resists. In both the individual and social cases, one runs into the elemental force. Each person, no less than each society, possesses a sum total of habits, dispositions, attitudes, and practices that, in their cumulative effect, frustrate any attempt simply to copy the virtues of another. Just as successful social reforms must proceed from the bottom up and develop potentials already present, so an individual can improve morally only by becoming a better version of who she already is.

Better practices must not depart too far from existing ones. Massive transformation cannot be achieved by a concerted act of will. For one thing, there is no single core to all our habits any more than there is a single underlying law accounting for all social practices. For another, will, like reforming ardor, flags. Each new set of habits must be acquired slowly. Once it takes, it may allow for unpredictable new opportunities for improvement, and so on, in a direction that is anything but straight or foreseeable.

Kitty does not understand these truths, and so she adopts Madame Stahl's views wholesale and copies everything Mademoiselle Varenka does. Kitty even imitates Varenka "in her manner of walking, of talking, of blinking her eyes"

(237). She tends to the sick and, like Madame Stahl, reads the Gospel in French. When Kitty's mother tells her (also in French) not to take things to extremes, Kitty thinks "that one could not talk about overdoing it where Christianity was concerned. How could one go too far in the practice of a doctrine wherein one was bidden to turn the other cheek when one was smitten, and give one's cloak if one's coat were taken?" (238). Change by copying tends to extremism because the restraining factor—consciousness of the impossibility of making any desired change at will—is absent. The dream of imitating Madame Stahl's niece by spending her life reading the Gospel to the sick, the criminals, and the dying, fascinates Kitty. Of course, such an occupation would run counter to her natural health, life force, and devotion to family, and she could not do it successfully, but she still imagines she can simply choose whatever ideal appears best. If it works for Aline Stahl or for Varenka, she thinks, why not for me?

Despite her enthusiasm, Kitty remains a Shcherbatsky, attentive to the details of life. In spite of herself, she notices contrary evidence. "Elevated as Madame Stahl's character was, touching as was her story, and exalted and moving as was her speech, Kitty could not help detecting some traits that perplexed her" (237). She sees Madame Stahl smile contemptuously, keep her face in the shadow when talking with a priest, and respond irritably to Mademoiselle Varenka. What most disturbs Kitty is that her own attempts to help one family, the Petrovs, have actually sown dissension between husband and wife. This outcome recalls Levin's insight that reform by copying often proves not just unproductive but counterproductive. In her philanthropic zeal, Kitty has made things worse, and she has begun to suspect as much.

When Kitty's father returns from a trip, he finds her new infatuations disturbing. His wisdom will serve as the catalyst for Kitty's insights, but Tolstoy characteristically describes the source of that wisdom as impure. The old prince is troubled by "his habitual feeling of jealousy of everything that drew his daughter away from him, and a dread that his daughter might have got out of the reach of his influence into regions inaccessible to him" (240). And yet, despite his jealousy, he cannot be false. He is eager to mock both Madame Stahl and Varenka, but when he meets Varenka he realizes that she is no fake. "Kitty saw that her father had meant to make fun of Varenka, but that he could not do it because he liked her" (242).

All of us may be troubled by jealousy, and many characters in this novel— Anna, Kitty, Levin, Karenin, and others—experience its effects. The old prince is honest and self-aware enough not to let jealousy find nothing but confirmation of its suspicions.

Madame Stahl is not Varenka, and Kitty's father has little trouble exposing her. Come, we will meet her if she sees fit to recognize me, he tells Kitty, and when Kitty asks in surprise if he already knows her, he replies that he knew

Madame Stahl and her husband before she joined the Pietists. "'What's a Pietist, Papa?' asked Kitty, dismayed to find that what she prized so highly in Madame Stahl had a name" (242).

Why should it matter that it has a name? The answer is that the behavior and attitudes Kitty has taken as sincere may have been put on like a uniform. If what Madame Stahl does and professes has a name, then it may have come ready-made, not from the heart but off the philanthropic shelf. Not only does this possibility add to Kitty's doubts about Madame Stahl, but it also implies that Kitty herself may have adopted Madame Stahl's beliefs readymade as Madame Stahl has adopted Pietism. Imitation begets imitation.

Just at this point, Kitty and her father run into the Petrovs, and Kitty grows painfully aware that in adopting something "with a name" she has wound up doing harm. When they at last meet Madame Stahl, Kitty is ready to see her as a none too skillful actress:

> "You are scarcely changed at all," the prince said to her [Madame Stahl]. "It's ten or eleven years since I had the honor of seeing you."
>
> "Yes; God sends the cross and sends the strength to bear it. One often wonders what the goal of this life is? . . . The other side!" she said angrily to Varenka, who had rearranged the comforter over her feet, not to her satisfaction.
>
> "To do good, probably," said the prince with a twinkle in his eye.
>
> "That is not for us to judge," said Madame Stahl, perceiving the shade of expression on the prince's face. (244)

After Kitty and her father leave Madame Stahl, the prince enters into discussion with a Moscow colonel who asks him if he knew Madame Stahl before illness left her unable to stand on her feet. The exchange that follows shows the prince taking a bit too much delight in unmasking an enemy and yet uttering a profound truth:

> "She doesn't stand up because her legs are too short. She had a very bad figure."
>
> "Papa, it's not possible!" cried Kitty.
>
> "That's what wicked tongues say, my darling. And your Varenka catches it too," he added. "Oh, these invalid ladies!"
>
> "Oh, no, Papa!" Kitty objected warmly. "Varenka worships her. And then she does so much good! Ask anyone! Everyone knows her and Aline Stahl."
>
> "Perhaps so," said the prince, pressing her hand with his elbow; "but it's better when one does good in such a manner that no one knows of it." (244)

The prince is reminding Kitty of a Gospel passage that she and Madame Stahl have evidently not taken to heart:

> Take heed that ye do not your alms before men, to be seen of them: otherwise ye have no reward of your Father which is in heaven. Therefore, when thou doest thine alms, do not sound a trumpet before thee, as the hypocrites do in the synagogues and in the streets, that they may have glory of men. Verily, I say unto you, They have their reward. But when thou doest alms, let not thy left hand know what thy right hand doeth: that thine alms may be in secret . . . (Matthew 6:1–4)

It would be hard to find a Gospel passage more in the spirit of this novel. Proper charity has no history. All genuine charitable acts resemble each other, but each fake charitable act is fake in its own way. Whatever proclaims itself, whatever is most dramatic and visible, is false. Goodness lies in deeds we do not even notice. It belongs not to Madame Stahl but to Dolly.

Dolly does not sound a trumpet. And readers of this novel need to seek important events not where they call most attention to themselves but where they are openly camouflaged. Indeed, despite its centrality to the novel, this very passage from the Gospel appears only by allusion. Unlike the epigraph, or the lines from the Sermon on the Mount spoken by Karenin, it is not cited. Just as this book's title names only the most dramatic story and omits the others, so its epigraph easily overshadows the Gospel passage that, in its significant absence, is so easily overlooked.

The Fake Way to Avoid Being Fake

Kitty becomes so disappointed in herself that she falls into a childish fury. It serves me right, she keeps saying, and when Varenka asks what she means, Kitty answers: "It serves me right because it was all false; because it was all pretense and not from the heart . . . it was all a fake! A fake! A fake!! [*pritvorstvo*]" (248). I was totally false, she repeats, "in order to seem better to people, to myself, to God, to deceive everyone. Now I won't descend to that. I'll be bad; but anyway not a liar, a cheat." (248)

Kitty has gone from one extreme to another. Of course she was not *totally* false. And the proper reaction to a failure to improve is not to resolve to be bad. Such "honesty," like Stiva's, is itself fake, and Kitty rapidly recovers from it. She calms down, and then Kitty "did not give up everything she had learned, but she became aware that she had deceived herself in supposing she could be what she wanted to be" (249).

Levin does not decide that because the usual methods of reform have failed he might as well give up, and Kitty understands that, although she has tried to improve herself in the wrong way, she can still become a better version of herself. She retains her skills at nursing, as we see when she helps Nikolai Levin. She has also learned a lesson about faith. In Part Eight, when Levin worries about being a nonbeliever, Kitty smiles at such a view because, regardless of what doctrines he professes, Levin lives a life of faith. Better an unbeliever like Kostya, Kitty says to herself, than a believer like Madame Stahl "or what I tried to be in those days abroad" (818).

Karenin and Christian Love

So far as I know, only two books in world literature have described a conversion to Christian love — in the full sense of actually loving one's enemies — in a way that is psychologically convincing. Tolstoy wrote them both.

In *War and Peace,* Prince Andrei comes to love his enemy Anatol Kuragin. Andrei has long sought an epic heroism that transcends ordinary human courage, and he at last finds a Christian heroism that leaves epic itself far behind. In *Anna Karenina,* the notably unheroic Karenin, who at first glance seems incapable of deep feeling, becomes the unlikely object of a conversion he has not sought.

Indeed, this kind of conversion cannot be successfully sought. If one resolves to love one's enemy out of principle or because one is a Christian, one will at best achieve a pretense of love. So Ivan Karamazov insists when he mentions a saint who took a loathsome beggar, putrid with some disease, into his arms: "I am convinced he did that from 'self-laceration,' from the self-laceration of falsity, for the sake of the charity imposed by duty, as a penance on him. . . . To my thinking, Christ-like love for men is a miracle impossible on earth. He was God. But we are not gods" (BK, 281). Dostoevsky repeatedly tried to disprove this argument against the possibility of Christian love. By describing a conversion that is psychologically plausible, Dostoevsky reasoned, he would show that Christian love is at least possible. For if it were not, then any psychological portrait would seem false. Unfortunately, as Dostoevsky well knew, he never could make a conversion ring true.

Dostoevsky at first planned *The Idiot* as a novel about such a conversion, but, unable to make the change believable, he at last abandoned this plot and started with an "idiot" who was already a Christ figure. His notebooks testify to his struggle with the perverse facts of human psychology he understood better than anyone. To Dostoevsky's dismay, his psychology kept triumphing over his Christianity. He declined to offer a less than plausible description of a conversion not only because he did not want to ruin his work but also because, by his own reasoning, to do so would be to admit tacitly that no more plausible description could be given. One can only imagine the mixture of emotions he experienced when writing his reviews of *Anna Karenina.*

One cannot become a saint by imitating *the* Lives of the Saints, and one cannot love one's enemies out of the conviction one should do so. Imitation and prescription lead not to love but to sanctimony. How then does such a conversion take place? Before considering how Levin's ideas illuminate why Karenin cannot maintain his Christian love, I would like to consider the extraordinary way in which Tolstoy makes that love believable in the first place.

Tolstoy uses two techniques, one of which appears in *War and Peace* and one of which is new. In both novels he extends his trademark method of describing the tiny, tiny alterations of consciousness. Each tiny step is plausible, and so we reach the end point without ever having to take a leap. Having granted each step, we grant the conclusion.

The Sound of Listening

In *Anna Karenina,* Tolstoy often employs a technique that fits his theme that looking and listening are actions. He invites us to imagine what one character experiences when listening to another. Or he encourages us to imagine a character's reaction if he or she could eavesdrop on another's thoughts. Whether the listening act is real or potential, we are asked to fill in what the author leaves tacit. Tolstoy uses this method with special effectiveness in describing Karenin's conversion.

How does an author extend an invitation to imagine how a character listens or would listen? One way is to paraphrase a mistaken guess about that reaction. As we identify the mistake, we may also fill in a more likely reaction.

When Karenin prepares to talk with Anna about how she behaved with Vronsky at Betsy's, he is comically wrong in guessing her response. As he enters her room, he shrinks in horror at the knick-knacks suggesting an inner life separate from his and at the awful possibility that she might love someone else. "To put himself in thought and feeling in another person's place was a spiritual exercise not natural to Aleksey Aleksandrovich" and he draws back; but we may imagine what he does not and the way she would react to these very thoughts.

In the opening passage where Stiva reflects on his "truthfulness," we not only hear what Stiva thinks but also imagine how Dolly would listen. Stiva supposes that he might have concealed his indiscretion more carefully had he anticipated Dolly's reaction. He has erred in guessing that she must have long known about his infidelities and chosen to view them as he would like. To his surprise, Dolly has reacted with horror to her discovery; and we may ask how she would react if she could overhear this very expression of surprise or the whole inner monologue in which it appears.

As we hear Stiva's musings, we may fill in Dolly's potential reactions:

> He could not at this date feel repentant that he, a handsome, woman-prone man of thirty-four, was not in love with his wife, the mother of five living and two dead children, and only a year younger than himself. . . . He had never clearly thought out the subject, but he had . . . even supposed that she, a worn-out woman no longer young or good-looking, and in no way remarkable or interesting, merely a good mother, ought from a sense of fairness to take an indulgent view. It had turned out quite the other way. (5–6)

"It had turned out the other way": the humor of the passage, and of the last line, depends on our imagining what Stiva has not. Think of Dolly becoming aware that Stiva is "not in love" with her, regards her as unattractive, thinks of the living and dead children in terms of their effect on her body, and, above all, understands good mothering as something to preface with "merely." If Dolly knew these thoughts, her reaction to them would be much stronger than her reaction to the infidelity itself. She would learn Stiva's contemptible values and so could not possibly accept the picture Anna paints of the incident. In fact, Dolly does eventually learn how Stiva thinks, so the potential in this passage becomes realized.

In describing Karenin's conversion, Tolstoy combines his psychology of small changes with a particularly effective invitation to imagine a series of listening acts. If we do not accept that invitation, we will not see how Tolstoy makes the conversation psychologically plausible.

The Terror of Pity

The chapter describing Karenin's conversion begins by mentioning Dolly's advice that, as a Christian, he should forgive an unfaithful spouse. This advice annoys Karenin: "The applicability or nonapplicability of the Christian precept to his own case was a question . . . that had long been answered by Aleksey Aleksandrovich in the negative" (430). The bureaucratic language, of course, indicates that this third-person passage paraphrases Karenin's own inner speech, which the author tinges with irony. Although Karenin has rejected responding with Christian love, the thought of it is present to him as the chapter begins.

Karenin has never sufficiently understood what he considers a "weakness, opposed to the general trend of his character" (294). "None but those who were most intimate" with him—his wife, the chief secretary of his department, his private secretary—know that Aleksey Aleksandrovich is so deeply moved by the sight of a woman's or child's tears that he cannot master his reactions. His secretary warns women with petitions not to give way to tears because Karenin, experiencing a severe emotional disturbance he cannot control, will become angry and throw the petitioner out of his office.

Karenin's reaction to the tears of others demonstrates yet again that he is not unfeeling, but unable to master his feelings. Karenin fears above all the loss of control, a condition he regards as a combination of madness, childishness, and shameful exposure of all that is most intimate. His fear of suffering doubles his suffering. In the same way, when he thinks of a duel, he experiences not just cowardice but also "dread of his own cowardice" (296) and not just terror but also terror of being terrified. Anna in childbirth fever asserts that although it is hard to understand Karenin, he feels deeply and is capable of real forgiveness. She knows that he maintains a cold surface precisely because of the deep emotionality that he conceals from himself as well as from others.

On the way home from the races, Anna bursts into tears and tells Karenin in as coarse a way as possible that she hates him and is Vronsky's mistress. Karenin experiences two contradictory emotions. He is predictably angry, but he also feels "a rush of that emotional disturbance always produced in him by tears" (295). Anger and pity strangely mix in a way he cannot understand. He reacts by trying to suppress "every manifestation of life" in himself so as to betray no feeling at all. His face assumes a death-like rigidity that testifies not to indifference, cruelty, or cold anger, but to the fear that an inappropriate pity will lead him to lose control of himself.

The Accompanying Message

Part Four, chapter 17 begins with Karenin's reflections about the dinner at which Dolly implores him to forgive.

At the dinner, Dolly at first reacts to Karenin as so many readers do: she views him as a "cold, unfeeling man who was so calmly intending to ruin her innocent friend" (413). But Karenin explains that Anna has herself declared her infidelity and then, giving way to his feeling so that his "tongue was being loosened in spite of himself," he tells Dolly from the heart that he would give anything for doubt still to be possible. Dolly's sympathies shift. "I am very unhappy," he says, but "he had no need to say that. Darya Aleksandrovna had seen that as soon as he glanced into her face; and she felt sorry for him, and her faith in the innocence of her friend began to totter" (414). The more he describes his experience, so similar to her own, the more she feels for him and the more her sympathies shift from Anna to him. "Darya Aleksandrovna at that moment pitied him with all her heart" (415). Because Dolly serves as the moral compass of the book, her shift in sympathies implicitly directs readers to reconsider any partiality for Anna.

When Karenin recalls the dinner, he sets aside Dolly's advice to forgive and thinks instead of a guest's thoughtless comment. Turovtsyn praised a husband who "acted like a man," challenged his wife's lover to a duel, and shot him. Karenin imagines that everyone tacitly shared this feeling, so he feels shame that he will not fight a duel. In his own eyes, his wife's behavior has demeaned his manliness and his fear of a duel lowers it still more. Karenin's shame fuels his resentment.

Karenin's secretary brings him two telegrams, the first about his political career and the second about Anna's severe illness. Other novelists would have avoided diluting the effect of Anna's dramatic message with another about a quite different topic, but Tolstoy knows that even the most important events never take place by themselves. They happen, as Auden writes, "While someone else is eating or opening a window or just walking dully along" (Auden, 198). In Part Five, Levin simultaneously receives two letters, an unsurprising one from Dolly and another saying that Levin's brother is dying. The same technique, which might be called the *accompanying message,* appears repeatedly in *War and Peace.* Even when facing execution, irrelevant thoughts occur to Pierre, and Tolstoy corrects those who imagine a commander can just contemplate the facts and then make a reasoned decision. Such a picture omits the interruptions that constantly take place, the requests that must be answered, and the many decisions that must be made at the same time. The most important news usually comes accompanied by noise. We hear the voice crying in the wilderness over a distracting tune from the radio.

The Stages of Comprehension

What links the two telegrams is Karenin's reaction to them. The emotion provoked by the first shapes the reception of the second. By chance, Karenin first opens the telegram informing him that his political enemy Stremov has received the post Karenin has coveted. Karenin reacts with disappointment and, perhaps, a further sense of humiliation. He opens the second telegram imagining it contains some similar message. Noticing that it is from Anna, Karenin must recall the resentment and shame he just felt when thinking about the dinner. The two telegrams have thus far contributed to Karenin's feelings of helplessness and impotence.

Anna's message is brief and clear enough that other novelists would have simply described Karenin's reaction, but Tolstoy divides that reaction into distinct steps. He therefore allows us to assess Karenin's emotions at each tiny moment of comprehension. Still thinking of the news about Stremov, Karenin first sees Anna's signature, which for some reason is in blue pencil, and realizes that the telegram is from her. We may guess the effect her name has on him and the vague sense of oddity evoked by the blue pencil. Only then does he read: "I am dying; I beg, I implore you to come. I shall die easier with your forgiveness" (431).

Karenin immediately judges the message to be a trick. "Of that there could be no doubt," he thinks, and so we realize that he does doubt. He is reacting out of anger and knows it. Unsure of his judgment, he must insist to himself that it is correct. If Karenin's suggestion of trickery seems gratuitous, we may recall that later in the book Anna sends Vronsky a telegram that falsely asserts that their daughter is ill in order to force his immediate return.

Karenin next justifies his guess that the telegram is a trick. He tells himself there is no deceit she would not try. But a trick requires a purpose and so he asks himself what Anna's aim could be? To legitimize the child, prevent a divorce, compromise him? But Karenin's journey would accomplish none of these things. Unable to answer his own question, his mind returns to the actual words of the telegram. "But something was said in it: 'I am dying . . .' He read the telegram again and suddenly the plain meaning of what it said struck him" (431).

Karenin has already read the line and understood it; if he had not, he could not have asked himself why she would be pretending to be dying. But although he has understood it, he has not really understood it until he reads it for the second time. Tolstoy knows that the process of comprehending even the simplest and most straightforward statement takes place in stages. Understanding the literal meaning, and then some of the significance, does not yet entail understanding even "the plain meaning" of the words, much less their implications. Each small deduction requires a modicum of attention, energy, and effort, and will not be drawn until that requirement is met.

Because Tolstoy describes the comprehension in stages, we can see how Karenin accuses Anna, suspects his accusation, accuses her again, and only then realizes what the words say. He has gone through a process in which he has angrily made what will turn out to be a false accusation, and the memory of this injustice will produce guilt. If Tolstoy had depicted Karenin understanding the plain meaning of the words at a glance, there would be no guilt over a mistaken guess.

Wishing Her Dead

At last understanding Anna's words, Karenin now entertains the possibility that they are true. He thinks: suppose that, approaching death, she is genuinely penitent and I, imagining a trick, refuse to go. That would be both cruel and stupid.

Karenin calls a coach. He decides that if her illness is a trick, he will say nothing and go away, but if she "really is ill and near death and wishes to see me before death," then "he would forgive her if he found her alive, and pay her the last duties if he came too late" (431). I quote these words, which trace the sequence of Karenin's thoughts, because double mention of the word death (missing in the English translation) leads Karenin to dwell on the prospect of her dying. We detect what he soon will realize: that he wishes her dead. Now he wants to believe the message is *not* a trick.

After spending the night on the train, Karenin takes a coach to the house. He tries not to imagine what he might find. "He could not think about it, because in picturing what would happen he could not drive away the reflection that her death would at once remove all the difficulty of his position" (431). Karenin has evidently several times pictured her death and found himself wishing for it. Knowing that such a wish is immoral, he has fought his own thoughts.

Because the phrase "remove all the difficulties of his position" sounds official, we may read this sentence as a paraphrase of Karenin's inner speech. If we do, then we may also reflect that Karenin does not ask himself how the birth of an infant not his own will affect his position. He is entirely focused on the death he desires and the effort not to desire it.

As Anna in her final coach ride notices all the shops, so Karenin sees the changing street signs. For her, everything says the same thing, and for him everything serves as a distraction from the one thing he is trying not to think about. When he arrives at the house, he first sees a sleigh and a carriage with a coachman asleep in it. He must be asking himself who is there. Of course, if she is ill, a doctor would be present, but who else? Could one of the vehicles belong to Vronsky? Such a thought must revive Karenin's feelings of jealousy while creating humiliation and simple fear that he will meet Vronsky. Karenin draws "resolution from the deepest corner of his brain," tells himself that if she is dying he must do what is proper, and enters.

The porter who opens the door looks strange without a tie and in an old coat and slippers; the night has evidently been busy. Karenin asks "how is your mistress?" and the sleepy porter answers truthfully, but misleadingly: "Safely delivered yesterday." By not mentioning the most important fact, that Anna is near death, this idiotic answer implies that she is well. Drawing this conclusion, Karenin turns white. "He felt distinctly now how intensely he had longed for her death" (432). He can no longer have any doubts about that wish or its intensity. When he is told that Anna is indeed very ill, Karenin feels "some relief at the news that there was still hope of her death" (432). This phrase tells us what

Karenin himself is experiencing: he is quite aware of the relief he feels. He has lost the struggle to suppress his wish that she die.

When he sees a military overcoat on the hatstand, Karenin learns, and the servant confirms, that Vronsky is in the house. Karenin next encounters the midwife, who leads him to the bedroom "with the familiarity given by the approach of death" (432), an expression it would take Tolstoy to note but which Karenin must sense. He must feel the wish for her death all the more strongly until the midwife tells him that Anna has been constantly asking for him. Can it therefore be true that she is penitent? If so, is it not wrong for him to be wishing her dead?

When Karenin enters the bedroom, his first sight is of Vronsky, "his face hidden in his hands, weeping." We know how much Karenin is affected by the sight of a woman's tears: how much more must he be moved to see a man cry, and not just any man but an officer, and not just any officer but his wife's lover. Vronsky draws his head into his shoulders as if he wants to disappear, tells Karenin that the doctors say there is no hope of Anna's recovery, and begs to be allowed to stay. What must Karenin be feeling at the sight of Vronsky's humiliating posture? He has anticipated that Vronsky might shame him, not that Vronsky himself would be humiliated, nor that Vronsky would be in his power, nor that Vronsky would actually beg. Everything has been turned upside down.

The sight of tears, especially these tears, must elicit an especially strong sense of pity in Karenin and the role reversal must provoke both confusion and triumph. The news that there is no hope must again make Karenin aware of his strong desire for his wife's death. These four emotions—pity, confusion, triumph, and hope for her death—overwhelm him. "Aleksey Aleksandrovich, seeing Vronsky's tears, felt a rush of that nervous emotion always produced in him by the sight of other people's sufferings" (432–33). He turns away and moves to the door of the bedroom.

As he approaches the door, he hears Anna's voice "saying something," a phrase indicating we are following Karenin's perceptions. He goes to her bed and sees her flushed face. "It seemed as though she was not only well and blooming, but in the happiest frame of mind" and she is speaking "with exceptionally correct articulation and expressive intonation" (433). Tolstoy alone would notice a stage in mortal illness that seems like health. It must add to Karenin's sense of confusion. Nothing seems to make sense or fit an expected pattern.

Eavesdropping on Vindication

Anna does not notice Karenin's presence, so she speaks about him as if he were not there. Karenin finds himself in the rare position of hearing what a person says about one in one's absence. An unwitting eavesdropper, he credits what Anna says as sincere because it has not been formulated with his reaction in mind. Imagine his emotional response to each of Anna's comments:

> "For Aleksey—I am speaking of Aleksey Aleksandrovich (what a strange and awful thing that both are Aleksey, isn't it?)—Aleksey would not refuse me. I would forget, he would forgive. . . . But why doesn't he come? He's so good, he doesn't know himself how good he is. Ah, my God, what agony! . . ."
>
> "Anna Arkadyevna, he has come. Here he is!" said the midwife, trying to attract her attention to Aleksey Aleksandrovich.
>
> "Oh, what nonsense!" Anna went on, not seeing her husband. . . . "You say he won't forgive me because you don't know him. No one knows him. I'm the only one, and it was hard even for me. His eyes I ought to know— Seryozha has just the same eyes—and I can't bear to see them because of it. Has Seryozha had his dinner? I know everyone will forget him. He would not forget . . ." (433)

"He doesn't know himself how good he is": at one time or another we all fantasize that some perfect judge who knows everything about us would accept our self-justifications. Anna does all this and more for Karenin. She knows him better than he knows himself and insists he is better than his most flattering moral self-assessments.

"You say he won't forgive me because you don't know him": we all internalize others' views of us, perhaps especially the negative views, and Karenin knows that he is regarded as cold and unforgiving. Anna rejects that mistaken impression, which arises from the difficulty in seeing past his outward manner.

We all hope, and grow wise enough to look ironically at our hope, that people who have wronged us will come to see their actions as we do and beg forgiveness. Again, Anna does that and more: she not only acknowledges she has hurt him but also credits him with the goodness to forgive.

"Seryozha has the same eyes": Karenin has told Dolly that he has even begun to suspect that Seryozha is not his son. Anna could not be making this comment if someone else were Seryozha's father.

"He would not forget": in this book, where evil is identified with absence and forgetting, the line rings powerfully for the reader. For Karenin, it recalls the pain he felt when telling Dolly that Anna has forgotten and counted for nothing their eight years of marriage. Not only does Anna remember, but she knows that he would never forget.

How does Karenin react to this succession of powerful and totally unanticipated vindications beyond his, or anyone's, dreams? In addition to joy at her words, to the shock of hearing something so unexpected, to the pity he feels at another's sufferings ("What agony!"), he experiences profound guilt. These vindications and this love come from the very person whom he falsely accused of trickery and of concealing Seryozha's paternity. Above all, they come from a person whose death he has been intensely desiring. For Karenin, each vindication is also an accusation. As she is praising him, he realizes that his thoughts have sinned against her.

He Did Not Think

When Anna at last notices her husband, she first shrinks back and then calls for him to come closer. In agony, she hurries to say what she understands before she dies. "Now I understand, I understand it all, I see it all!" (433).

Tolstoy at last makes Karenin's reaction explicit, but reveals only what could be seen from outside Karenin's consciousness:

Aleksey Aleksandrovich's wrinkled face wore an expression of agony; he took her by the hand and tried to say something, but he could not utter it; his lower lip quivered, but he still went on struggling with his emotion and then glanced at her. And each time he glanced at her, he saw eyes gazing at him with such passionate and triumphant tenderness as he had never seen in them. (433–34)

Karenin's "wrinkled [or pinched] face wore an expression of agony": this expression is visible only to others. Tolstoy has switched from an internal view, when Karenin was himself aware of how intensely he has been longing for his wife's death, to a purely external view. He does so because the confusion of emotions Karenin experiences—pity, guilt, joy, love, triumph, surprise—leaves almost no room for him to observe his feelings. Karenin experiences them without being explicitly aware of them. This lack of awareness suggests the proximity of a complete loss of control. His feelings will soon go their own way without any direction from his will.

In the passage that follows, Anna describes how she deliberately misperceived Karenin: "there is another woman in me, I'm afraid of her; she loved that man [Vronsky], and I tried to hate you [*ia khotela voznenavidet' tebia*], and could not forget the woman who used to be. That one is not me" (434). She expresses her physical pain in vivid ways. She says how bad she has been and that she wants only one thing, Karenin's forgiveness, even though she does not deserve it: "'I know it can't be forgiven! No, no, go away, you're too good!' She held his hand in one burning hand, while she pushed him away with the other" (434).

These lines express the essence of her whole speech, with its simultaneous acceptance of all blame and assurance that he will forgive the unforgivable, an almost supernatural ability. At the same time, Karenin's guilt over wishing her death makes him sense that he is no less sinful and in need of forgiveness than she.

Anna's burning hand makes her suffering tangible. Karenin has always handled his intense emotional reaction to others' suffering by banishing them or escaping, but now he can do neither. He must for once let his emotions play themselves out. When he does, he at last experiences Christian love:

> The nervous agitation [*dushevnoe rasstroistvo,* confusion of soul] of Aleksey Aleksandrovich kept increasing, and had by now reached such a point that he ceased to struggle with it. He suddenly felt that what he had regarded as nervous agitation was on the contrary a blissful spiritual condition that he had never known. He did not think that the Christian law he had been all his life trying to follow enjoined him to forgive and love his enemies; but a happy feeling of love and forgiveness for his enemies filled his heart. He knelt down, and laying his head in the curve of her arm, which burned him as with fire through the sleeve, he sobbed like a little child. (434)

"He did not think . . .": this line makes absolutely clear that the forgiveness is not contrived but comes from the heart. It also indicates that the change takes place because Karenin has surrendered to the feeling. He does not will the forgiveness, and such forgiveness cannot be willed. As the stiff official sobs like a little child, we accept the result of a process we have been tracing step by tiny step.

Christian Love and the Elemental Force

Karenin really does forgive both Anna and Vronsky, and he is quite sincere when he tells Vronsky that "I forgive completely. I would offer the other cheek, I would give my cloak if my coat be taken. I pray to God only not to take from me the bliss of forgiveness!" (436).[5]

I suppose that if any other writer, even Dostoevsky, had ever created a scene that made Christian love psychologically plausible, he would have ended the novel right there. What would not be anticlimactic after accomplishing the impossible? And think what an amazing ending this scene would make.[6] In the serialized version of the book, one installment does end here (Todd, 53–60), but Part Four continues and in the version published in book form, the novel simply proceeds to the next chapter of Part Four.

In addition to avoiding melodrama, Tolstoy wants to show not only that Christian love is possible but also that it may not be a good thing. The problem is not that the expression of such love is always fake, or that, as is often said, Christianity would be wonderful but it has never been tried. The problem is that even unsanctimonious, real Christian love leads to destructive results.

At first, Karenin gives himself over wholly to his new feeling. Two months after his return from Moscow, he realizes that he had not known his own heart until he gave way to that compassion for the suffering of others he had always regarded as a weakness. "And pity for her, and remorse for having desired her death, and most of all the joy of forgiveness" gave him "a spiritual peace he had never experienced before. He suddenly felt . . . that what had seemed insoluble while he was judging, blaming, and hating had become clear and simple when he forgave and loved" (440).

The author warrants that Karenin forgives and pities his wife, both for her sufferings and from remorse; forgives Vronsky, especially after hearing of his attempted suicide; and takes a renewed interest in his son. Karenin also feels a special interest in the little girl who is not his daughter.

It is at this point that we are told, in a subordinate clause buried in a long sentence, that the girl would have died but for his concern. This crucial information is presented as mere supporting evidence for the main point of the passage, the remarkable interest that this stiff bureaucrat takes in a baby. Karenin would go into the nursery several times a day, gaze "at the saffron-red, downy, wrinkled face," and watch all her movements. "At such moments particularly, Aleksey Aleksandrovich had a sense of perfect peace and inner harmony, and saw nothing extraordinary in his position, nothing that ought to be changed" (440–41). Think how far he has come in two months and how believable Tolstoy has made this transformation.

Karenin "saw nothing extraordinary in his situation": since Karenin experiences true Christian love, forgiveness of one's enemies, love of a child not his own, and change from a bureaucrat to a doting parent are all perfectly in order. But from the perspective of everyday human life, Karenin's feelings and actions contradict all received patterns of behavior. Karenin consequently runs straight into the elemental force, here called the "brutal force" because its relentless workings are destructive: "He felt that besides the blessed spiritual force controlling his soul, there was another, a brutal force, as powerful, or more powerful, which controlled his life, and this force would not allow him that humble peace he longed for" (441).

Just as one cannot introduce new agricultural methods that run counter to the habits of the peasants, cannot make reforms take when they do not fit with established practices, and cannot improve oneself simply by copying an ideal, so one cannot live a life so exalted that it contradicts all social mores. One can love one's enemies, but one cannot keep loving them if no one else understands.

Karenin finds that everyone looks at him "with questioning amazement" and that his worldly acquaintances, especially women, take a particular and voyeuristic interest in his situation. To them, he is not a saint but a ridiculous cuckold, all the more so for his weird forgiveness. Just as Karenin has always appeared socially inept, now he seems totally uncomprehending about sex, love, and his social position. There could hardly be a better formula for ridicule, and so Karenin keeps seeing that his acquaintances have difficulty concealing a sort of mirth. "Everyone seemed, somehow enormously delighted, as though they had just been to a wedding. When they met him, they inquired about his wife's health with undisguised glee" (441).

These acquaintances are not especially cruel. They simply give in to the natural human interest in a tantalizing story. No one, except perhaps Princess Betsy, means him any harm. Given Karenin's strange feelings and behavior, his political prominence, and the sexiness of his story, people can resist it no more than, in our day, inbound drivers can resist slowing down to gape at a bloody accident in the outbound lane.

No Escape

We see the brutal force at work when Karenin investigates why Annie seems to be in pain. The English governess confides that the baby is not ill but hungry because the wet nurse has no milk. When Karenin asks the nurse about the wet nurse's milk, she agrees with the governess:

> "Then why didn't you say so?"
> "Who's one to say it to? Anna Arkadyevna still ill. . . ." said the nurse resentfully.
> The nurse was an old servant of the family. And in her simple words there seemed words there seemed to Aleksey Aleksandrovich an allusion to his position. (442)

Anna is ill, Vronsky would not understand and is not there, so who is one to say it to? The implication is that Karenin cannot be told because, despite his obvious interest in the baby, he is not the father. The comment marks the difference between his feelings and every one else's assumptions.

Just as Levin's peasants do not intend sabotage, so this old family nurse means no harm. She wounds Karenin because the way she thinks is the way everyone thinks.

Karenin constantly encounters similar incidents. There is no one to resent and no single source of the problem to correct, and yet the pressure never ceases. One cannot escape the elemental force.

Christian Love and Prosaic Goodness

After Anna leaves for Italy with Vronsky, Karenin finds the pressure almost too much to bear. The story of his life no longer makes sense because "he could not in any way connect and reconcile his past with what he was now" (531). The break that makes his life nonsense is not the discovery of his wife's infidelity or even her departure. Those facts are painful, but by themselves they would not have left him in a hopeless, incomprehensible position. The past he cannot reconcile with the present is the recent past in which he forgave Anna, loved his enemies, and doted on the other man's child, only to find himself "alone, put to shame, needed by no one and despised by everyone" (531).

Karenin suffers especially strongly precisely because he has truly loved his enemies. Left alone, he strains every nerve to preserve the appearance of composure, but when the valet Korney hands him a bill from—of course—a fashionable clothing store that Anna had—of course—forgotten to pay, Karenin reaches his limit and can no longer speak. Now he discovers a new reason people despise him: not for anything he has done, but simply because he is so unhappy. He is utterly powerless to do anything about their reaction.

Karenin's very pain leads to its increase. He suffers still more because he has no one to turn to. Now we learn for the first time about his earlier life. Karenin was an orphan, and his only close friend was his brother, who is now dead. Anna's aunt trapped him into marriage by first inviting him and then insinuating he has compromised Anna, a situation (as the aunt describes it) resembling what we see with Vronsky and Kitty. Unlike Vronsky, Karenin acts honorably and marries Anna. He concentrates on her all his feelings and capacity for intimacy. When she leaves, he has no real friends and no one with whom to share his sorrow. The only possible confidante is his private secretary, whom he likes but with whom he has never spoken except about business. Tolstoy describes how Karenin attempts to begin, "So you have heard of my trouble?" but instead ends up saying, as usual, "So you'll get that ready for me?" (533).

Perhaps because he is now an object of ridicule, or perhaps just "for some reason," his career effectively comes to an end. When he goes to a public reception, he is perfectly aware that everyone is laughing at him, and as he looks across that sea of hostile eyes, he finds in his loneliness one person who cares for him, the awful Countess Lydia Ivanovna. He falls utterly into her hands. Her fake religiosity replaces the real Christian love that no one wanted. It offers him a sense of elevation necessary for him in his humiliation (537).

Karenin now becomes a moral monster. He becomes as bad as Anna once falsely described him. He descends so far precisely because he was exalted so high. Christian love, though initially beautiful, leads to moral disaster because it cannot be reconciled with ordinary life. It is utopian, and like political utopias, it makes matters much worse. Although he does not know it, Levin's book about the elemental force serves as a theological warning.

Far better the sort of prosaic love and lowly wisdom we see in Dolly. Dolly may advise Christian love, but she understands it in a prosaic way, as overcoming feelings of resentment so that one can forgive an injury. She does not think of something superhuman. She takes care of her family and is suspicious of any thought or feeling that departs too much from the wisdom of the Shcherbatskys. In this novel, Christian love produces monstrosity, and real saintliness, if the term can be so used, is inconspicuous. It does not sound a trumpet.

Any doctrine that defies human nature and everyday practices will, if backed by sufficient force, create much greater suffering than it sets out to alleviate. A movement that is truly "revolutionary" — that, like Bolshevism, sets out to change human nature entirely — will create evil on a scale not seen before the twentieth century. Tolstoy saw Christian love, revolutionism, and all other utopian ways of thinking as related errors. If so, they are errors of our time, and perhaps prosaic goodness offers the best hope of correction.

Counterfeit Art. What Is Interesting?

As reforms that do not proceed from experience are bound to fail, so artworks that do not proceed from experience are bound to be fake.

For Tolstoy, real art derives from a finely observed experience that evokes an emotion unlike any other. In *Anna Karenina,* the painter Mikhailov knows for certain that the painting on his easel is unique, "that no one had ever painted a picture like it. He did not believe that his picture was better than all the pictures of Raphael, but he knew that what he had tried to convey in that picture no one had ever conveyed. He knew this positively" (494). Since he has obviously not seen all paintings, how can he be so sure? The answer is that all experiences, if observed finely enough, are unique. They seem identical only if one's eye cannot discern the particularities with sufficient precision.

Mikhailov has spent his whole life learning to see. When he meets a shopkeeper who sells him cigars, he notes the face and stores it in his mind without even realizing he is doing so. He has painfully acquired the habit of careful observation until it operates spontaneously. If one were to describe the creative process leading to his works, it would be coterminous with his daily life.

For this reason, Anna, Vronsky, and their friend Golenishchev annoy Mikhailov by attributing the quality of his work to "technique," or mechanical facility, and to "talent, by which they meant an inborn and almost physical aptitude apart from brain and heart, and in which they tried to find an expression for all the artist had gained from life" (501). Mikhailov knows that his art depends not so much on his merely passable mechanical ability as on his trained eye: "If to a little child or to his cook were revealed what he saw, it or she would have been able" to paint as well or nearly as well.

Mikhailov paints because he needs to convey emotions that his fine observations have evoked in him. By contrast, Vronsky paints because he has nothing else to do and has begun to feel "a desire for desires" (488). Painting becomes one of a series of activities, along with hospital building and engaging in local politics, that Vronsky seizes upon. Without a compelling need to express a particular experience, Vronsky begins to paint by choosing a school of painting:

> He had a ready appreciation of art, and for accurately and tastefully imitating it. . . . and after hesitating for some time about what kind of painting to select—religious, historical, realistic, or genre painting—he began painting. He appreciated all kinds, and could have felt inspired by any of them; but he had no conception of the possibility of knowing nothing at all of any school of painting, and of being inspired directly by what is within the soul, without caring whether what is painted will belong to any recognized school. Since he knew nothing of this, and drew his inspiration not directly from life, but indirectly from life embodied in art, his inspiration came very quickly and easily, and as quickly and easily came his success in painting something very similar to the sort of painting he was trying to imitate. (489)

"The sort of painting he was trying to imitate [*podrazhat*]": Vronsky is producing not art, which demands keen observation of unrepeatable experience, but counterfeit art, which can be made by applying mechanical facility according to one or another recipe. Counterfeit art is the artistic analogue of Madame Stahl's piety, which tries to pass itself off as a real feeling but is actually a role learned by imitation.

In his treatise *What Is Art?*, Tolstoy enumerated several ways in which one can produce counterfeit art. One may simply copy by formula and rely on people mistaking for art something that recalls art they have experienced in the past. In that case, one typically employs "poetic" subject matter—one or another school's equivalent of "nightingales." Or one can try to rivet interest by "striking" effects, such as the excitement of disgust or the violation of a taboo, which has the added advantage of flattering the audience's self-image as "progressive" people. Or one can include the "interesting," by making the work a sort of riddle and including "difficult" material that only the initiated can understand. These methods win prizes.

When Levin goes to a concert in Part Seven, he hears "interesting" music explained by intellectuals who appreciate it by assigning it to a school. "Levin felt like a deaf man watching people dancing" (713). If there is one thing that cannot be said about Mikhailov's painting and Tolstoy's novel, it is that they are, in this sense, "interesting."[7]

Counterfeit Thinking and Sergey Ivanovich's Beliefs

In the same way that art and philanthropy can be fake, so can ideas. Real thinking, like real art, derives from serious reflection on finely observed experience. As his experience accumulates and his powers of observation sharpen, Levin is always changing his mind.

Unlike so many intellectuals in this novel and in our own world, Levin does not begin by subscribing to one or another theory or political position and then seek arguments to counter opponents. Although it may require study, such "thinking" expresses not experience, but the desire to be accepted by a certain sort of people. It is almost useless for understanding its purported subject matter.

Anyone really interested in reforming agriculture, reducing crime, or mitigating poverty would not rule out but would seriously entertain opposing arguments. When encountering evidence that seems to contradict one's preferred reforms, one would not engage in damage control by learning the proper way to refute opponents, but would consider how to modify one's recommendations. If one does not take contrary evidence and opinions seriously, then one does not really care about crime, agriculture, or poverty, but uses these charged issues to further the success of the party one has selected in advance. With no possibility of recognizing a mistake or changing one's mind, one can maintain one's social connections and one's self-image as a friend of beneficent causes. No matter how much evidence accumulates that one's prescriptions have failed in practice, one can safely deem opponents sinful and selfish or uncaring and mean-spirited. And with a bit of finesse, one can even smugly accuse them of being "closed-minded." Chekhov, no less than Dostoevsky and Tolstoy, found such practices disturbing.

Anna Karenina offers a gallery of counterfeit thinkers. Sergey Ivanovich, Katavasov, Pestsov, Metrov, the irascible professor, Golenishchev and others all live by theories, and Svyazhsky, Stiva, Vronsky and others learn and profess them. In almost every intellectual exchange, Levin encounters one or another variety of fake thinking. Tolstoy tries to teach us to recognize and avoid engaging in fakeness of all kinds.

This novel is concerned at least as much with *how* we think as with *what* we think.

Levin thinks from experience up, but Sergey Ivanovich from theory down. Levin's half-brother holds quite definite beliefs in favor of the peasantry. He derives them from theory, from contrast with town life, and from other abstract principles. Sergey Ivanovich likes to talk with peasants and "from every such conversation he would deduce general conclusions in favor of the peasantry and in confirmation of his knowing them" (251). The only way to arrive at generalizations that readily is to know them in advance and to ignore all particularities. And the only way in which every conversation could confirm one's views is to think so as to make counterevidence impossible. By contrast, Levin, who lives among the peasants, holds no definite views about them. He is "continually discovering new traits, altering his former views of them and forming new ones. With Sergey Ivanovich it was quite the contrary" (252).

Sergey Ivanovich professes a concern for the public good and Levin does not, but Levin actually does good. Sergey Ivanovich's views come easily because he is not "led by an impulse of the heart to care for the public good, but reasoned from intellectual considerations that it was a right thing to take an interest in public affairs, and consequently took an interest in them" (253). Like philanthropy derived from religious or political injunctions, such interest in the public good usually accomplishes nothing or does positive harm. By contrast, a concern with specific problems and particular people may not only help them but also lead to insights that, with suitable modification, might help others elsewhere. Levin's book does not at all resemble Sergey Ivanovich's.

How Stiva's Opinions Change

Unlike Sergey Ivanovich, Stiva does not choose his political views. "These political opinions and views had come to him of themselves," just as his dress reflects whatever happens to be in style (9). In a remarkable sentence, Tolstoy explains that Stiva "firmly held all these views held by the majority and by his paper and changed them only when the majority changed them — or, more strictly speaking, they seemed to change of themselves within him" (9).

Any group or party gradually changes its positions, and over time, may reverse them. John F. Kennedy advocated a more muscular defense, lower taxes, and more free trade, while Republicans disagreed; and when exactly did these positions reverse themselves? If a person always agrees with his party no matter how its positions vary, then we can safely conclude that that person is not really thinking through the issues. Rather, a process of change taking place outside is being tacitly accepted. Strictly speaking, the person is not changing his views, but his views are changing within him.

Stiva chooses liberal opinions not because they are more reasonable but because they are "closer in accordance with his manner of life" (9). The liberal party maintains that everything in Russia is bad, and Stiva is decidedly short of money. It holds that marriage is an out-of-date institution, and "family life certainly afforded Stepan Arkadyevich little gratification and forced him into lying and hypocrisy, which were so repulsive to his nature" (9). The liberal party regards religion as nothing more than a way to keep the lower classes in check, and Stiva "could never make out what was the object of all the terrible and high-flown language about another world when life might be so very amusing in this world" (10).

Far from proving sincerity, the coincidence of Stiva's views and life indicate hypocrisy. Nikolai Irtenev, the narrator of Tolstoy's *Boyhood,* remarks that "the incongruity between a man's situation and his mental activity is the surest sign of his sincerity" (CBY, 167). The point shocks, because we usually think of hypocrisy as the divergence of opinions from behavior, and sincerity as their coincidence, but Irtenev argues the opposite. He exaggerates, but his essential idea is correct: the only way to make one's views and life coincide is to choose one's views so as to justify how one lives. Levin's life and opinions do not coincide because he is always questioning his beliefs and choosing new ones, whether they justify him or not. He cares about the truth. He changes his mind in response to experience, so his views on different subjects may prove inconsistent while his behavior lags behind. Stiva, like Sergey Ivanovich, can therefore best him in argument. In debates with intellectuals, sincerity and a concern for truth usually prove a hindrance.

Svyazhsky and Magic Words

Svyazhsky's opinions do not accord with his life, yet he is no hypocrite. Despite the failure of his costly agricultural reforms, he maintains progressive views and explains failure by insisting that still more expense is needed. This excuse for failure is always available to reformers, because no matter how much is spent, more could have been. As there are unfalsifiable propositions, there are universal excuses, and success in partisan debate depends on a solid mastery of them.

Levin can find no reason for Svyazhsky's interests. Svyazhsky cares about the partition of Poland even though the issue has no connection to anything else that really concerns him. Levin wonders why Svyazhsky cares. What's Poland to him, or he to Poland?

Because authentic ideas come from experience, one can learn from them even if one disagrees. One can read back from the idea to the experience and consider it in light of one's concerns. Levin does not agree with the reactionary landowner, but he easily grasps what sort of incidents have shaped his views. Reflecting on the landowner's words, Levin in effect adds the landowner's experience to his own. As a result, Levin's views become more complex.

By contrast, Svyazhsky's views are entirely counterfeit. Or to be more precise, they are genuine, but in a hidden way. Svyazhsky is a warm, decent man and a good host, and his views reflect not their ostensible topic but the experience of giving hospitable dinners. When Svyazhsky discourses on Poland, one can learn nothing about Poland, but one can learn about dinnertime conversation.

When Levin points out that progressive agricultural reforms fail, Svyazhsky at one point maintains that they would succeed if the peasants were better educated. "But how are we to educate the people?" Levin asks (356). Svyazhsky replies: "To educate the people three things are needed: schools, schools, and schools" (356). Even at over a century's distance, we sense that this witticism must have been constantly repeated, like our own real estate comment about "location, location, and location." The word "schools" serves as a sort of magic word, which one intones as if it were an answer and required no further thinking. Who could be against schools?

Levin, who does not think by intellectual magic words, replies with the same questions that Prince Andrei asks about Pierre's proposal to build schools. What kind of schools? What will they teach? How precisely will that curriculum help the peasants? Has anyone asked the peasants what they want? Levin's point is that the peasants do not want the intellectuals' and aristocrats' schools, even beg to have their children released from them, because they see no connection between what is taught and what they need to know. Of course, intellectuals are likely to reply that peasants argue this way only because they are ignorant, so their very objections to schools really confirm their need for them. Such reasoning not only presumes what it purports to prove but also denies the peasants any voice whatsoever. Only intellectuals have a say, which may be why these arguments seem so persuasive to them.

Svyazhsky praises the new schools because they "give the peasant fresh needs" (356), but Levin asks how those needs are to be satisfied. No one has thought of providing work for peasants who have gone through such an education. So in our time, Third World countries produce university graduates who cannot find jobs, and then intellectuals wonder why so many of them become Trotskyites, fanatic nationalists, religious extremists, or terrorists.

Levin's key argument, and Tolstoy's, concerns the *process* of reasoning intellectuals use. Levin tells a story:

> The day before yesterday I met a peasant woman in the evening with a little baby, and asked her where she was going. She was going to the village sorceress; her boy had screaming fits, so she was taking him to be doctored. I asked, "Why, how does the wise woman cure screaming fits?" "She puts the child on the hen roost and repeats some charm . . ." (357)

Svyazhsky interrupts to say that the story shows that peasants need schools, but in so doing he misses Levin's point: intellectuals do the same thing as this peasant woman. The only difference is that their magic words come from a different lexicon. The peasant woman cannot state the connection between charms and screaming fits and intellectuals often cannot state the connection between their proposed reforms and improved conditions. Neither looks at contrary evidence and neither alters views as a result of failure.

One's Own Thought

These passages did not make Tolstoy popular with the intellectuals of his day, and they have the same effect today when intellectuals do not entirely ignore them. Tolstoy sharpens his point by making the only genuine thinker Levin meets a reactionary. As the reactionary landowner states his views, Svyazhsky makes "a faint gesture of irony" to Levin as if to say, "get a load of him!" For Svyazhsky, as for similar people today, the mere fact that the landowner's conclusions are not the ones thought of as progressive precludes serious consideration of anything he says. One laughs, not listens, and so one is both amused and insured against disconfirmation.

Levin does not react as Svyazhsky does. He listens carefully. "The landowner unmistakably spoke his own thought—a thing that rarely happens—and a thought to which he had been brought not by a desire of finding some exercise for an idle brain, but a thought which had grown out of the conditions of his life, which he had brooded over in the solitude of his village, and had considered in its every aspect" (350). This passage expresses the author's highest praise.

From a Tolstoyan perspective, one might say: As Vronsky learns to imitate schools of painting, today students learn that reading without a theory is either reactionary or impossible. To assert otherwise is to proclaim oneself, at best, a dilettante. It is therefore not surprising that so many bright undergraduates become well educated but unimaginative doctoral candidates. Such students may have "talent," but too many have all but lost their own originality and the ability to recognize it in others. But they might still, like Kitty, Mikhailov, or Levin learn instead to become better versions of themselves and speak their own thought.

Meaning and Ethics

The real discovery is the one that makes me capable of stopping doing philosophy when I want to.
— WITTGENSTEIN (*Philosophical Investigations,* paragraph 133)

The Svyazhsky Enigma

Levin works out his ideas about agriculture while another question grows increasingly urgent. Every time he encounters his tubercular brother Nikolai, and most acutely when he watches Nikolai die, Levin experiences an existential fear of death that threatens to make nonsense of everything.

Levin tries not to face this question, but it forces itself upon him. When he discovers that he must confess and take the sacrament in order to be married, he realizes that he can neither do so sincerely nor regard the obligation as a mere formality. He cannot just go through the motions without feeling he is lying and committing blasphemy. Horrified by his own effrontery, Levin honestly tells the priest that he doubts the existence of God, but the priest replies that doubt is natural and that even the holy fathers doubted. The priest asks rhetorically: who but God could have made the world, and what will you say to your children when they ask who made it? Levin is ashamed to answer with metaphysical arguments, so he simply says that he does not know. To Levin's surprise, that answer turns out to be a good one, because the chief question for the priest is not whether one doubts, but whether one seeks faith in spite of doubt. He admonishes Levin to seek, and Levin realizes that he already does.

As Levin leaves, he thinks

that what the kind, nice old fellow had said had not been at all so stupid as he had thought at first, and that there was something in it that must be cleared up.

"Of course, not now," thought Levin, "but someday later on." Levin felt more than ever now that there was something not clear and not clean in his soul, and that in regard to religion, he was in the same position he perceived so clearly and disliked in others, and for which he blamed his friend Svyazhsky. (464)

The reference to Svyazhsky concerns a state of mind that Levin has discovered in his friend and that he has come to recognize in himself. Most critics have taken the portrait of Svyazhsky as entirely satiric, but to do so is to miss the real complexity of his character and the reason that the "Svyazhsky enigma" continues to disturb Levin until the novel's end.

This enigma concerns the divergence between Svyazhsky's principles and his life. The two seem to be not just different but totally separate. Svyazhsky holds quite liberal views on all current issues, but his life proceeds openly in an entirely traditional manner. Svyazhsky despises the nobility, but serves as their marshal; "he believed in neither God nor the devil" but assiduously applies himself to the welfare of the local clergy; he listens with respect to the peasants even though, as a good Westernizer, he regards them as somewhere between ape and man (346). Though an extreme feminist and believer in women's right to labor, he "arranged his wife's life so that she did nothing and could do nothing but share her husband's efforts to make her time as agreeable as possible" (346). And she, and he, and all around them seem the happier for it.

Levin knows that it would be easy to dismiss Svyazhsky as a fool or a hypocrite. But Svyazhsky is unmistakably intelligent and clearly decent. He understands both his life and his views, and he deceives neither himself nor others. Despite the shallowness of his ideas, he may even be wise. But what is this wisdom and how is one to explain the contradiction in his life?

Accepting two contradictory philosophies at once: this paradoxical state of mind is what Svyazhsky symbolizes for Levin. The enigma is how such acceptance is possible without either stupidity, self-deception, or hypocrisy.

Levin imagines that there is a secret here, some hidden set of principles that explains the enigma, but he cannot get at it. Whenever he tries to go beyond the "antechambers" of Svyazhsky's mind, he detects a faint sign of alarm, which Levin interprets as fear that the hidden secret will be discovered. But Levin is entirely mistaken. There is no secret in the sense Levin imagines. Svyazhsky's wisdom does not entail a philosophical truth reconciling opposites.

An Unbeliever's Prayer

When Levin confesses, and still more when Kitty is in labor, he finds himself in Svyazhsky's position. Levin's materialist convictions run counter to his spiritual experience and he cannot reconcile the two.

While Kitty is suffering, time slows down for Levin to the point where her screams seem endless. He recognizes his feeling as analogous to his experience of his brother's death.

> But that had been grief—this was joy. Yet that grief and this joy were alike beyond the ordinary conditions of life; they were openings, as it were, in that ordinary life through which there came glimpses of something sublime. And in the contemplation of this sublime something the soul was exalted to inconceivable heights of which it had before had no conception, while reason lagged behind, unable to keep up with it. (742)

Levin suddenly finds himself praying, "feeling, in spite of his long and, as it seemed, complete alienation from religion, that he turned to God just as trustfully and simply as he had in his childhood and first youth" (742–43).

Every time Levin hears Kitty shriek, he tries to justify himself, remembers he is not to blame, longs to help her, and falls again to praying without ceasing. His prayer has been utterly sincere, indeed more than sincere, since it has come from his soul without any assessment of its appropriateness. Yet it contradicts his professed convictions. How is he to understand this contradiction? He faces a version of the "Svyazhsky enigma."

Two Problems

Part Eight concerns above all Levin's encounter with ultimate questions. This encounter is especially pertinent today because the materialist paradigm with which Levin struggles has become still more dominant.

Ever since his brother's death, Levin has grown increasingly horrified by the way in which mortality sharpens the problem of life's meaning. How is he to live without knowing "whence, and why, and how, and what it [life] was"? (818). His new convictions—"the organism, its decay, the indestructibility of matter, the law of the conservation of energy, evolution"—seem utterly useless for understanding the questions that perplex him (818). These "convictions" are surely necessary for doing science, but do not touch the sense of existence. Science explains causes, but when problems of meaning arise Levin "felt suddenly like a man who has changed his warm fur cloak for a muslin garment, and, going out for the first time into the frost, is immediately convinced, not by reason, but by his whole nature that he is as good as naked, and that he must inevitably freeze. . . . He was in the position of a man seeking food in a toy shop or at a gunsmith's" (819).

The progress of science since Tolstoy's time does not resolve Levin's dilemma in the slightest, because scientific explanations per se cannot address problems of meaning. In Tolstoy's time and ours, scientists sometimes pretend otherwise, but when they do, they are covertly presenting their metaphysics as if it were part of science. No conceivable causal accounts can answer noncausal questions. Regardless of what we may learn about genetics or subatomic particles, the problem of how to live or what is good and meaningful will remain.

We, and Levin's friends, often miss this point, because one set of questions may "almost touch" on the other. In our time, sociobiologists and sociologists may present an account of why we regard certain actions as good or bad as if that account explained whether they *are* good or bad. Knowing what evolutionary function a given way of thinking serves does not give it persuasive force when we are perplexed by questions of ethics or meaning.

Levin sees through, or rather directly senses, the fallacy in such explanations. When he reads or speaks with up-to-date people, they give him a "mechanistic explanation of the soul" (820) or, as we would say today, "a neurological explanation of consciousness." Levin realizes that such explanations may serve to discredit religion, but cannot replace any part of it except the one that sounds like primitive science.

To make matters still more perplexing, Levin's dilemma becomes tied to "the Svyazhsky enigma" that he recognizes in himself. During Kitty's confinement, Levin not only prayed but "at the moment he prayed he believed. But that moment had passed, and he could not make his state of mind at that moment fit into the rest of his life" (820). He cannot dismiss his act of praying as a mere effect of terror, like a nightmare, hallucination, or groundless fear of the dark recalled from childhood, because he truly believed when praying. Moreover, the moment he prayed remains precious to him, and to regard it as mere weakness would be to desecrate it. On the other hand, Levin cannot accept that his belief at that moment is true and everything else he knows is false.

So Levin now faces two problems dividing him against himself. First, the scientific explanations that have replaced his former religious convictions cannot address what disturbs him. Second, he apparently believes sincerely and consciously in two opposing things. Anna believes in opposites—that Karenin is an unfeeling puppet and that he can feel deeply even if he cannot express his feelings—because she resorts to self-deception. Others would use Stiva's method for dealing with contradictions and simply forget what they do not wish to remember. For the very reason that Levin thinks through his ideas about agriculture rather than accept prevailing opinions, he cannot but face his spiritual self-divisions. His honesty leads him to despair.

Why There Are Many Problems

When philosophers use a word—"knowledge," "being," "object," "I," "proposition," "name"—and try to grasp the *essence* of the thing, one must always ask oneself: Is the word ever actually used in this way in the language game which is its original home?

What *we* do is to bring back words from their metaphysical to their everyday use.

— WITTGENSTEIN (*Philosophical Investigations,* paragraph 116)

Tortured by doubt, Levin reads the great thinkers. To answer the doubts raised by materialism, he reads Plato, Kant, Schelling, Schopenhauer, and other nonmaterialist philosophers. At first, these thinkers impress him because they provide strong arguments against the materialists, but he soon realizes that they are of no use except in the game of refuting other theories. So long as Levin follows the "fixed definitions of obscure words" like spirit, will, freedom, and substance, and lets himself "enter the verbal trap set by the philosophers or himself, he seemed to comprehend something" (821). But as soon as he turns to life itself, and forgets "the artificial train of reasoning," the entire edifice falls apart like a house of cards and turns out to be built of nothing but words "apart from anything in life more important than reason" (821).

Levin realizes a Tolstoyan truth quite difficult for intellectuals then and now to grasp: some dilemmas that appear philosophical cannot be answered philosophically. No more than science is philosophy an overarching form of reasoning. It is no more accurate to say that all questions are "ultimately" philosophical than to say they are all reducible to physics. Philosophy is just another form of reasoning, good for particular purposes but bound to mislead when presumed to be universal. In the *Philosophical Investigations,* Wittgenstein develops Tolstoy's skeptical attitude to philosophy. Wittgenstein likely had Levin in mind when he pointed out that arguments have a meaning in a particular language game but may generate unsolvable problems when taken outside their "original home." Then "language goes on holiday" and the engine is merely "idling" (*Philosophical Investigations,* paragraph 132).[8]

Levin discovers that nonmaterialist philosophy has its proper use in the game of "doing academic philosophy," the game that Sergey Ivanovich plays as well as chess. But it falls apart just as quickly as materialist philosophy when Levin applies it to real problems of life. Levin has tacitly regarded philosophy and science as sublime and pure inquiries that, like logic or Euclidian geometry, reach truth before being applied to any particular sphere of life. In fact, like every other form of speaking and acting, they have meaning only where genuine problems must be solved. Problems are not solved in a pure and crystalline realm before specific activity; they are solved where things are impure and where there is always "friction." Without friction there is no traction. When we seek purity, "we have got on to slippery ice where there is no friction and so in a certain sense the conditions are ideal, but also, just because of that, we are unable to walk. We want to walk; so we need *friction*. Back to the rough ground!" (*Philosophical Investigations,* paragraph 107).

Wittgenstein explains his and Tolstoy's insight: "Problems are solved (difficulties eliminated), not a *single* problem. There is not *a* philosophical method, though there are indeed methods, like different therapies" (*Philosophical Investigations,* paragraph 133). Wittgenstein concludes, as Tolstoy's novel does, that "the real discovery is the one that makes me capable of stopping doing philosophy when I want to." In agriculture, social reform, and practical life, Levin rejects out of hand the notion that there is a single problem to be solved and a single method for solving it, but when questions of meaning arise, he still seeks to overcome the "inconsistencies" of his own "Svyazhsky enigma" as if a single system of thought had to apply everywhere.

The Svyazhsky Enigma in Its Sharpest Form

Tolstoy loves to analyze issues by showing what all positions share and must share, however much they may differ in other ways. If that commonality contains an error, then no variations on current theories can do any good. An entirely new orientation is needed.

Levin discovers that any science or philosophy must arrive at some form of the following proposition: "In infinite time, in infinite matter, in infinite space, is formed a bubble-organism, and that bubble lasts a while and bursts, and that bubble is I" (822). I think it is clear that today's science, or whatever future science we can imagine, must leave this formulation untouched in any way that matters.

Tolstoy immediately comments:

> It was an agonizing fallacy, but it was the sole logical result of ages of human thought in that direction. This was the ultimate belief on which all the systems elaborated by human thought in almost all their ramifications rested. . . . But it was not merely a fallacy, it was the cruel jest of some wicked power, some evil, hateful power, to whom one could not submit. (822)

For Levin, it is impossible to live without meaning, and theory makes meaning impossible. Suicide is therefore the only possible course of action. He must escape from the jest of this wicked power, and so from life itself. In twentieth-century terms, we could say: he senses the absurd and recognizes suicide as the one escape. "And Levin, a happy father and husband, in perfect health, was several times so near suicide that he hid a rope so that he might not be tempted to hang himself, and was afraid to go out with his gun for fear of shooting himself" (822).

It is especially important that what drives this happy and healthy man toward suicide is not sadness, illness, guilt, regret, or depression. It is the chain of philosophical reasoning itself. His daily happiness provides some sort of counterargument to his reasoning, though Levin does not yet see how anything so unphilosophical as everyday living could help. He goes on living, not knowing why. This contradiction is yet another version of the Svyazhsky enigma. Now his ideas go one way and his life the other, not because of how he lives, but because he lives at all.

The Sole Solution to All the Riddles of Life and Death Is Untrue

Although he does not see how, Levin's life offers a clue to his dilemma. Usually in Tolstoy, the sense of meaninglessness is a symptom of a life badly led. When in *War and Peace* Pierre, in a state of total despair, meets the Freemason Bazdeev, he confesses that he abhors his life. Bazdeev quite justly answers:

> "Look at your life, my dear. How have you spent it? In taking everything from society and giving nothing in return. . . . You have spent your life in idleness. . . . A man offended you and you shot him, and you say you . . . abhor your life. It is hardly surprising, my dear sir!" (W&P, 430)

In "The Death of Ivan Ilych," the hero's despair also reflects the way he has lived. In his relentless psychological agony, he at last recognizes this possibility: "'Maybe I did not live as I ought to have done,' it suddenly occurred to him . . . and immediately he dismissed from his mind, this, the sole solution of all the riddles of life and death, as something quite impossible" (GSW, 295).

This "sole solution" does not apply to Levin. Tolstoy explicitly states that Levin is living as he should. His despair must have some other cause. What is it?

Fleming

The author begins chapter 10 with a puzzle. Whenever Levin thinks about what he is living for, he finds no answer and despairs, but when he stops asking, "it seemed as though he knew both what he was and why he was living, for he acted and lived resolutely and without hesitation," more so than at any other time in his life (822). He successfully manages his sister's and half-brother's property as well as his own estate, improves his relations with the peasants and neighbors, gets a new beekeeping hobby to prosper, and gets on better and better with his wife and child.

Strangely enough for Levin, these activities occupy him not because he justifies them with any "general principles" as he would have in the past (823). On the contrary, disappointed with his former efforts for the general welfare and too busy to think of anything but his countless responsibilities, he occupies himself with work simply because "it seemed to him that he must do what he was doing—that he could not do otherwise" (823).

In contrast to what he has always thought, and to what intellectuals like his half-brother routinely assume, Levin grasps that principle is a poor motive for action. In the past, whenever he tried to do something "for the good of all, for humanity, for Russia . . . he had noticed that the idea of it had been pleasant, but the work itself had always been clumsy" (823). The results of the work were poor because "he had never been fully convinced of its absolute necessity." Projects that began with high ideals lessened and vanished into nothing. By this point in the novel, we understand that the same is true of all such attempts at change. As Kitty discovers from her infatuation with philanthropy, ideals and principles that come from above are bound to flag in the face of daily habits and the elemental force. Revolutionary and reformist energy also flag. Begin with Trotsky, end with Brezhnev. Start with moral zeal and end with a faceless bureaucracy.

Levin now works without any thought of principles, but simply because he feels absolutely convinced of his work's necessity. He experiences no delight at the thought of his work, but it succeeds far better than ever before.

Levin works as he does just because he cannot do otherwise. The sense that what one does is "incontestably necessary" (823) and requires no reasons offers not only a strong possibility of success but also an excellent chance to accomplish moral good. Levin acts as if he cares only for himself and his family but the result benefits many others. The point is not that some alchemy converts sheer selfishness into altruism, or that an invisible hand turns greed into virtue. Rather, work that continues without appeal to abstractions succeeds whereas work based on ideals alone will not only fail but also tend to do more harm than good.

The great idealists of our time include Mao, Hitler, Pol Pot, and Khomeini. For every Gandhi or Martin Luther King there are two Kim Il Sungs. But Fleming discovered penicillin, which led to the development of more antibiotics and the greatest conquest of disease ever known, not because he set out to save humanity but because, in his dogged work, he noticed the effect of an accidentally growing mold. It says a great deal that many more people know of Mother Theresa than of Fleming.

What Is "Incontestably Necessary"

Levin thinks: to take care of his family, to live the life of his forefathers, and to preserve the land so as to pass it on to his children, are all as "incontestably necessary" as eating. He cannot *not* look after the affairs of his sister and half-brother, and he cannot not attend to the needs of peasants who come to him for help and advice. To refuse would be "as impossible as to fling down a baby one is carrying in one's arms" (823).

One does not ask for *reasons* or principles not to fling down a baby. I would not trust my child to someone who would invoke or remind himself of such principles. Memory fails, and principles can always be set against other principles. The sense of what just must be done or simply cannot be done is much more important than any reasons one could give for that sense.

The very idea that one needs principles not to do something manifestly wrong is misguided. Aristotle liked to point out that whereas in geometry axioms and theorems are more certain than specific applications of them, in practical affairs the reverse is usually the case. There are some things we know more surely than any reason we can give. To use Aristotle's example, we may theorize why chicken is good to eat, but we will be less sure of those theories than of the fact that chicken is good to eat. One danger in thinking one needs to justify all actions by principles is that we can always find principles to justify any behavior. Whenever possible, we are far better off relying on a sense of what is "incontestably necessary." That sense of necessity derives from our whole lives, from everything we have learned, felt, and reflected on, even if we cannot formalize it as a chain of propositions.

Levin's ability to work better than ever before implicitly contains a lesson that accords with his book's emphasis on daily practices. His doubts derive from philosophy, but his activity succeeds without philosophy. He prays without reasoning, and he works in disregard of principles. Are such divergences hypocritical or do they contain a kind of wisdom?

Levin's Casuistry

These divergences give birth to another. Levin now makes moral, as well as practical, decisions better than ever before. "Besides knowing thoroughly what he had to do, Levin knew in just the same way *how* he had to do it all, and what was more important than the rest" (824). Tolstoy then gives us a list of decisions Levin makes with confidence. I abbreviate a long passage:

> He knew he must hire laborers as cheaply as possible; but to hire men in bond, paying them in advance less than the current rate of wages, was what he must not do, even though it was very profitable. Selling straw to the peasants in times of scarcity was what he might do, even though he felt sorry for them; but the tavern and the inn must be ignored. . . . To Piotr,

who was paying a moneylender ten per cent a month, he must lend a sum of money to set him free. But he could not let off peasants who did not pay their rent. (844)

And the list goes on. Readers who miss Tolstoy's point may ask: What is the underlying principle behind these decisions? The answer is that there is none and that it is a mistake to look for one. Levin comes to the right decision not by deducing actions from general principles but by relying on his moral sensitivity, developed over a lifetime.[9]

Tolstoy consciously attacks an important tradition of Western ethics, which has existed since antiquity and which has predominated in recent centuries. This tradition, which can be traced to Plato, views ethics as a kind of moral geometry. The central idea is that one can make particular ethical perceptions clearer by demonstrating how they exemplify more general rules, which, it is presumed, can be known with greater certainty. The most general rules function as absolutely certain axioms. This approach has aspired to transform ethics into a kind of science, a general, systematic account that our intuitive moral perceptions and judgments can only hint at. (See AoC, 19.)

In the *Nichomachean Ethics,* Aristotle rejects this approach because it overlooks the crucial differences between theoretical and practical reasoning. In some forms of reasoning, like mathematics, certainty is achieved by proceeding from first principles. In others, it is best to begin with something different in kind, a moral character possessed by a person "brought up in good habits. For the fact is the starting point" (Aristotle, 937–38) and one needs good habits to appreciate the moral facts of daily life. Platonists may object that reliance on things as vague as "character" and "good habits" can yield only persuasiveness but not proof. That objection is quite true; but in moral questions persuasiveness is all that we can hope for and it yields better results than what appears to be proof.

In matters of ethics, as in every practical pursuit, unforeseeable particulars make too great a difference for certainty to be had. We must be content "in speaking about things which are only for the most part true and with premises of the same kind to reach conclusions that are no better. . . . it is the mark of an educated man to look for precision in each class of things just so far as the nature of the subject admits" (Aristotle, 936).

The best laws and general principles often fail in particular instances because they envisage a paradigmatic case, but particular cases vary, and differ more or less from the paradigm. Principles must fail at times because "it is impossible to make a universal statement that will be correct" (Aristotle, 1000). The problem is not that the principle is faulty, in which case one could come up with a better one, but that no principle can envisage all possibilities. When it is manifest that the result of applying principles is monstrous, then we must forsake the principle for "the equitable, a correction of law where it is defective owing to its universality. In fact, this is the reason why all things are not determined by law, viz. that about some things it is impossible to lay down a law" (Aristotle, 1020). One needs something more respectful of the local situation, a sort of moral "leaden rule" that "adapts itself . . . to the facts" (Aristotle, 1020).

Aristotle's idea gave birth to the tradition of case-based reasoning, or casuistry in the nonpejorative sense. In casuistry, one examines particular cases to improve one's ethical sensibility. As late as Montaigne, the idea that facts are too various to be subsumed by universal rules seemed obvious. But Pascal's famous attack on casuistry in the *Provincial Letters* stressed how easy it is to manipulate this kind of thinking for the purposes of special pleading. Pascal's book left the approach in disrepute, all the more so since moral Newtonianism in general was gaining ground.

The fact that case-based reasoning can be abused does not mean that, when used honestly and sensitively, it is inferior to deductive approaches. After all, is there any way of thinking immune to abuse? Casuists know, as would-be moral scientists often forget, that no rule is self-interpreting, and that judgment must always come into play at some point if monstrous results are to be avoided. Casuistry does not reject rules, but gives them a role quite different from axioms and theorems. Properly conceived, rules function as maxims or general reminders of situations that have occurred frequently. They allow us to bring these situations to mind either because the present case is similar or because we can reflect on the significance of its differences. Such maxims serve to raise questions, not to dictate answers.

Aristotle insists that, unlike mathematics, ethics is not an entirely teachable subject because one must begin with good habits, a good character, and moral sensitivity. Many lack the first two and the third requires time, so cannot belong to young people. Often enough, moral sensitivity is insufficient to decide an issue, and it is then that one resorts to case-based argument and debate.

Without the possibility of mathematical proof, casuistry by its nature allows for reasonable difference of opinion among moral people. It favors dialogue. If ethics is a science, however, one can no more differ reasonably than one can reasonably dispute the law of gravity or the Pythagorean theorem. If one imagines ethics mathematically, then, as Bakhtin liked to say, "only error individualizes" (PDP, 81). The idea of a moral science is inherently intolerant.

Under the sway of the "Newtonian" paradigm of knowledge, thinkers often tend to one or another extreme: to dogmatism, when the rules are presumably known, or to absolute relativism, when the impossibility of resolving cultural differences by logic becomes manifest. Radical skepticism arises from disappointment with a mistaken model of knowledge and therefore testifies to the assumption that that model is the only possible one. Social scientists and humanists are attracted to both positions, much as Pierre alternates between these extremes in *War and Peace*. Stephen Toulmin observes: "Once we accept rules and principles as the heart and soul of ethics, no middle way can be found between absolutism and relativism" (AoC, 6).

Either there is certainty or nothing: that is the heritage of moral Newtonianism. But surely most of the knowledge on which we rely every day has not been scientifically proven. Anyone who tried to rely only on what has been proven would not survive more than a few days, if that. Our very behavior demonstrates that, even without proof, we believe some practices work better than others, on the whole and for the most part. Casuistry is the art of reasoning better, not perfectly. It is inherently nonutopian.

The Moral Wisdom of the Realist Novel

Casuistry did not disappear from European culture. Abandoned by philosophy, it found a home in the novel. Defoe's fiction began as casuistical articles in the *Athenian Mercury*. Like a "Dear Abby" column in our time, Defoe's essays would present complex cases as occasions for moral reflection and debate. Because casuistic arguments and conduct manuals tended to provide an abundance of detail in presenting cases, they favored the sort of rich description we associate with the realist novel. When Defoe got the idea of stringing hypothetical cases together, he arrived at his episodic novels. (See Starr, AoC.) In *Moll Flanders,* for instance, we are constantly presented with the heroine's apparently plausible justification of her immoral behavior. We need to engage with her, to see what is right and wrong in what she says, and in the process to educate our own moral discernment. Reading becomes an occasion for moral education, for hypothetical debate with the heroine, and for real dialogue with other readers.

From Defoe on, the novel developed increasingly complex examples of moral situations far beyond the reach of any philosophical system. Just compare the complexity and density of moral problems in *Middlemarch* with those in the examples given by philosophers. In Eliot's novel, Mary Garth acts with a fine moral sensitivity and Farebrother reasons, casuistically and wisely, about particular situations. When, in his two great novels, Tolstoy undertook to defend case-based reasoning explicitly, he was recapitulating the origin of the genre and making visible the wisdom inherent in its very form.

We may say: Levin gives up the truth of philosophy for the truths of novels. His wisdom is the realist novel's wisdom.

The Wisdom of Behavior

Levin realizes that deliberation brings him to despair but that "when he did not think, but simply lived, he was continually aware of the presence of an infallible judge in his soul, determining which of two possible courses of action was the better" (825). Whenever he makes a mistake, he *senses* it at once. This awareness of error does not result from any process of deduction but from an immediate feeling of wrongness.

When despairing, Levin feels that he must either answer unanswerable questions or commit suicide. Yet he lives better than ever before. This paradox implicitly raises the question: Which is wiser, ideas or behavior? If the former, why does Levin not kill himself, and if the latter, what does it mean to say that behavior has wisdom?

Behavior has wisdom in the same way that habits can be appropriate, skills can work without our attending to each step, and social institutions can perform their function without conforming to some formalizable set of principles. Wise behavior, good habits, and effective institutions implicitly reflect the entire process of trial and error, correcting and tinkering, and balancing current advantage against long-term flexibility, that have produced them over lengthy periods of time. Although we cannot give a specific reason for the resulting behavior, it is usually better than anything we could give a reason for. Since we live in a world of friction, contingency, and uncertainty, the best testimony is not conformity to timeless criteria but a long history of adaptation.

Wisdom Does Not Come from the Peasant

We see Levin supervising work in the granary. As he wonders why the old woman laboring there does not despair as he does, he checks his watch so as to calculate how much work can be done that day. Philosophy and practical work compete in his mind and he still cannot imagine how they can coexist. With this dilemma before him, Levin falls into conversation with one of the peasants, Fyodor, and asks him why the peasant Fokanych will not rent a certain piece of land while another peasant, Kirillov, rents it and makes it pay. The answer, says Fyodor, is that Kirillov "flays the skin off" the men who work for him while Fokanych does not treat people that way. Why doesn't Fokanych behave as Kirillov does? asks Levin, and Fyodor replies, simply enough, that Fokanych "is a righteous man. He lives for his soul. He remembers God" (827).

Levin suddenly becomes excited. He knows that these words suggest the answer to his dilemma because undefined but clearly significant ideas come whirling in his mind. Levin senses a clue.

This passage is so often misread that I cannot insist too strongly that Tolstoy is not saying that peasants are all wise and that in these simple words they express their superior wisdom. It is Sergey Ivanovich, not Tolstoy, who idealizes peasants in this way. If all Tolstoy had to offer was the advice that we should be righteous and live for our souls, who would need him? We would have a bad novel.

It ought to be a critical maxim that when a wise author seems to be saying something shallow or stupid, we ask ourselves whether we might not be misreading.

Fyodor's words are not the answer but the catalyst—or as Tolstoy says, "the electric shock" (838)—for Levin's process of discovering the answer. I say discovering, because Levin's behavior has already implicitly contained the answer. What he now does is make the wisdom of his behavior present to his mind. By themselves, Fyodor's words mean nothing. They acquire meaning because of the life Levin leads and the meanings he assigns to them in the process of applying them to his own dilemmas.

Sayings and proverbs favor the prepared mind.

Given Without Proof

The electric shock suddenly transforms Levin's disjointed thoughts into a meaningful whole. He has not learned a new fact or arrived at a proposition, but has come to see the world differently *as a whole.*

The meaning of life cannot be a proposition, or we would all already know it. It would be the first thing we were taught. But it isn't; it is a sense of experience as a whole. Wittgenstein expresses Tolstoy's thought: "In short, the effect must be that it becomes an altogether different world. It must, so to speak, wax and wane as a whole. The world of the happy man is a different one from that of the unhappy man" (Wittgenstein, *Tractatus,* 6.43).

So close is the conclusion of Wittgenstein's *Tractatus* to the conclusion of *Anna Karenina* that it probably constitutes Wittgenstein's conscious interpretation of Tolstoy's novel. At times, the interpretation seems to follow Tolstoy's original almost line by line. It is as if Wittgenstein had set himself the task of arriving at Tolstoy's conclusions by a different route. Each work can serve as a gloss on the other.

What strikes Levin is not what Fyodor says but the fact that he, and everyone, immediately grasps and grants it. Those vague and senseless words of Fyodor, proved by nothing and hard to clarify further, are not at all stupid or inexact. In fact, Levin reflects, "I understood them more fully and clearly than I understand anything in life, and never in my life have I doubted nor can I doubt about it" (828). The same thought is understood by almost everyone, the educated and ignorant, the simple and wise, people in our part of the world and in any other. We must live not for our belly but (however this may be expressed) for our soul, for God.

Levin thinks:

"I and all men have only one firm, incontestable, clear knowledge, and that knowledge cannot be explained by reason — it is outside it, and has no causes and can have no effects.

"If goodness has causes, it is not goodness; if it has effects, a reward, it is not goodness either. So goodness is outside the chain of cause and effect.

"And yet I know it, and we all know it." (828–29)

Goodness cannot have causes because a cause is simply a fact in the world, subject to natural laws. It cannot give meaning to the chain of which it is a part. Whatever natural laws cause, they *simply* cause, and nothing more. If goodness were a matter of effects, of earning a reward, then it would be merely an economic calculation about advantage, but not something good in itself. Goodness and meaningfulness are not instrumental. Wittgenstein puts the point this way:

6.372. Thus people today stop at the laws of nature, treating them as something inviolable, just as God and Fate were treated in past ages. . . . the modern system tries to make it look as if *everything* were explained.

6.41. The sense of the world must lie outside the world. In the world everything is as it is, and everything happens as it does happen; *in* it no value exists — and if it did, it would have no value.

If there is any value that does have value, it must lie outside the whole sphere of what does happen and is the case. For all that happens and is the case is accidental. (Wittgenstein, *Tractatus*)

The world does have value, and so that value — what Fyodor clumsily but clearly expresses — is *given.* "I looked for an answer to my question. And thought could not give me an answer to my question — it is incommensurable with my question. The answer has been given me by life itself, in my knowledge of what is right and what is wrong. And that knowledge I did not arrive at in any way, it was given to me as to all men, *given [dano],* because I could not have gotten it from anywhere" (830; italics in original).

Scientific or philosophical thought is incommensurable with the question of meaning because such thought must lead to explanations that are beside the point. The real answer is "given" because one cannot derive it either logically or empirically. No axioms could be more sure than this knowledge of right and wrong, and no deductive process could make it more certain than it already is.

It cannot be derived empirically because the way people do live does not by itself tell us how they should live.

Although he has never seen it, meaning has always existed right before Levin's eyes. In *War and Peace,* Pierre senses the meaning of things only when he "throws away the telescope" with which he has been looking over the heads of men and surveys the ever-changing world immediately around him.

Meaning is openly camouflaged. It is hidden in plain view.

Miracle and Narrative

To discover meaning, we need no miraculous revelation but an awareness of what we have known since childhood. This absence of the need for a miracle is itself the miracle:

> "And I watched for miracles, complained that I did not see a miracle that would convince me. A material miracle would have persuaded me. And here is a miracle, the sole miracle possible, surrounding me on all sides, and I never noticed it." (829)

What obscured Levin's vision and led him to despair? It was his belief that to be meaningful, life must be justified by theory. Death, suffering, and the impossibility of understanding them had made Levin believe "that he must either interpret life so that it would not present itself to him as the evil mockery of some devil, or shoot himself" (830). Looking for a theory to justify life, he realized that there neither is nor could be one.

The search for such a theory leads logically to suicide. Levin's own book argues that theory must never dictate to practice, but he did not apply this lesson to his ethical dilemma.

Levin now reflects that he went on living anyway because somewhere he dimly sensed that he was either asking the question wrongly or asking the wrong question. The wisdom of his good life saved him. "What did this mean? It meant that he had been living rightly but thinking wrongly" (830). Levin now understands: he was rescued from suicide by the habits that led him to live for the right things no matter what he thought. Levin recognizes those habits as first acquired in childhood. Once again, *Anna Karenina* insists on the crucial importance of parenting.

Levin could not clearly state to anyone else what he has discovered, and when he momentarily tries, the intellectual Katavasov just laughs at his vagueness. For Tolstoy, narrative is so important because it can illuminate how a person finds meaning even though the meaning itself cannot be stated. Among

Tolstoy's later works, brief stories collected in the anthology Wittgenstein knew as *Twenty-three Tales,* as well as novellas such as "Father Sergius" and "The Death of Ivan Ilych," portray a successful quest for meaningfulness.

Pierre, Father Sergius, Ivan Ilych, and other heroes discover meaningfulness not when they answer existential questions but when those questions disappear. Wittgenstein paraphrases Tolstoy's repeated point:

> 6.521. The solution of the problem of life is seen in the vanishing of the problem.
>
> (Is not this the reason why those who have found after a long period of doubt that the sense of life became clear to them have been unable to say what constituted that sense?)
>
> 6.522. There are, indeed, things that cannot be put into words. They *make themselves manifest.* (Wittgenstein, *Tractatus*)

Levin could never have reasoned himself to meaningfulness because meaningfulness is unreasonable. He has been hindered by pride, "and not merely pride of intellect, but the stupidity of intellect. And most of all, the deceitfulness, yes, the deceitfulness of intellect" (831).

Why Vision Is Not Singular

The "deceitfulness" of intellect consists above all in the claims that scientific theories can in principle account for all experience, and that, outside them, there is only superstition. This deceit, which prevails no less strongly today, is itself a superstition of the intelligentsia.

Why must there be a *single* theory of everything? We assume there must be some unifying theory of theories, but that assumption may be entirely mistaken.

Levin prays sincerely but cannot give up a scientific explanation of nature. He concludes that an enigma lies behind this apparent contradiction. But perhaps the enigma does not exist.

What if science is not some sort of universal theory? What if, instead, it is more like a set of crafts or, as Wittgenstein would say, a language game that misleads when applied outside its proper domain? In that case, there would be nothing wrong with holding two visions, or speaking two languages, on different occasions and for different purposes. We do not insist that we use words the same way when writing wills, gossiping, discussing art, outlining construction projects, and talking with children. We need not think of everything in the same terms.

Lying on his back, Levin gazes up at the sky:

"Do I not know that that is infinite space, and that it is not a rounded vault? But however I screw up my eyes and strain my sight, I cannot see it but as round and finite, and in spite of my knowing about infinite space, I am incontestably right when I see a firm blue vault, far more than when I strain my eyes to see beyond it." (833)

Astronomical concepts are for doing astronomy. For understanding daily life, the rounded vault makes more sense. This pluralistic insight resolves the Svyazhsky enigma.

Dostoevsky Answers Tolstoy

Just as Levin once imagined that his book would have utopian consequences, so he anticipates that his new faith will entirely change his life. Perhaps any significant discovery, even one about the impossibility of understanding everything, easily leads to the hope that everything can be understood. We readily take anti-extremism to an extreme, make an all-encompassing theory out of skepticism, and dramatically proclaim the value of the prosaic. Levin readily falls into these traps.

"He thought now that his relations with all men would be different" (834). Levin imagines that he will no longer be aloof with his half-brother, that "with Kitty there shall never be quarrels," and that with servants, like the annoying Ivan the coachman, he will always be friendly. Always, never, entirely different: Levin draws extraordinary conclusions from belief in the ordinary. Almost immediately, he quarrels with Ivan the coachman and, when he meets Sergey Ivanovich, the same old aloofness returns. Even so, Levin can recall the train of thought that led him to faith and knows that, somehow, that faith is still intact.

The conversation among Levin's guests turns to the Eastern War. Part Eight begins with a description of soldiers going off to fight the Turks and liberate the Slavs under Turkish rule, with Vronsky among the volunteers. Sergey Ivanovich and Katavasov, who advocate the war, insist that for once Russians agree. The uneducated feel for their suffering Orthodox brethren and the educated of all political persuasions justify Russian intervention theoretically. Nevertheless, Levin and Kitty's father differ from the others. One of the most remarkable moral discussions in the book follows.

Dostoevsky reacted angrily to this discussion, and his views sharpen the issues at stake. A Writer's Diary, Dostoevsky's monthly periodical, breaks its rule against including literary criticism and devotes some forty pages to Tolstoy's novel. Most of these pages offer truly extraordinary praise. Dostoevsky proclaims that *Anna Karenina* justifies the very existence of the Russian people. Perhaps only a Russian would imagine that the existence of a people required justification or that a work of literature could provide it. Dostoevsky was therefore all the more enraged by the political discussion in Part Eight, which seemed to him profoundly immoral.

Levin mounts a number of arguments against the war. No awakening of the Russian people's spirit is taking place: there are always ruined people like Vronsky who will enlist in any campaign, newspapers love wars because they sell papers, and the common people neither know nor care about this war. Levin doubts that intellectuals understand the people because he himself is one of the people and he feels no spirit of combat. Like Dostoevsky, Katavasov and Sergey Ivanovich find it presumptuous that Levin, an aristocrat, should consider himself one of "the people," a concept that was typically identified with the supposedly authentic Russians, the peasants. Levin replies: "that word 'people' is so vague" (841).

Levin's reply violates the key intellectual taboo of the time. All parties claimed to be speaking for "the people," the way everyone today claims to favor "progress" and "social justice," and the word carried a kind of sacramental resonance. For that very reason, it seems to Levin like just another "magic word" substituting for real thought. Its use conceals counterfeit ideas.

Dostoevsky responds: Turks are massacring Bulgarians with unspeakable cruelty and Levin does not seem to care. Could it be because the atrocities are happening far away? We may recognize the pertinence of Dostoevsky's question when we consider the weak reaction to the atrocities in Rwanda and the Sudan in our day. Dostoevsky voices a timeless concern here. Tolstoy has anticipated this objection and faces it squarely.

Sergey Ivanovich, who is "practiced in dialectics" (841), poses a hypothetical question. Suppose you were to see *right in front of you* drunken men beating a woman or child:

> "I think you would . . . throw yourself on them, and protect the victim."
> "But I would not kill them," said Levin.
> "Yes, you would kill them."
> "I don't know. If I saw that, I might give way to my impulse of the moment, but I can't say beforehand." (839)

Dostoevsky entitles one chapter of his response: "Levin's Agitation. A Question: Does Distance Have an Influence on Love for Humanity?" (AWD, 1093). Levin would throw himself on drunken men beating a child directly in front of him but neglects suffering abroad. Why?

Dostoevsky understands this apparent inconsistency psychologically. "Is it simply the distance that influences the matter?" he asks (AWD, 1095). If we examine this "*psychological* peculiarity" (AWD, 1095), Dostoevsky reasons, we might ask whether we would care if someone was torturing infants on Mars. People do tend to feel, without ever quite saying so even to themselves, that atrocities happening somewhere else do not need to be considered, at least not urgently. If so, Dostoevsky concludes, then a new question arises: "at what distance does love of humanity end?" (AWD, 1096).

Strengthening Sergey Ivanovich's hypothetical example, Dostoevsky describes the atrocities taking place in the Balkans. We may easily substitute horrors from Bosnia, Cambodia, or other killing fields in our time: "The skin is stripped from living people while their children watch; children are tossed in the air and caught on the point of a bayonet while their mothers watch," and a two-year-old boy has "his eyes pierced with a needle while his sister watched and was then impaled on a stake so that he did not die quickly but screamed for a long time" (AWD, 1095).

Now imagine Levin "right there" when the Turk is about to pierce the child's eyes. Dostoevsky supposes that Levin, if consistent with his professed beliefs, would just stand there, thinking and hesitating:

"I don't know what I'll do. I don't feel anything. I'm one of the People myself. . . ."

But seriously . . . would he really not snatch him [the child] from the hands of the villainous Turk?

"Well, yes, I'd snatch him away, but suppose I had to give the Turk a good hard push?"

"Then push him!"

"Push him, you say! And if he doesn't want to let the child go and draws his saber? Why, suppose I had to kill the Turk?"

"Well then, kill him!"

"But how can I kill him! No, I mustn't kill the Turk. No, it's better to let him pierce the child's eyes and torture him; I'll go home to Kitty." (AWD, 1096)

It does not take much imagination to appreciate Dostoevsky's point. Conversations more or less like this must have taken place when the Holocaust was in process. I remember similar discussions regarding Pol Pot, Idi Amin, and Slobodan Milosevic. I cite Dostoevsky's response to Tolstoy because the dialogue between these two authors is perhaps even more relevant to our time than to theirs.

The First Tolstoyan Reply: Moral Distance

Tolstoy understands Dostoevsky's position, or he would not have given a version of it to Sergey Ivanovich. He rejects it for multiple reasons:

Distance really does affect responsibility. Moral Newtonians with their universal laws presume that ethics does not respect persons. The moral law treats everyone as of equal value. Tolstoy regards such a view as monstrous. No one is a disembodied agent lacking connections to particular people. Do we really want to say that we owe no more to our own children than we do to strangers half-way around the world? Is a mother morally wrong in her partiality to her own child? Should Dolly spend less time with Tanya and Grisha in order to raise money for the suffering Slavs?

For Tolstoy, morality may be described in terms of concentric circles. We owe our greatest responsibility to our family, then to our neighbors, relatives, or co-workers, then to people in our community, and, only several circles later, to people we have never met on the other side of the world; and only beyond that to "Martians." When someone bids us to do unto others, ask them *which* others. Because time and energy are limited, demand to know unto which others we will consequently do less. Responsibility never entirely evaporates at any distance, but it does diminish. To be precise, it diminishes not with physical but with what might be called *moral distance.*

The Second Tolstoyan Reply, and Three Maxims about Social Judgments

When we view a distant hilltop, all we see is trees, and so we conclude that the region contains nothing but trees. An analogous fallacy distorts our moral judgments. When we consider distant places, problems seem simple, good and evil clearly delineated, and solutions obvious precisely because we do not really know what is going on. We see the problems in our own family as complex because so many particularities strike us and the obstacles impeding any course of action can be easily imagined. Here is a Tolstoyan maxim: the less we know about a situation, the simpler it seems.

People tend to hold firm views about distant places or different social groups because it is easy to pass moral judgment when we know little and are immune from the consequences of our judgments. We can feel morally superior without cost. Intellectuals typically imagine that, unlike those whose views are distorted by self-interest and self-deception, they see clearly. It rarely occurs to them that the belief in the disinterestedness of intellectuals is itself self-interested. Here are two more Tolstoyan maxims: the more an opinion makes oneself or one's favored groups morally superior, the more suspicious one should be of it. And the more cost-free to ourselves a given policy seems, the more we should suspect the arguments for it.

The Third Tolstoyan Reply: Theoretical Illustrations vs. Novelistic Cases

Sergey Ivanovich and Dostoevsky each offer to clarify a moral problem with a hypothetical example. But anyone who understands case-based reasoning ought to recognize what is wrong with these examples. To begin with, they are extreme. In part, the extremism derives from the need to illustrate a theory. To do so, one seeks a maximally clear example, and so illustrations of this sort tend to extreme formulations with obvious conclusions.

It is a difficult question whether Mary Garth in *Middlemarch* should have torn up Featherstone's last will, as the dying man demanded, and she herself never fully decides whether she was right to refuse. How Karenin should react when he suspects, and then knows, of Anna's affair is a question hard to resolve, which is one reason that no matter what he does Anna can find reasons to fault him. We can be seduced by Moll Flanders's self-justifications, and maybe some of them are right. Real moral questions are hard and are usually presented as such in great realist novels (Dostoevsky's included).

From a Tolstoyan perspective we might say: Be suspicious of hypothetical examples that resemble theoretical illustrations more than novelistic cases. When the conclusion is unique and obvious, ask what has been omitted. Be all the more suspicious when the course of action justified by the example is itself extreme. People rarely justify war with nuance; and no one recommends leaving murderous tyrants in power by acknowledging the case for stopping them.

It is almost always easy enough to formulate illustrations that make the opposite conclusion equally unavoidable. Since examples of this sort can justify anything, they should always be treated with skepticism. When it is easy to formulate opposite and equally extreme illustrations, suspect that weak moral thinking is taking place.

The Fourth Tolstoyan Reply: Galileo and Dolly

Notice how little context is provided in theoretical illustrations. They are short and leave out "extraneous" details. It is as if their model were Galileo's experiments with gravity that proceeded by *abstracting* the essence of the situation from the distracting details. Perhaps the astonishing success of this abstracting method exercised as much influence as Newton's laws in shaping the modern preference for theoretical over practical reasoning not just in physics but also in social and moral matters. We should perhaps speak of moral Galileans.

By contrast, casuistical examples and novelistic portraits are often criticized for containing too much detail. Suspicious of the abstracting method, casuists and novelists believe that in life the details often make all the difference in ways that cannot be specified in advance.

When Sergey Ivanovich asks how Levin would react in the case of the drunken men beating a woman or child, Levin answers that he does not know, and would have to decide on the moment. For Sergey Ivanovich, Katavasov, and philosophers generally, such an answer is no answer at all, because it does not provide the criteria for decision or explain why those criteria cannot be weighed beforehand. But from Tolstoy's perspective, Levin's answer is correct. The particularities of the situation make all the difference. What sort of beating, under what provocation, and for what reasons (to save a life, perhaps?); and what alternatives are available for stopping it? The consequences of a wrong decision either way are too great for one to decide how to respond without knowing the answers to these and many others questions unimaginable in advance.

Complex moral decisions by their very nature do not lend themselves to abstraction, or they would not be complex in the first place. Reacting properly is not a matter of applying a theory, or of deciding which theory best pertains to the given situation. It depends on responding as Levin and Dolly do. They *perceive* at a glance countless particulars. And they rely on their *moral sensitivity.*

As we saw with Mikhailov, sensitive perception requires training. It takes work to see more wisely. That requirement pertains no less to moral discernment than to painting. In both cases, the process of improvement is in principle endless. One develops moral acuity over a lifetime by constantly asking oneself questions about situations and people, real or fictional. One discusses those situations and people with others. The realist novel began as a lengthy prompt for such dialogues, and one of its most important functions is to educate our moral sense. Levin stages internal moral dialogues and takes both sides of each question, in part because he can find so few people willing to engage in a real discussion. His weighing of opposing complexities weakens him in "dialectics" but strengthens his perceptiveness.

We learn the process of moral questioning and improvement in childhood when fundamental habits develop. In language that may seem quaint to us, Dolly thinks of her children's growth not in therapeutic but in moral terms. Perhaps we might do well to add Dolly's approach to our own?

The Fifth Tolstoyan Reply: Presence

Time and timeliness matter in moral decisions. Dostoevsky asks about spatial "distance" but temporal distance may be as important. To decide too early — before one knows the particulars, for instance — can be as bad as deciding too late. Often, one needs to be *present,* in both senses. In *War and Peace,* the wise general Kutuzov recognizes that battle is so complex that the people who really make a difference are the line officers taking advantage of the opportunities of the moment. To do so, they need not a strategic plan but a good night's sleep. When Pierre learns to make decisions as well as Levin does, Tolstoy describes his state of mind as "moral alertness" (W&P, 1209).

Moral alertness allows one to decide on the instant. Dostoevsky imagines Levin "hesitating" while the atrocity is taking place. Tolstoy would reply: Hesitation is much more likely when one relies on theory, because one has to process a great deal of information to decide which theory applies and how. It is only moral sensitivity combined with moral alertness that allows one to act wisely on the moment.

When a fireman who rushes into a building to save a child is asked what passed through his mind, he typically answers that nothing passed through his mind. He just saw and acted. In such situations, he does not need to consider: perception, sensitivity, and training lead to an action that is simply "incontestably necessary." It is performed more quickly than any theoretically induced action could be.

A Still More Senseless Prayer and a New Mistaken Question

In the discussion about the Eastern War, Levin soon realizes that he cannot convince anyone. He turns, as Svyazhsky would, from the topic to the present situation where "one thing could be seen without doubt—that is, at the actual moment the discussion was irritating Sergey Ivanovich and so it was wrong to continue it" (844). Seeing a storm coming, he leads everyone home, where he learns that Kitty and the baby are still somewhere in the woods. Annoyed and afraid, he goes in search of them and suddenly sees lightning strike a familiar oak tree, which uncannily changes its position and falls. "My God! My God! Not on them!" he finds himself saying. He instantly realizes that this prayer is even more senseless than his earlier ones because he is asking that something not have already happened, as if the past could be altered. And yet he can "do nothing better than utter this senseless prayer" (845).

For the rest of the day, Levin experiences disappointment that his discovery of faith and meaning has not led to the total change in himself he expected. Yet the change is taking root. He no longer has to recall the whole chain of thought that led him to the feeling of meaningfulness, but can fall at once into the feeling. That chain of thought was really negative, a clearing away of earlier thoughts that had obscured what his way of living meant. As Mikhailov would say, Levin has "removed the coverings" (493), and now he can access the feeling directly. In fact, "thought could not keep pace with the feeling" (847).

Levin has not derived but recognized a truth. "I have discovered nothing. I have found out only what I already knew. . . . I have been set free from falsity" (829).

Remembering a thought interrupted by Sergey Ivanovich's arrival, Levin asks himself about other religions. If Levin's faith comes from recognizing his given sense of right and wrong, then how is he to regard non-Christians? Can it be that Jews, Muslims, and Buddhists do not have this sense? If they do, how is Levin to understand the contradiction of religions, each of which claims the others are false?

Dolly and Kitty have long known the answer to this question. Dolly has a strange set of religious beliefs all her own but she takes her children to the Orthodox church anyway. Although her Orthodoxy condemns Levin to hell as an unbeliever, Kitty nevertheless knows that her husband's life already expresses the faith that matters. Levin at last understands: Religious doctrines and practices do not matter in themselves. They are ways in which various peoples express their sense of the same "given." Of course those expressions differ, because the histories that give rise to them differ. Each culture expresses faith in a form that corresponds to its way of life. In tending his bees, Levin has just remarked to himself that each hive has its own history (836). Viewed in this way, the different religions do not in fact contradict each other.

Moreover, Levin understands that he is once again asking the wrong question. He has no duty, right, or need to resolve doctrinal differences. He reflects: to my heart "has been revealed a knowledge beyond all doubt, and unattainable by reason, and here I am obstinately trying to express that knowledge in reason and words" (829).

The Meaning of Meaningfulness

Levin considers telling Kitty about his new feeling but he immediately realizes that it must remain his own secret. It cannot be put into words. Doubtless, her own sense of meaningfulness is just as unique to her. Meaningfulness is not a proposition that can be explained and shared. "Propositions can express nothing that is higher" (Wittgenstein, *Tractatus,* 6.42). Those who sense the meaning cannot express it. Those who do not cannot benefit from the recital of theses, although they may be inspired by the story of someone who has found meaning—a story like Levin's in *Anna Karenina*.

Life is a plurality. There is no universal answer, only a sense of faith that differs from person to person. That sense of faith solves no problems. The facts remain the same. Faith changes nothing in the world, but the world as a whole changes. All the sources of friction that existed for Levin before discovering faith still exist, but they now exist in a meaningful world.

Levin needs not to solve problems but to retain the sense of meaningfulness. To do so is within his power. He must continue to live rightly and he must avoid letting theoretical abstractions obscure the feeling that expresses this life. He must attend to and recall this feeling. The novel concludes as Levin thinks:

> This new feeling has not changed me, has not made me happy and enlightened all of a sudden, as I had dreamed. . . . I shall go on in the same way, losing my temper with Ivan the coachman . . . there will still be the same wall between the holy of holies in my soul and other people, even my wife; I shall still be as unable to understand with my reason why I pray, and I shall still go on praying; but my life now, my whole life apart from anything that can happen to me, every minute of it is no longer meaningless, as it was before, but it has an unquestionable meaning of the goodness which I have the power to put into it. (851)

The world as a whole has become different, even though nothing in it has changed, because Levin sees it differently. He must still work at moral discernment and resist the intellectual blinders that once obscured the wisdom of his behavior. But Levin has the power to put meaning into the world because he has learned how to see it more wisely.

One Hundred Sixty-Three
Tolstoyan Conclusions

These conclusions, which paraphrase Tolstoy's thought or draw dotted lines from his thought to the present, are offered not as so many truths but as prompts for dialogue.

1. We live in a world of uncertainty. Assured prediction is impossible. History and individual lives contain contingent events that might just as well not have happened. No account that tries to think contingency away can be adequate.

2. There can never be a social science, in the sense that nineteenth-century physics is a science.

3. We need not only knowledge but also wisdom. Wisdom cannot be formalized or expressed adequately in a set of rules. If it could, it would not be wisdom at all. Wisdom is acquired by attentive reflection on experience in all its complexity.

4. Because the world is uncertain, presentness matters. The present moment is not an automatic derivative of the past. In human life, more than one thing can happen at any given moment. Theories that assume otherwise mislead.

5. Because presentness is real, alertness matters. The more uncertain a situation, the greater the value of alertness.

6. Numerous biases distort our perceptions of our lives. We must understand these biases to minimize their effect.

7. The idea that truth lies in the extreme is not only false but also dangerous. Even extraordinary moments are largely the product of what happens at ordinary ones.

8. The road of excess leads to the chamber of horrors.

9. True life takes place when we are doing nothing especially dramatic. The more drama, the worse the life.

10. Plot is an index of error.

11. Our lives, properly understood, consist mainly of tiny, tiny alterations of consciousness. Small changes shape the social world as well.

12. Most of what we do, we do by habit. Habits are the product of countless small choices at ordinary moments.

13. The decisions that result in an action are often located not right before the action but at countless earlier moments when small choices shaped habits.

14. We often act at a remove. Such action can feel like subjection to fate if we look only to proximate decisions. In the same way, a small range of freedom may be sensed as no freedom at all if we imagine that real choice can exist only at major turning points.

15. Actions may also be traced to the failure to acquire certain habits. Evil does not require malice.

16. We may do good, as well as evil, without setting out to do so. The most effective good actions are performed in this way.

17. The real saints do not know they are saints and are never canonized.

18. We acquire most habits in childhood. Life is not long enough to acquire enough good habits later. Even the ability to acquire better habits depends on habits of learning acquired much earlier.

19. The importance of habits and ordinary life establishes the importance of parenting and the family.

20. Goodness and evil pertain above all to ordinary moments. We usually do not notice what makes life better or worse.

21. Evil consists primarily of negative actions—what we fail to do. It usually resembles criminal negligence.

22. The greatest immorality often pertains not to the actions we commit but to our failure to imagine how they will feel to others. That is one reason that great immorality may not be intended. Those who commit it may be sincerely surprised if told what they caused others to suffer.

23. A key source of evil is the failure to acquire habits of identification with others. To avoid adulterating our pleasure, we look the other way. The less we learn to put ourselves in another's place, the more evil we may unwittingly commit.

24. We may wittingly learn to commit unwitting evil.

25. Honesty involves more than not telling conscious falsehoods. It includes checking to see whether anything we know or have done shows what we say to be untrue.

26. We must *learn* to be honest. Honesty is active, a skill acquired through hard work.

27. We can become more honest by understanding the various and complex ways we deceive ourselves.

28. We mistake sincerity for honesty when we fail to appreciate that honesty is not passive. One can sincerely state what a moment's thought would tell one is untrue. Dishonest people can sometimes pass lie detector tests.

29. The best tool for being dishonest with sincerity is a good forgettory. A forgettory does not work by repressing inconvenient information. Rather, it insures that one does not acquire habits of checking. Repression is a positive action, but the actions of a forgettory are negative. Each act of non-seeing requires little or no effort. Repression demands energy and easily betrays itself in feelings of discomfort. Forgettories work much better than repression.

30. Censorship is less effective than absence of thought.

31. The better one's forgettory, the less one is capable of remorse. Guilt is a poor index of immorality. Those who feel the least guilt are not the guiltless but those who can best forestall feeling, those with excellent forgettories. Conversely, truly moral people often feel the greatest guilt precisely because they constantly monitor their behavior. They have a habit of trying to detect and correct anything they may have done wrong. That monitoring, that use of guilt to correct bad actions, is what makes moral people moral in the first place.

32. The more a belief justifies our way of life, the more we should suspect our reasons for believing it.

33. One can lie by looking and practice falsehood in silence.

34. Lying is not limited to false speaking. False listening and false seeing are also forms of lying.

35. Looking and listening are actions. We choose how to perform them. We can look and see morally or immorally, honestly or dishonestly, skillfully or carelessly, foolishly or wisely.

36. The most important, because most frequent, action we perform is directing our attention. We can deceive ourselves by choosing to notice or overlook what we wish. We can exaggerate or diminish our perceptual biases.

37. Self-deception is not passive, not a matter of holding two divergent beliefs at once. Because experience is varied, no one's beliefs are totally consistent. But not all inconsistency involves self-deception. To think of self-deception in terms of belief is to err, because self-deception is active. It involves an attempt to see certain things and not see others.

38. The most meaningful moments of our lives do not fit life stories. We either do not see them at all, or we merely glimpse them. They may be found but not sought. They appear like gold in sand.

39. Real heroism does not look heroic in the usual sense. As charity does not puff itself up, heroism works quietly in the background. Epics, saints' lives, opera, and high drama all mistake the nature of heroism.

40. Because real heroism is prosaic, we are likely to look for it in the wrong place.

41. Romantic love is only one kind of love. We too often think that if love is not romantic it is not "true love."

42. We must overcome the myth of romantic love, which is a version of extremist thinking. True life is not lived at moments of greatest intensity.

43. The myth of love as passion—as something that happens entirely apart from our will—disables us from choosing.

44. We often describe actions as passions so as to avoid responsibility for them.

45. We sometimes choose to create situations in which something we wish for but know is wrong can happen "against our will."

46. Fatalism provides us with a fake alibi for responsibility. It fosters and is fostered by the myth of romantic love.

47. Fatalism comes in many forms. It speaks different languages at different times and in different cultures. It conceals itself so we do not easily recognize it. Those who laugh at omens may fall prey to other signs from the future. They may disbelieve in the gods but ascribe agency to elements of their unconscious that "compel" them to act one way or another.

48. The inability to choose may be attributed to natural or supernatural, psychological or sociological, remote or proximate forces. Regardless of its form, its sign is the plea that one could not but have chosen as one did. Fatalism also works in the present, not just to excuse an action after the fact, but also to allow us to perform it in the first place. I cannot refrain from doing it; it is beyond my power to resist.

49. Fatalism is a choice and freedom is ineluctable.

50. Myths often bedevil us through language: We may base our choices on what is *called* true love or true life even if our values and feelings would otherwise lead to different choices.

51. Romantic love, with its cult of mystery, is ultimately incompatible with marriage and family. If a family is to survive, romantic love must change into prosaic love. Otherwise it leads to a sense that life is empty, to a feeling of having been betrayed, and to adultery.

52. Prosaic love values intimacy above all. It cultivates closeness, knowledge of the other, and better communication. Marriage and family love require it. It does not make a good story.

53. Prosaic love has its own kind of intense eroticism different from romantic eroticism. This eroticism comes from knowing another, emotionally and physically, extremely well.

54. Prosaic love is above all a way of paying attention.

55. The deepest love often feels like a source of vulnerability. Love for an infant does not feel as it is conventionally supposed to feel because it includes pity and disgust.

56. There exists a prosaic sublime, in which the conditions of ordinary life

allow us to feel what reason cannot grasp and reach places where reason lags behind.

57. Marriage is not an idyll in which one simply "enjoys love." It demands the constant work of knowing oneself and another as changing people in changing circumstances.

58. As a valuable life demands meaningful work, boredom and the need to fill time are signs that a life is lived badly. When life is lived well, there is never enough time.

59. One can estimate the value of a given kind of work by its similarity to parenting.

60. When events resemble a well-plotted story, it is usually because we are imitating that story or misperceiving reality so as to omit everything else.

61. Suspect that critical moments are fabricated. The feeling of "now or never" is often mistaken and prevents us from trying again. It is typically a concealed form of fatalism. "Now or never" occurs rarely, if ever.

62. Whenever events feel as if they were somehow "meant to be," recognize this feeling as a temptation to fatalism. Ask oneself whether one truly believes that an author is planning the details of one's life the way novelists plan the lives of their characters.

63. Imagining oneself as a tragic, romantic, or novelistic hero or heroine may deprive one of freedom, but it confers a spurious sense of importance. It feeds narcissism.

64. Life is not a work of any genre.

65. Pure and perfect sorrow is as impossible as pure and perfect joy.

66. No emotion, no personality, and no social situation can ever be pure. When art represents them as all of a piece, it misleads. We believe the world resembles such art at our peril.

67. We are not coherent wholes. All our traits do not fit together in some deep way. We negotiate among clusters of habits acquired in contingent circumstances. We do not coincide with ourselves. That is why characters in fiction feel more real when they are not overly consistent and why lies can be more persuasive when they do not account for everything.

68. One sign of forgery is total consistency or typicality.

69. Like individual people, society does not coincide with itself.

70. Important news is usually accompanied by less important news as well as sheer noise.

71. As dishonesty may be sincere, so naturalness may be contrived, spontaneity may be studied, and simplicity may be fake.

72. Deceivers know: If one would successfully deceive others, learn to perform at will actions usually assumed to be involuntary, like crying, blushing, or

laughing. If we can forget our choice to perform these actions, or choose at a remove, we may deceive ourselves as well.

73. Every perceptual bias can be and is manipulated for purposes of deceit and self-deceit.

74. It is often when nothing special is happening that lives are being smashed.

75. We often confuse the repetition of a thought with its truth or logical necessity. Obsession is no proof.

76. One may lie about not wanting to lie. It is easy to apply the idea of "truth to oneself" to justify anything. Because truth to oneself is an important value, one must be careful to invoke it truthfully.

77. No matter what divorce laws or gender roles may prevail, infidelity will always cause pain. When children are involved, divorce will always involve difficult moral problems.

78. Whenever we feel we have the key to everything, we are leaving something out.

79. All formulae, philosophies, or emotional states that promise a totalism of meaning significantly misrepresent reality and cause severe harm.

80. Narcissism feeds the belief we have the single key.

81. The body has a mind of its own.

82. Bodily actions sometimes derive not from thought, whether conscious or unconscious, but from physical habits. Or they may respond to perceptions of which we are not aware.

83. Bodily actions that do not arise from thought may call thoughts to mind.

84. We always know more than we know.

85. The most horrible moment of a suicide's life may be the very last, when regret at self-destruction comes too late.

86. Russia was the first country to choose rapid modernization. Russian debates explore patterns of argument subsequently followed elsewhere. That priority constitutes one significance of Russian history when viewed from a global perspective.

87. Attempts to modernize cannot succeed if they conflict too much with the elemental force, the sum total of habits and practices of people.

88. The elemental force is the product of countless contingent circumstances and cannot be reduced to one or a few forces.

89. Most attempted reforms fail or make the situation still worse.

90. Conspiracy logic teaches people to attribute the resistance of the elemental force to sabotage. If a regime has enough force at its disposal, the most horrible human calamities may result from such thinking.

91. Because the world is uncertain, we are always scanning.

92. If life were essentially predictable, our hands would not have an inbuilt tremor and our minds would not wander. Antelopes would have wheels and communism would work.

93. What often makes a machine last or break is what the operator does when his or her mind wanders.

94. What often makes reform succeed or fail is what happens when enthusiasm flags and habits take over.

95. There are always unintended consequences, which in turn have consequences. Successful reformers therefore constantly monitor, adjust, and tinker with their reforms in response to experience.

96. Great leaps forward take us backward.

97. No one who really cares about the professed goal of a reform silences criticism. The more deeply one cares, the more one invites criticism.

98. When a reformer refuses to credit opponents with insight or knowledge, he or she demonstrates greater concern for identifying with other reformers than with having the reform succeed.

99. Successful reforms are neither copied from a model nor imposed by template. They come from the bottom up.

100. The root cause of the greatest social evil is the belief that one has found the root cause of social evil.

101. The simplest changes are often very difficult because of "friction." Friction in this sense is how the elemental force's resistance is experienced. One cannot identify precisely what the obstacle is, because the friction results from countless small pressures.

102. The fundamental state of the social world is mess. Order is not given, and it does not lie beneath surface disorder. One does not discover it but makes it. It requires work.

103. Left to themselves, things tend to "messify." A social analogue of entropy governs.

104. Potholes do not fix themselves.

105. Self-improvement resembles social reform in this respect: one cannot make oneself a better person by copying another or imposing a template. One cannot become a saint by imitating the Lives of the Saints.

106. One becomes better one habit at a time. Changes in habits that are to work must not conflict too much with the elemental force of one's personality, the sum total of one's habits.

107. Beware of belief systems that can be adopted whole, the way one puts on a uniform. Suspect people who wear such a uniform.

108. As goodness does not sound a trumpet, it does not offer all the answers nor lead to the same answer time and again.

109. Life requires practical wisdom. Practical wisdom is not a mere substitute for theoretical wisdom when the latter is not yet available. In practice theorists rely on practice.

110. The more uncertainty and the more complexity, the more flexibility pays.

111. As chance favors the prepared mind, opportunity favors the heterogeneous situation.

112. Some kinds of knowledge advance by abstraction, as Galileo abstracted principles of motion by imagining an ideal situation without friction. In other kinds of knowledge, abstraction would necessarily omit the very factors one most needs to know.

113. As one may slow oneself down by hurrying, one may stupefy oneself with philosophy.

114. Intellectuals have developed an arsenal of means for avoiding contrary evidence: the argument by bibliography (not answering a questioner but referring him to a reading list), the argument by disciplinary exclusion (treating questions as too naïve to be asked), and the argument by association (a form of name-calling). Intellectuals and professionals need to remind themselves of basic questions asked by laymen.

115. Christian love is possible but not necessarily desirable. It runs so strongly against the elemental force that it may easily turn into a form of sanctimonious cruelty, all the more for having been true and sincere at the start.

116. Genuine art is made from experience observed with great sensitivity. Each experience differs from all others, but one can detect the differences only if one has trained oneself to see.

117. One cannot make genuine art by copying a model, by including currently fashionable subject matter, or by relying on striking effects. Such methods produce only counterfeit art.

118. The more an artwork resembles a statement of beliefs currently favored by the intelligentsia, the more one should suspect it is a counterfeit.

119. The more pleasingly "transgressive" a work is, the more likely it is to be a cliché of the present moment.

120. Real thinking, like real art, derives from serious reflection on finely observed experience.

121. A person who agrees with all the opinions favored by most intellectuals of the day is probably simply accepting those beliefs wholesale. Real thinking is bound to depart from received intellectual truths.

122. It is possible to coin a cliché. We celebrate discoveries of what we already know.

123. One can learn from those with whom one disagrees if their ideas have

been arrived at authentically. Because authentic ideas come from sensitively observed experience, one can, so to speak, graft that experience onto one's own.

124. If one is interested in the truth, one seeks, not avoids, authentic ideas that contradict one's own.

125. Real thinkers are not afraid to be called behind the times. They suspect evaluation by temporality (locating ideas on a time line).

126. Genuine education does not teach students to learn a prescribed method of thinking. It shows them examples of authentic thinking so they recognize it when they see it, in others and in themselves.

127. Some people change their views. With others, their views change within them.

128. If one cannot imagine an honorable and decent person holding opinions differing from one's own, one is not really thinking.

129. Holding beliefs without discovering the best opposing beliefs is like trusting a trial with only a prosecution.

130. Intellectuals have their own superstitions and think by their own magic words.

131. One sign of a magic word is that one cannot imagine opposing what it purports to stand for. Is there anyone against education, justice, and progress?

132. Another sign of a magic word is that those who invoke it do not ask how exactly to achieve the purpose it names.

133. We usually assume that divergence between one's beliefs and behavior necessarily signifies hypocrisy, but sometimes the opposite is the case. The only way to get one's beliefs and behavior to coincide totally is to choose one's beliefs so as to rationalize one's behavior. Divergence may signify hypocrisy but it may also indicate an honest attempt to find the truth even at the cost of self-criticism.

134. It is a mistake to think that there is a master discipline—physics, philosophy, economics or any other—that enunciates fundamental truths to which all other truths must conform. One often needs different ways of thinking in different spheres of life.

135. Think of each discipline as a way to approach certain kinds of problems, not as a model for all thinking. The earth is the center of the moral universe.

136. Science explains causes but cannot provide meaning.

137. Scientific explanation of meaning can only arrive at some version of the following statement: "In infinite time, in infinite matter, in infinite space, is formed a bubble-organism, and that bubble lasts a while and bursts, and that bubble is I."

138. The sense that life is meaningless is usually a symptom of a life badly

lived. In these cases, one needs not to answer a philosophical question, but to change one's life. Then the question is not answered, but it disappears.

139. In other cases, the sense of meaninglessness derives not from a life badly lived but from trusting theories more than lived experience. Even if one lives well, one can despair if one seeks an answer that cannot be given.

140. The meaning of life cannot be a proposition or we would all already know it.

141. The meaning of life cannot be a fact in the world of cause and effect.

142. When one senses the meaning of things, one cannot formulate it so that others will sense it, the way one can demonstrate a theorem in Euclidian geometry. But one can tell a story about how one arrived at a sense of meaningfulness. That story can help others to recognize when a similar process is taking place in themselves.

143. Meaningfulness changes one's sense of the world as a whole. But it does not solve the specific problems of the world.

144. Work that is truly meaningful feels "incontestably necessary." One feels that one could not do otherwise.

145. In choosing an occupation, look not for what conforms to one's theory of justice in the abstract. Rather, find one in which the day-to-day work feels necessary and so engages one's energies.

146. In matters of ethics, we know some things more surely than any reasons we can give to justify them.

147. Fostering sensitivity to particular cases is the best ethical training. Morality is not a matter of applying a theory to a particular situation. Because sensitive reflection on cases develops one's ethical insight, experience matters.

148. We do not owe the same treatment to everyone. Attention and effort are limited resources, and we owe the greatest responsibility to those who are closest to us.

149. Responsibility diminishes with moral distance.

150. To behave morally, one must be able to imagine oneself in another's place: there but for the grace of God go I. Each person is a natural egoist who sees the world as if it were a novel in which he or she were the hero or heroine, but morality begins when a person can see the world as if he or she were a minor character in someone else's novel.

151. The ability to see and feel the world from another's perspective is necessary, though not sufficient, for morality.

152. Real ethical training must include practice in transcending one's own perspective.

153. The richest cases we have are to be found in realist novels. If psychologists, sociologists, or philosophers understood people as well as the great realist

novelists, they would be able to describe people who seemed as real as characters in George Eliot or Tolstoy.

154. No other art form or discipline describes moral situations, as well as individual people, with the richness and complexity of the great realist novels.

155. Realist novels make clear that simple solutions to complex problems are absurd.

156. The process of identifying with a novelistic character is itself a form of moral education. One sees the world with a different set of eyes.

157. The contention that realist novels have outlived their day and can no longer speak to us is mistaken. We need to explore the people and situations of our world as much as earlier ages needed to explore theirs.

158. An important ethical task of the critic is to "translate" the wisdom of the great novels into our own terms.

159. Instead of presuming that our values are superior, suspend that sense of superiority and let the novel interrogate us.

160. Do not treat *Anna Karenina,* or any other great novel, only as a document of its times, as sugar-coated philosophy, or in any other way that diminishes its moral import for ourselves.

161. Let each person open himself or herself to a genuine moral dialogue with the work. If successful, that dialogue will be valuable not only for yielding propositions but also for the dialogic process itself.

162. We must cast away the telescope and learn to see the world of tiny alterations right before our eyes.

163. To understand life more deeply we must learn to see more wisely.

Notes

Introduction

1 BoG, 39. My characterization of literature was indebted to Ellis, chapter 2, who writes: "Literary texts are defined as those that are used by the society in such a way that *the text is not taken as specifically relevant to the immediate context of its origin*" (italics in original). I explained that my formulation differed from Ellis's in that (a) his definition is evaluative as well as interpretive, and (b) he is concerned with the use of the word literature and I with identifying a specific class of text.

Chapter One. Tolstoy and the Twenty-first Century

1 Donna Orwin observes that Tolstoy's "opposition to philosophizing in the novel was itself part of a principled philosophical position" and that "the novel imitates life before it analyzes life, which therefore is never completely explained by analysis" (Orwin, "Antiphilosophical Philosophy," 95, 99).

2 I owe this parable to a conversation with Aron Katsenelinboigen.

3 For a reply to "prosaics" in this novel, see Mandelker, 70–73.

Chapter Two. Dolly and Stiva: Prosaic Good and Evil

1 The French saying—"Les peuples heureux n'ont pas d'histoire"—connects *Anna Karenina* to *War and Peace,* where the saying appears (see Orwin, *Art and Thought,* 179 and Babaev, 133). In a draft of the novel, gossipers remark that one must speak ill of people in order to have something to say, because happy people have no history (see Orwin, *Art and Thought,* 244, and Babaev, 133).

In fact, this thought was not unusual. The *Oxford Dictionary of Quotations* lists as an early nineteenth-century proverb: "Happy is the country which has no history" (621). It refers the reader to Montesquieu, or rather, to Carlyle citing Montesquieu: "Happy the people whose annals are blank in history books!" (545).

Brewer's Famous Quotations, which offers commentary to each entry, quotes George Eliot in book 6, chapter 3 of *The Mill on the Floss* (1860): "The happiest women, like the happiest nations, have no history." *Brewer's* explains that Eliot was adapting a proverbial expression and cites Carlyle (1838) citing Montesquieu: "Carlyle had written: 'A paradoxical philosopher, carrying to the uttermost length that aphorism of Montesquieu's "Happy the people whose annals are tiresome," has said, "Happy the people whose annals are vacant.""" In *Poor Richard's Almanack* (1740) we find: "Happy that Nation,—fortunate that age, whose history is not diverting." We may guess at how commonly the saying was invoked by the fact that Theodore Roosevelt felt compelled to contest it (speech of 1899): "It is a base untruth to say that happy is the nation that has no history. Thrice happy is the nation that has a glorious history. Far better it is to dare mighty things. . . ." (*Brewer's*, 185).

The *Yale Book of Quotations* includes as a proverb: "Happy is the country which has no history." It cites Thomas Jefferson (letter of 1807): "Blest is that nation whose silent course of happiness furnishes nothing for history to say" (610).

What I identify as a "Yiddish curse" is sometimes given as a Chinese curse. One suspects the national attribution to be not a factual ascription but a rhetorical part of the saying itself.

2 A notable exception is Helen Edmundson's adaptation to the stage. Edmundson describes how when she first read the novel, she found the Levin story to be "an irritant," but eventually decided that the presence of the Levin story is what makes the novel "something great." "Watching the films of the novel, all of which deal solely with Anna and none of which get beyond melodrama and cliché," she resolved to find a way to do both stories (see Edmundson, v).

3 Amy Mandelker questions my reading of Dolly as heroine (in one of my articles) in Mandelker, 47–57 (a section entitled "Who Is a Heroine?"). Despite his commitment to polysemy, Vladimir Alexandrov maintains that "Any [*sic*] analysis of Dolly has to consider that she is a secondary character with a relatively limited role in the novel" (Alexandrov, 211). I differ.

4 Interestingly enough, Kropotkin found Anna "not as living a creation as she might have been; but the more ordinary woman, Dolly, is simply teeming with life" (Kropotkin, 366).

5 With some exaggeration, we may say: the more likely a passage is to be omitted by an anthologizer or left undramatized by an adapter, the more important it is likely to be.

6 This passage is especially difficult to interpret in today's terms because the equivalent of birth control in Dolly's culture is not birth control in ours. One could hardly imagine an educated American woman of Dolly's social class unaware of birth control. And marriage has changed so much that birth control does not have the same significance.

What is disturbing here is the *reasons* Anna uses birth control and those reasons, no matter what behavior they affect, betray Anna's despair, values, and patterns of behavior.

7 Including the reader, whom he often charms. Orwin comments: "The opening sally in the novel is especially daring, because Tolstoy maneuvers readers into identifying with Stiva when this character is behaving unfairly" (Orwin, "Antiphilosophical Philosophy," 101). Gina Kovarsky traces a pattern by which the novel shapes readers' reaction to Stiva: "enforcing attraction, creating ambivalent feelings of kinship, and establishing moral distance" (Kovarsky, 168).

8 The classic discussion of Stiva in English, Kathryn Feuer's, sees Stiva as "an unusual character in Tolstoy's fiction, a man of flawed morality whom the reader is nevertheless encouraged to like" (Feuer, 348). She sees Stiva's dilemma in the novel's opening as the conflict between his honesty and the inborn zest for life he shares with

Anna, for whom the same conflict becomes tragic. "Honesty makes Stiva and Anna acknowledge their faults, but the conviction that they cannot go against their innermost nature tells them they are not to blame" (Feuer, 350). Although I do not agree with this portrait of Stiva and Anna, I find Feuer's close readings illuminating and her conclusion, about Stiva's phrase *obrazuetsia* [things will shape themselves] profound: "The idea [of this phrase], however, in opposition to the human delusion of deciding and settling, lies close to the 'labyrinth' of *Anna Karenina*" (Feuer, 354). John Bayley, who is sympathetic to Stiva, shrewdly observes: "Another role of Stiva is no less important. It is to identify us, at the outset, as if it were in play, with the situation of an adulterer. The immediate and involuntary sympathy we feel for him—perhaps identification rather than sympathy, for it is something physical rather than moral—will stay with us in all such situations throughout the book. . . . though his sex-life is presumably more complicated and sordid than that of any other character, it seems innocent to us because it seems so to him" (Bayley, 206–7).

Chapter Three. Anna

1   Martin Price observes: "Characters like Anna are tragic figures because, for reasons that are admirable, they cannot live divided lives or survive through repression" (Price, 202). Harold Bloom replies: "That sentence of Martin Price is the best I have read about Anna, but I wonder if Anna can be called a tragic figure, any more than she can be what Schopenhauer grimly would have called her, a traitor. Tragedy depends upon division and repression, and Anna is betrayed by nature itself, which does not create men as vital as herself, or, if it does, creates them as savage moralists, like Tolstoy" (Bloom, 8). Julie Buckler observes: "Tragedy is the dramatic mode most frequently associated with Anna's story. . . . Still, students should be encouraged to question the tragic reading of Anna as potentially reductive" (Buckler, 133). Svetlana Evdokimova, like Buckler, explores the generic bases of the novel; she sees it as a novelization of the Platonic dialogue (Evdokimova, 141).

2   Amy Mandelker asserts that, on the contrary, the majority reading is critical of Anna: "Despite recognition of the novel's complexity and the ambivalence of Anna's characterization, the critical consensus is that the novel condemns Anna with heavy-handed didacticism" (Mandelker, 40). Sydney Schultze observes: "Perhaps of all the issues [discussed by readers of *Anna Karenina*], the question of Anna's guilt, or the 'wrongness' of her actions, has generated the greatest amount of discussion. Most readers consider Anna not guilty, but the reasons for acquitting her vary widely" (Schultze, 10). Evidently, there is no clear consensus on majority and minority. Moreover, it is not always clear whether readers are speaking of author or implied author; or whether, regardless of what either author or implied author may mean the reader "acquits" Anna. My own classification of majority and minority refers to opinions about what the "implied author" (or the work itself) does. It does not refer to my own opinion of Anna's actions.

3   Gustafson's interpretation of the novel as "a parable of self-indulgence" (Gustafson, 131) remains powerful even without invoking Tolstoy's theology.

4   I largely agree with Gustafson: Anna "thinks she hates falsehood, but that is only how it seems to her that she thinks. Falsehood is her fatal flaw. Anna is not honest with others or herself, however, because she has suppressed her guilty conscience. . . . She

sees, disapproves of what she sees, and therefore cannot let herself see. . . . Anna's drama results from the suppression of her guilty conscience. . . . Anna lies, especially to herself" (Gustafson, 120–21).

5 One of the most powerful and theoretically sophisticated readings also sees the novel as critical of Anna from a nonreligious point of view. Edward Wasiolek observes that we want to exonerate Anna and that Tolstoy gives us many ways to do so, but nevertheless "Tolstoy is convinced that she is wrong" (Wasiolek, 150). By "Tolstoy" here he means the implied author in the text, and the weight of the structure as he has designed it. Nevertheless, Wasiolek writes, the text will support other readings. "Tolstoy has drawn a powerful portrait of a woman tortured and torturing, loving and hurting and being hurt. The portrait moves us as powerfully as it did Tolstoy's contemporaries, but for different reasons—reasons supported by structures in the text" (Wasiolek, 155).

6 Andrea Lanoux notes: "*Anna Karenina* has inspired over twenty film adaptations around the globe, including seven silent films, a ballet version, several made-for-television miniseries, two Hollywood film classics starring Greta Garbo and Vivien Leigh, plus more recent versions starring Jacqueline Bisset and Sophie Marceau" (Lanoux, 180). On the different kinds of adaptations, see Makoreeva.

7 Consider Gina Kovarsky's paraphrase of Tolstoy's method and her quotation from Tolstoy: "In Tolstoy's view, the artist teaches best who imparts a deeply felt experience of moral conflict, succeeding better than a polemicist who presents ready truths. As Tolstoy wrote in 1852, morally effective literary works elicit empathy only if readers 'recognize in [a character] as many of their own weaknesses as they do their virtues; the virtues are optional; the weaknesses necessities'" (Kovarsky, 169). Such a strategy runs the risk that the reader will want to apologize for the character.

8 Describing Anna's passion, Harold Bloom writes: "What Tolstoy does show us, with overwhelming persuasiveness, is that there is no choice involved" (Bloom, 1).

9 Orwin points to the significance of the full title: *Anna Karenina: A Novel.* The word for novel, *roman,* can also mean a romance or a love affair. See Orwin, *Art and Thought,* 179.

10 Gary Jahn sees the novel and Anna illustrating a universal human dilemma: we "must live perpetually in the space between the Charybdis of an inescapable (determined) fate as a social being . . . and the Scylla of unrestrained gratification of the spontaneous ego, of freedom. . . . Thus, Anna truly is, as she says again and again, both guilty and yet not to blame" (Jahn, 8).

Stiva also participates in the novel's consideration of Plato's theory of love, which Stiva and Levin discuss in the restaurant. On this debate, see Gutkin.

11 Wasiolek offers a shrewd psychological analysis of why Anna refuses a divorce and prefers to stay a mistress.

12 Commenting on the scene where Anna does not punish Seryozha for his naughtiness, as Seryozha expects, Orwin explains: "Anna fails to punish Seryozha because, knowing herself to be guilty of a greater sin, she is more concerned that he love and forgive *her* than that she do what is best for *him*" (Orwin, *Art and Thought,* 145). Olga Karpushina comments on Anna's attitude to her children: "Serezha, who so resembles Karenin, is a permanent reminder of lies, deceit, and adultery—all those things that Anna tries to bury and forget. Yet in the depths of her heart Anna knows that what she is doing is wrong, and she cannot love Annie because she cannot forgive herself

that the child is Vronskii's. Anna gave to her son all the energy of her unspent love; in her relations with Vronskii Anna expends all her love on him, and so cannot give Annie something she no longer possesses" (Karpushina, 73).

13   Iseult is an adulteress and so is Anna Karenina, whom de Rougemont, interestingly enough, interprets as if Tolstoy exalted, rather than exposed, the romantic ideal. De Rougemont himself sometimes tends to extremism, and in his embrace of a total interpretation of European culture, cannot recognize the most outstanding counter-example.

14   In her adaptation, Edmundson has Anna say of the novel she reads: "I can hardly bear to read it because his story is mine" (Edmundson, 17). Edmundson opens her adaptation with a conversation in which Anna confronts Levin to "banish" him from the play:

> ANNA.   You are Levin. You are Constantine Levin. Why are you here? . . . This is my story (Edmundson, 1).

15   Orwin observes: "Characters in *Anna Karenina* are necessarily imperfect, but they are capable of moral choices. Moral choice is the lynchpin around which *Anna Karenina* turns" (Orwin, *Art and Thought*, 178). All the more striking, then, is the choice of a heroine who is a fatalist.

16   Martin Price comments: "The ludicrous sight of Karenin's ears seems to precipitate a new way of looking at him. He ceases to be a familiar presence, someone seen as all but part of herself. Instead, he has become a distinct figure, seen from a distance and very much from the outside. The observation of his ears is not, of course, the cause of what follows; it is simply the first detail registered by a new analytic view made possible through the withdrawal or absence of the usual feelings" (Price, 185).

17   In Edmundson's metanarrative, Levin reminds Anna that she is falsifying the past by quoting back her earlier words to her.

18   We may also be inclined to see the story through Anna's eyes if we detect a parallelism between Karenin and Casaubon in George Eliot's *Middlemarch*. For a subtle analysis of the many connections between the two novels, see Blumberg. After enumerating several ways in which Karenin and Casaubon resemble each other, Blumberg notes two differences: Casaubon makes no progress on his book, but Karenin accomplishes a great deal as an administrator (even if such accomplishments are worthless in Tolstoy's view); and Karenin "loves his wife with far greater feeling than Casaubon, with his 'exceedingly shallow rill.'" (Blumberg, 566).

19   Gustafson comments on Anna's dismissal of Vronsky's desire to "end it" by "mimicking Karenin's imagined response. . . . The Karenin she creates in her dramatic rendering is the Karenin she needs" (Gustafson, 123).

20   Harriet Murav observes: "Karenin can be all too readily dismissed as a mere creature of Petersburg officialdom. Encouraging a more sympathetic reading is important. By getting a better understanding of Karenin's transformation—regardless of his subsequent reversal—students come closer to understanding the dilemma of divorce in *Anna Karenina*" (Murav, 77–78).

21   Malcolm Jones alludes to this passage in his description (with which I am largely sympathetic) of Anna's marriage: "But if Anna is sensible of the pretense in her relations with her husband, it is possible to exaggerate the discomfort which this affords her. Of its kind, the marriage seems to have been a moderately successful one. . . .

With Karenin she has always been open about her deepest joys and anxieties and he has always listened sympathetically, even if he does decline to identify with her imaginatively, believing as he does that to put oneself in thought and feeling into another being is a harmful and dangerous exercise" (Jones, 99).

22 Enumerating ways in which Anna parries Karenin, Gustafson comments: "Throughout this scene, the second one between Anna and Karenin, Anna is lying to herself and to Karenin—only now she knows that she is. She is 'amazed at her own capacity for lies' and feels herself 'dressed in an impenetrable armor of lies' . . . she finds a new mechanism for evading responsibility. She trivializes Karenin's emotions and turns them against him" (Gustafson, 123).

23 Bayley notes that the race is described twice, a device he attributes to Tolstoy's attempt to show the "separation" of Anna and Vronsky (Bayley, 219).

24 Wasiolek comments: "We must feel sympathy for him [Karenin] here. . . . Anna adds no qualification, no excuse, and makes no extenuation of the facts. She makes the declaration with total disregard for Karenin's feelings" (Wasiolek, 142).

25 Malcolm Jones aptly observes: "She sees him now not as a remarkable man, but as a hypocrite who cares only about pretense and propriety and has no feelings. It is, after all, but a short step from a refusal to discern another's feelings to a denial that he has any" (Jones, 103).

26 Harriet Murav observes: "In part 4, Anna refuses Karenin's offer of a divorce, even though he tells Stiva that he is willing to give up their son. . . . To agree to Karenin's offer of a divorce is to put herself utterly in debt to him" (Murav, 80).

27 Gustafson observes that "Anna turns her son into a weapon in her battle for love" (Gustafson, 124).

28 John Bayley is very good on impurity as it leads to characters who are not too consistent. Tolstoy "does not forget that most human beings are incapable of feeling one thing for long. . . . He makes us realise how dependent most novelists are on the obsessiveness, or at least the unusual singlemindedness, of their characters. He makes us wonder whether George Eliot's Tito Melema and Rosamund Vincy, or Henry James's Gilbert Osmond, would have been *quite* so unremitting in their selfishness or their vindictiveness" (Bayley, 227). "The difficulty of coming to any conclusions about life is that the body does not remain in the same state for long" (228). This thinking also leads Bayley to his shrewd comment about Tolstoy's "narrating by two 'positives,' where one might have expected a positive and a negative" (Bayley, 224).

29 I discuss the logic of foreshadowing in N&F, 42–81.

30 In the restaurant scene, Stiva tells Levin: "you're very much all of a piece. That's your strong point and your failing. You have a character that's all of a piece. And you want the whole of life to be all of a piece—and that's not how it is. You despise public work because you want the reality to be invariably corresponding all the while with the aim—and that's not how it is. You want a man's work, too, always to have a defined aim, and love and family life always to be undivided—and that's not how it is. All the variety, all the charm, all the beauty of life is made up of light and shade" (47). From the perspective of the novel, Stiva is right in his description of how the world is— not all of a piece. Where he is wrong is in his moral reaction to this fragmentation. Instead of trying to make work more closely correspond with its aim, and family life less divided, he simply takes pleasure in the discrepancy. Orwin justly observes: "In fact, although there is indeed much to criticize in Stiva, at this point in the discussion he is right" (Orwin, *Art and Thought,* 173); "Stiva's conclusion that the variety of life

is a good thing is correct, but his reason for drawing that conclusion—merely that it makes life charming and beautiful—is not" (Orwin, *Art and Thought*, 176).

31   Helena Goscilo refers to "Frou-Frou's death in the overly allegorized horse race" (Goscilo, 86).

32   Mandelker points out the parallel with the scene in Trollope's *Can You Forgive Her?* in which Burgo Fitzgerald (who occupies a place in the plot roughly analogous to Vronsky's) "recklessly rides a horse to death, destroying a creature 'much nobler than himself'" (Mandelker, 155–56). Given the importance of Trollope's novel in *Anna Karenina,* I agree that Tolstoy might well have had this scene in mind. Of course, Burgo kills the horse out of recklessness and ignorance, his basic character traits, whereas distraction is not Vronsky's basic character trait.

33   And if readers are like me, they identify with Anna, find her suffering acutely painful and wince at her unreasonableness, which can only make her suffering worse.

34   Commenting on the difference between Anna at the novel's opening and the end of Part Seven, Wasiolek comments: "What appalled him [Tolstoy] about Anna's fate and what appalls us in its reading is the change that occurs in her person. She changes from a beautiful warm person, to one who becomes increasingly querulous, petty, and vicious. We are so moved by compassion for her suffering that we tend to over-look the fund of sheer nastiness in her by the end of the novel" (Wasiolek, 130). William Dean Howells long ago noticed the degeneration, which he attributes to Anna's own behavior: "It is she who destroys herself, persistently, step by step . . . and yet we are never allowed to forget how good and generous she was when we first met her" (Howells, 79).

35   The use of this epigraph commands attention and demands explanation even more than we might at first assume. Andrew Wachtel points out that "in Russian realism the epigraph is practically unknown. The first major Russian novel since the time of Pushkin to have an epigraph was Dostoevsky's *The Devils*. . . . Thus, a serious, even cruel epigraph, such as 'Vengeance is mine; I will repay' must have been rather shock-ing for Tolstoy's contemporary reader" (Wachtel, 111).

36   Kate Holland comments that "critics have traditionally fallen into two camps: those who see the epigraph's roots in Old Testament vengeance and those who see in its Pauline context a different inflection." She raises questions about traditional read-ings: "Quick to suggest a particular interpretation of the epigraph, Tolstoy is as quick to violate it. Is the epigraph really a clue to reading the novel, or is it a narrative stooge? A sphinx? Tolstoy's last laugh on us?" (Holland, 147).

37   I agree with Alexandrov: "Furthermore, one of Anna's motivations in committing suicide is to avenge herself on Vronsky for what she believes she has suffered because of him, which means that she usurps a divine prerogative, according to the epigraph" (Alexandrov, 189).

38   On the image of light, Michael Holquist observes: "Society (*svet*) has cast him [Vron-sky] partially, and Anna completely, out of its light (*svet*). And the world (*svet*) looks completely different in the resultant darkness. How very different, we will know only in Anna's last day on earth, when—in a paradox whose daring is matched only by Melville's chapter on 'The Whiteness of the Whale' in *Moby Dick*—light (*svet*) will be used as the controlling metaphor for blackness" (Holquist, 183).

39   In an essay devoted to this passage as a culmination of the novel's meditation on language and communication, Justin Weir observes that Anna "serves as a focal point in the novel for what is often considered the central 'modernist' paradigm: that the

traditional relation between the subject and the outside world, constituted by language's capacity to represent the world logically and transparently, is no longer tenable" (Weir, 109).

40 Barbara Lönnqvist points out that these lines echo Anna's earlier defense of her decision not to have any more children: "What is reason given me for, if I am not to use it to avoid bringing beings into the world" (Lönnqvist, 86).

41 Donna Orwin observes: "Like Levin, Anna is a seeker. In this sense, for Anna as for him, the future is 'open' to the very end. Anna's options end with her suicide, of course, but that she draws back at the last moment from this fatal step is a testimony to the fact that spiritual (if not physical) choices remain for her" (Orwin, *Art and Thought*, 186).

42 The novel and its eponymous heroine also bear an interesting relationship to other genres, such as the society tale. Joan Delaney Grossman observes: "Certain characters in Tolstoy's novels serve a metonymic function in relation to segments of society. One of these is the old Countess Vronskaya. Her appearance early in the novel alerts the reader to the presence of a society tale 'overlay' on the beginnings of a family novel" (Grossman, 117). In my terms, Countess Vronskaya is a genre expatriate (what I used to call a generic refugee) from the society tale.

Logan Speirs contends that "the essential reason for the waste of Anna's life is the artificiality of her existence" (Speirs, 119).

43 Lönnqvist, who traces the references to Anna's bag, sees this scene in symbolic terms: "The red bag, having followed Anna on her journey of passion, has become a symbol of her earthly, bodily existence, and only when she has freed herself of it is she ready to go" (Lönnqvist, 89).

44 Lönnqvist points out that the peasant pays no attention to her—*ne obrashchaet na nee vnimanie*—the very words used when Vronsky, frustrated by all his attempts to deal with Anna, decides that he will pay no attention to her (Lönnqvist, 87).

Chapter Four. Levin

1 Japan's debate over Westernization in the sixteenth and seventeenth centuries and the initial decision to avoid it would perhaps give Japan priority in considering the question. But for Japan at that time, Westernization did not mean all that we now think of as modernization.

2 Edmundson's adaptation dramatizes Stiva's appeal to Karenin at such a moment as morally horrible, even chilling, and (I think) it can easily be read that way. It is probably both comic and morally disturbing at the same time (Edmundson, 81).

3 Tkachev suggested a continuation of the Levin story in which, combining his domestic and agricultural obsessions, he falls in love with his cow, Pava (Tkachov, 259–60).

4 Mary Helen Kashuba and Manucher Dareshuri use *Anna Karenina* to help students explore difficulties in introducing technologies to underdeveloped countries. "Lack of cultural preparedness, skilled labor, adequate markets, and compatible infrastructure hinders the use of these techniques in an underdeveloped country, whether it is nineteenth-century Russia or twentieth-century Iran" (Kashuba and Dareshuri, 94).

5 On this point I differ from Gustafson: "He forgives only because he believes Anna has changed. His forgiveness is given forth conditionally" (Gustafson, 127). Alexandrov believes (as I and most readers do) that "the change in Karenin is to be taken as

a genuine embodiment of the Christian ideal in its pure form" (Alexandrov, 123); but we disagree on the reason that Karenin cannot retain this state of soul. For Alexandrov, the reason is that Karenin is "a weak man" (128).

6   In fact, this possibility has occurred to critics. Shortly after the novel first appeared in book form, it was reviewed (1878) by A. V. Stankevich. Commenting on the scene in which Anna begs forgiveness and Karenin experiences Christian love, Stankevich writes: "The novel could have ended here with Anna's death. A pitiful Anna, in a late but complete repentance and in death paying for her conscious and unconscious guilt, would have retained her moral, albeit sad, beauty not only in Vronsky's memory but also in Karenin's and the readers'." However, such an ending would not have been as satisfying as one in which death is "the inevitable result of inner struggle and the outcome of the moral process within a person's soul" (Stankevich, 300). Julie Buckler considers Stankevich's suggestion in her discussion of the novel's relation to melodrama (Buckler, 134).

7   A fine study of Tolstoy's aesthetics is Silbajoris.

8   Martin Price traces significant parallels with Wittgenstein's works (see Price).

9   Alexandrov does not accept these passages as reflecting the perspective of the novel. He compares Levin's revelation to Karenin's fake Christianity when he is under the influence of Countess Lydia Ivanovna: "Levin's reasons for suddenly believing in God also reflect the narrator's critique of Karenin's faith. In effect, each character believes that God's truth lies in his heart and that he can determine the strength of his faith by himself. . . . it is hard to differentiate Karenin's complacency from Levin's certainty" (Alexandrov, 166). Levin's case-based ethics do not seem to Alexandrov to be ethics at all: "Whether or not this can really be called 'ethics' is questionable, however, because Levin's behavior is entirely unreflecting" (Alexandrov, 162).

Index

In this index an "f" after a page number indicates a separate reference on the next page; an "ff" indicates separate references on the next two pages. A continuous discussion is indicated by two page numbers separated by a hyphen. *Passim* indicates a cluster of references in close but not consecutive sequence.

This index uses the following abbreviations: A = Anna, C&P = *Crime and Punishment*, K = Karenin, L = Levin, SIK = Sergey Ivanovich Koznyshev, T = Tolstoy, V = Vronsky, and W&P = *War and Peace*.

Magic words, 195–96, 215, 231
Majority reading, 38, 57–61, 64, 86–97, 120, 136; of epigraph, 127–30; of horse race, 123–24; of K, 59f, 87, 93–95, 113; of letterbox proposal, 77; overlooks A's refusal of divorce and custody, 113–17; seven reasons for, 60–61; vs. T's 59–60, 62
"Make the stone *stony*," 59
Make work, 46
Makoreeva, Irina, 238
Malice, evil and antagonism without, 50, 97–98, 158, 224, 238
Malinowski, Bronislaw, 18
Mandelker, Amy 236, 241
"Manifest at a particular moment," 24–25
Mathematics, 16–20, 207
Mao Zedong, 204
Marceau, Sophie, 238
"Marriage of Heaven and Hell" (Blake), 36, 62
Marriage of two existentialists, 72
Mars and Martians, 25, 216f
Master disciplines, 18–20, 197, 199–202, 211–12, 231
Marxism-Leninism, 19
Materialism and antimaterialism, 170–71, 198–201
Matryona Filimonovna, 39, 41
Matthew, key passage for *Anna Karenina*, 175
Maxims vs. laws, 17. *See also* Aphorisms and maxims
"May you live in interesting times!," 35
Meaning and meaningfulness, 197–222; and the incontestably necessary, 204–5, 232; L discovers, 209–14, 220–22; and master disciplines, 197, 199–202, 211–12; and plurality of perspectives and problems, 200–202, 221–22; and stories, 225, 232; and Sviazhsky enigma, 197–200, 202–23; as symptom, 203, 231–32; and vanishing of the problem, 213, 231–32; and wisdom of behavior, 203–13
"Mechanical explanation of the soul," 200
Medicine and knowledge, 14, 17
Mediocre, Rostov as, 10
Melville, Herman, 241
Mengistu, Haile, 165
Merchant crossing himself, 132
Mere breeders, 65
"Merely a good mother," 53–54, 178
Merezhkovsky, 118–19, 120, 123
Merkalova, Liza, 65
Mess, 26–27, 155f, 163–64, 229
Messify, 229

Metrov, 192
Middlemarch (Eliot), 27–28, 57, 208, 218, 239; prologue and ending to, 29; title of, 37, 66
Midges, 124
Midwife at A's, 183
Mikhailov and Mikhailov scene, 12, 45, 190–91, 196, 219f
Mill on the Floss, The (Eliot), 235
Milosevic, Slobodan, 216
Milton, John (*Paradise Lost*), 36
Military ethos, 97–98
Mimicry, 88, 109–10, 239
Minor character in someone else's novel, 232
Minority reading, 58, 60, 237f
Miracles, 20–21, 212
Mirrors, 43–44, 65, 105
Mistaken: guess at a reaction, 177; turn in history of ideas, 5
Moby-Dick (Melville), 241
Modernization, 1, 143–46, 159, 161, 228, 242
"Modernization and distortion," 4–5
Mole, Darwin's, 22
Moll Flanders (Defoe), 208, 218
Monads, view of people as, 131
Money, 43, 105, 109
Montaigne, Michel de, 14, 27, 119, 168, 207
Montesquieu, Charles de, 235
Moral: alertness, 220; compass, 60, 102, 180; facts, 206–7; Galileans, 218; monster, 59,87; Newtonianism, 18–20, 26, 156–57, 206–8, 217; relativity, 83–84; sensitivity, 206–7, 209, 219f; superiority, 233
More, Henry, 14
"More like a bargeman than a philosopher," 171
Moscow colonel, 174
Moscow vs. Petersburg, 145, 148, 260
Mother Theresa, 203
Mowing, 10f, 157–58
Mozambique, 161
Mozart, Wolfgang (*Don Giovanni*), 52
Multiple paths, 20
Multiplot novel, 96
Murasaki Shikibu (*The Tale of Genji*), 4
Murav, Harriet, 116, 239f
Mushroom, 157
"Muslin garment," 199
Mystery and romantic love, 68
Myth, 63, 116, 226

Name, 174, 200
Napoleon, 21, 64
Narcissism, 46, 116, 227f, 239; and reading, 82; and romantic love, 65–68

RUSSIAN LITERATURE AND THOUGHT

Strolls with Pushkin
Abram Tertz (Andrei Sinyavsky)

Untimely Thoughts: Essays on Revolution, Culture, and the Bolsheviks, 1917–1918
Maxim Gorky

Abram Tertz and the Poetics of Crime
Catharine Theimer Nepomnyashchy

Dostoevsky and Soloviev: The Art of Integral Vision
Marina Kostalevsky

Toward Another Shore: Russian Thinkers Between Necessity and Chance
Aileen M. Kelly

Liberty, Equality, and the Market: Essays by B. N. Chicherin
Edited and translated by G. M. Hamburg

Pushkin's Historical Imagination
Svetlana Evdokimova

Rereading Russian Poetry
Edited by Stephanie Sandler

View from the Other Shore: Essays on Herzen, Chekhov, and Bakhtin
Aileen M. Kelly

See No Evil: Literary Cover-Ups and Discoveries of the Soviet Camp Experience
Dariusz Tolczyk

Philosophy of Economy
Sergei Bulgakov
Translated, edited, and introduced by Catherine Evtuhov

The Little Tragedies
Alexander Pushkin
Translated, with Critical Essays, by Nancy K. Anderson

A Voice from the Chorus
Abram Tertz (Andrei Sinyavsky)

1920 Diary
Isaac Babel

Earthly Signs
Marina Tsvetaeva

Problems of Idealism: Essays in Russian Social Philosophy
Translated, edited, and introduced by Randall A. Poole

Five Operas and a Symphony: Word and Music in Russian Culture
Boris Gasparov

"Anna Karenina" in Our Time: Seeing More Wisely
Gary Saul Morson